Home Theater For Dummies®

Surround format	Number of channels	Type of channels	Type of media with which the format may be used
Dolby® Pro Logic®	4	• 2 discrete, full-bandwidth channels (front left and right) • 1 matrixed, full-bandwidth channel (center) • 1 matrixed, limited-bandwidth surround channel (sent to left and right surround speakers)	• VHS movies • Broadcast TV • Dolby Digital sources downmixed to analog stereo (DVDs, DTV, DBS, digital cable)
Dolby Pro Logic II™ DOLBY SURROUND PRO LOGIC II	5.1	• 2 discrete, full-bandwidth channels (front left and right) • 3 matrixed, full-bandwidth channels (center, surround left and right) • 1 subwoofer channel via Pro Logic II's bass management	• All the same Dolby Surround sources as Pro Logic (VHS movies, broadcast TV) • All stereo sources including music CDs, MP3s, broadcast TV
Dolby Digital™ DOLBY DIGITAL	up to 5.1	• 5 discrete, full-bandwidth channels (front left and right, center, surround left and right) • 1 discrete LFE channel (subwoofer)	• All DVDs • Some broadcast DTV • Some DBS
DTS™ dts DIGITAL SURROUND	5.1	• 5 discrete, full-bandwidth channels (front left and right, center, surround left and right) • 1 discrete LFE channel (subwoofer)	• Some DVDs are DTS-encoded • Some CDs are DTS-encoded

Home Theater For Dummies®

Cheat Sheet

Surround format	Number of channels	Type of channels	Type of media with which the format may be used
Dolby Digital EX™ **DO DOLBY DIGITAL SURROUND·EX**	6.1	• 5 discrete, full-bandwidth channels (front left and right, center, surround left and right) • 1 matrixed, full-bandwidth channel (back surround) • 1 discrete LFE channel (subwoofer)	• Some DVDs are Dolby Digital EX-encoded • Regular Dolby Digital 5.1 DVDs can also be played with a Dolby Digital EX decoder
THX Surround EX™ (a THX-processed presentation of Dolby Digital EX) **THX®**	6.1	• 5 discrete, full-bandwidth channels (front left and right, center, surround left and right) • 1 matrixed, full-bandwidth channel (back surround) • 1 discrete LFE channel (subwoofer)	• Dolby Digital EX-encoded DVDs • Regular Dolby Digital 5.1 DVDs can also be played with a THX Surround EX decoder
DTS-ES™ **dts ES™**	6.1	• 6 discrete, full-bandwidth channels (front left and right, center, surround left and right, and back surround) • 1 discrete LFE channel (subwoofer)	• Some DVDs are DTS-ES-encoded • Regular DTS 5.1 DVDs can also be used with a DTS-ES decoder

Source: Crutchfield Corp. www.crutchfield.com

Logos courtesy of Dolby, THX, and Digital Theater Systems. (Dolby, Pro Logic, and the double-D symbol are registered trademarks of Dolby Laboratories. Surround EX is a trademark of Dolby Laboratories.)

Wiley, the Wiley Publishing logo, For Dummies, the Dummies Man logo, the For Dummies Bestselling Book Series logo and all related trade dress are trademarks or registered trademarks of Wiley Publishing, Inc. All other trademarks are property of their respective owners.

For Dummies: Bestselling Book Series for Beginners

Home Theater
FOR
DUMMIES®

by Danny Briere and Pat Hurley

WILEY

Wiley Publishing, Inc.

Home Theater For Dummies®

Published by
Wiley Publishing, Inc.
909 Third Avenue
New York, NY 10022
www.wiley.com

For general information on our other products and services or to obtain technical support, please contact our Customer Care Department within the U.S. at 800-762-2974, outside the U.S. at 317-572-3993, or fax 317-572-4002.

Wiley also publishes its books in a variety of electronic formats. Some content that appears in print may not be available in electronic books.

Library of Congress Control Number: 2002114820

ISBN: 0-7645-1801-1

Manufactured in the United States of America

10 9 8 7 6 5 4 3

1B/SW/QT/QT/IN

WILEY is a trademark of Wiley Publishing, Inc.

About the Authors

Danny Briere founded TeleChoice, Inc., a telecommunications consulting company, in 1985 and now serves as CEO of the company. Widely known throughout the telecommunications and networking industry, Danny has written more than 1,000 articles about telecommunications topics and has authored or edited eight books, including *Internet Telephony For Dummies* and *Smart Homes For Dummies*. He is frequently quoted by leading publications on telecommunications and technology topics and can often be seen on major TV networks providing analysis on the latest communications news and breakthroughs. Danny lives in Mansfield Center, Connecticut, with his wife and four children.

Pat Hurley is a consultant with TeleChoice, Inc., specializing in emerging telecommunications technologies. Pat currently concentrates on the field of home and wireless networking and is also TeleChoice's DSL industry analyst. Pat is the coauthor of *Internet Telephony For Dummies* and *Smart Homes For Dummies*. He lives in San Diego, California, with his wife.

Authors' Acknowledgments

Danny wants to thank his wife, Holly, and kids, who had to endure a blobby dad during 20 inches of prime sledding snow during the Holidays in 2002. Holly still remains the smarter one of the family, but Danny is certainly gaining in stature as his success rate with getting the new puppy to go to the bathroom outside is unparalleled in the family. Danny also thanks his Mom and Dad, whose unfailing support has been special throughout the years, but especially in 2002. And his Mom who made him take those typing lessons as a kid with all those yucky girls at the all-girls school — it's really come in handy.

Pat, as always, thanks his wife, Christine, for her infinite patience. (Is it patience when one refrains from bonking his or her spouse over the head with a cast iron skillet?) He also thanks her for gamely smiling and nodding when he introduced, over and over again, pictures of the newest future member of the Hurley family home theater, only to change his mind when he discovered the next silicon (not silicone!) laden object of his desire. Pat also thanks his parents for letting him spend entirely too much time during his Christmas visit hunched over his Powerbook. Pops — I'm working on that big screen for you!

Danny and Pat want to thank the following people and organizations for their support in writing this book: Joel Silver at Imaging Science Foundation, Jeff Denenholz at X10 Ltd., Larry Becker at Crutchfield, Nick Carter and the rest of the crew at AudioRequest, Kaleo Willess and Roger Dressler at Dolby Laboratories, Shawn Gusz at G-NET Canada, John Dahl and Amy Brighouse from THX, Ltd., and all those people manning the booths at CES '03 in Las Vegas who let us stare and gape at their rear-projection, plasma, and LCD screens for hours on end. We'd thank them personally, but none of them gave us one.

Special thanks to Sandy Daniels at TeleChoice for her dogged help in tracking down the untrackable, and her just great attitude and work ethic over the last several books.

Publisher's Acknowledgments

We're proud of this book; please send us your comments through our online registration form located at www.dummies.com/register/.

Some of the people who helped bring this book to market include the following:

Acquisitions, Editorial, and Media Development

Project Editor: Kala Schrager

Senior Acquisitions Editor: Steve Hayes

Copy Editor: Rebecca Huehls

Technical Editor: Mike Knapp

Editorial Manager: Kevin Kirschner

Permissions Editor: Carmen Krikorian

Media Development Manager: Laura VanWinkle

Media Development Supervisor: Richard Graves

Editorial Assistant: Amanda Foxworth

Cartoons: Rich Tennant, www.the5thwave.com

Production

Project Coordinator: Regina Snyder

Layout and Graphics: Karl Brandt, Seth Conley, Tiffany Muth

Proofreader: TECHBOOKS Production Services

Indexer: TECHBOOKS Production Services

Publishing and Editorial for Technology Dummies

    Richard Swadley, Vice President and Executive Group Publisher

    Andy Cummings, Vice President and Publisher

    Mary C. Corder, Editorial Director

Publishing for Consumer Dummies

    Diane Graves Steele, Vice President and Publisher

    Joyce Pepple, Acquisitions Director

Composition Services

    Gerry Fahey, Vice President of Production Services

    Debbie Stailey, Director of Composition Services

Contents at a Glance

Table of Contents

Introduction

The on-screen image looks crisp and sharp, like a huge moving photograph. You feel entranced. More to the point, you feel the immediate urge to own this video projector, provided it works with the DVD player and the rest of your fledgling home theater gear.

An enthusiastic salesperson sees your look and enters the demonstration room. "It's really beautiful," the salesperson proclaims. "That's the first DLP unit with a built-in line doubler that works in true 1080i at 16:9. Yup, she's a dream."

Moments like that make you wish that people came with a pause button — or at least an instant replay and color commentary.

For all the fun they bring and the good times they facilitate, home theaters (and their sundry technologies) come with a bewildering blizzard of terms and acronyms. Worse yet, it seems like everybody involved with the industry either knows what the terms mean but can't explain them, or has no clue about the true meanings but spouts the terms anyway. And neither of those cases helps *you* make any sense of the whole thing.

That's where *Home Theater For Dummies* makes its heroic entrance. (We'd cue up a low fog, some dramatic lighting, and that mysterious "something cool might happen anytime now" music to enhance the moment, but there's only so much you can do in a book.) Even without the special effects, this book still rescues you from all kinds of home theater perils. Read on to find out how.

About This Book

The book takes you through the world of home theater from the bottom to the top. Starting with a broad look at the basics of home theater concepts and technology, *Home Theater For Dummies* presses onward with more detailed information about source devices, surround sound gear, video display equipment, and PCs. The book even advises you about the theater room itself, giving guidance about everything from furniture to popcorn bags.

Best of all, this book delivers the information in the friendly, patient, and easy-to-understand manner that you know and expect from a title in the *For Dummies* line.

Get ready for one of the most enjoyable trips of your life. With this book at your side, you're ready for anything and everything that the industry (and those questionable salespeople at the local equipment store) can throw at you.

Conventions Used in This Book

Unlike its famous and prolific computer-oriented brethren, *Home Theater For Dummies* keeps things pretty simple in the "conventions" department. We use just a single bit of textual oddness that relates to Web sites. Any time the book talks about a World Wide Web address, you see the site address formatted in a special font, like this: www.dummies.com.

Why? For one thing, the font makes the text stand out so that you know exactly what to type. (Besides, we think the production department got a special deal on that font, so they just like seeing it in the books as much as possible.)

Just the (Techie) Facts, Ma'am

Although everything in the book meets rigorous standards for comprehension, usability, and lack of pointless geekiness, a few technical tidbits slipped in accidentally. Well, they didn't slip in accidentally. We wrote them that way.

At some point in the home theater process, you come face-to-face with technical tripe whether or not you want to. It's better that you hear this stuff from us than from some name-tagged human on a sales floor.

Foolish Assumptions

In writing a book, we have to spend a lot of time in malls, video stores, and movie theaters (that's the hard part) doing research. While doing so, we ponder all kinds of questions concerning our readers. Who are you? Where are you? What did you eat for lunch? Which movies tweak your interest? How do your home theater desires line up with your budget? Queries like that fill our minds constantly, much to the consternation of our spouses, who prefer more useful thoughts like, "Shouldn't you take the trash out?"

Because we never get to meet you in person, we end up making a few assumptions about you and what you want from this book. Here's a peek at our thoughts about you:

- You love movies, television shows, or video games — or perhaps all three.
- You've experienced wide screens and surround sound at the theater, and you liked it.
- For one reason or another, a 19-inch TV set with a single built-in speaker doesn't adequately meet your audio or video entertainment desires.
- You probably own a computer, or will soon.
- You don't shy away from high-tech products, but you also aren't the first person on the block with the latest electronic goodie.
- The weird technicalities of home theater circle around you like planes buzzing King Kong.
- You know something about the Internet and the Web.
- You (or someone in your family) enjoy watching movies, listening to MP3 audio, playing games, and possibly making movies on your computer.

If that describes you in detail or at least catches some of your shadow in passing, then this book is for you.

How This Book Is Organized

Rather than haphazardly fling information at you and hope that some of it sticks, the book clumps related topics together into six parts. Here's a peek at what they cover.

Part 1: Welcome to the World of Home Theater

With home theater, the trek begins here, in Part I, which covers the basics of the basics, starting with a look at what home theater really means, includes, requires, and offers. From there, it looks at what it takes to get into a home theater, in terms of space, timing, budget, and equipment. In Chapter 4, this part gets a little techie, but necessarily so, by giving you some solid insight into the terms and technologies that you will encounter. You need this baseline knowledge for the rest of the book, so read Chapter 4 closely. In fact, read it twice. (It's even better the second time around.)

Part II: What Are You Going to Watch?: Source Devices

Home theater installations really contain two parts: source and presentation. Part II covers all kinds of sources, ranging from the prerecorded offerings of DVD players and VCRs to the over-the-air-and-through-the-sky action of broadcast TV and satellite dishes. As an added bonus, this part even takes you on a tour of the personal video recorder (PVR), possibly the most ground-breaking entertainment device since the VCR itself, as well as state-of-the-art gaming platforms. (Pat performed that excruciating gaming research.) We also talk about your PC and the growing role it plays in sourcing audio, video, gaming, and other content for your system.

Part III: Watching and Listening: Display and Control Devices

Part III focuses on the control and presentation aspects of your system, with in-depth looks at your receivers, controllers, speakers, and video displays. We look at all-in-one receivers and separates, such as controllers and power amps. On the video side, this part explores the strange world of television sets (which looked pretty simple until a few years ago when HDTV arrived on the scene) and video projection systems, which are home theater's answer to the movie house's silver screen. Then, all eyes — er, ears — turn to audio for details about surround sound systems, speakers, and more. Finally, we talk about remote controls — an often overlooked area that deserves more attention. A remote control is your single biggest interface to the system, so we give you some options here.

Part IV: Putting It All Together

With your location selected, your gear picked out, and your walls trembling in fear, it's time to install your theater, and Part IV guides you through the process. In fact, hooking up your home theater is one of the harder parts of the experience. We start with the basics — the different types of cabling — and work our way up to connecting all the different components into a working system. Toward the end of Part IV, we give you advice on how to link your home entertainment system to other TVs and systems in the house. After all, you paid a lot of money for your theater — why not get the most use from it that you can?

Part V: Let Your Home Theater Be All It Can Be

You might think that your home theater equipment is out-of-the-box ready to be plugged together and to start playing movies, but it's not that simple. Almost every part of your system needs to be tuned, like a nice grand piano. Although we use big words and phrases such as *calibration* and *bass management* in this part, these merely relate to fine-tuning your system to itself and its environs. We also give you ideas for sprucing up your home theater with fancy lights and soundproofing (the latter of which is great for those late night sleepovers the kids have). We end the part with a cool look at the higher end of home theater — the things you can dream about during those long trips to Grandma's.

Part VI: The Part of Tens

Like the other *For Dummies* books, *Home Theater For Dummies* closes with a look at life from the humorous side with perky Part VI, the Part of Tens. Each chapter counts off a bunch of goodies that help you show off, troubleshoot, and generally accessorize your theater.

Icons Used in This Book

Packing so much stuff into such a small space makes the book easy to carry, but it also shrinks the important details until they're easily overlooked. To point out the important stuff (and highlight the technicalities you might want to avoid), the book relies on several helpful icons. Each icon identifies a particular type of information. Here's a quick field guide to what each of these little billboards means.

Whenever you see the Remember icon, grab a handy mental highlighter (and maybe a real one, too) and mark the section, because this information might come in handy at any moment, either now or in the future.

Everybody looks for tips (particularly in the stock market, the race track, and at your favorite restaurant). When a Tip icon shows up here in *Home Theater For Dummies,* it points out information destined to simplify your life. You can't go wrong with a Tip!

When a topic includes technology, then technical tripe always finds its way into the book. At some point or another in the home theater experience, you need to know the geek-speak. Don't fear paragraphs with these icons, but don't rush to them, either. Just brace yourself for the technical onslaught, secure in the knowledge that this book protects you from the worst of the techno-drivel.

Nothing in your home theater really threatens personal peril — at least no more peril than you get from plugging in a toaster or accidentally watching a bad movie at your local theater. In those rare moments when inserting the right plug in the wrong socket could spell doom for your gear, the Warning icon hops into action. When you see one of these, stop for a moment, read the text, and double-check your progress before continuing.

Where to Go from Here

Apart from the pleasing shade of yellow on the cover, the best part of a *For Dummies* book is its open and available layout — you can start anywhere you want. If you already know the stuff in Chapter 1, dive in somewhere else instead. Where you start and what you read depends entirely on what you need to know right now.

Read over the Table of Contents to see if any topics really jump out at you. If nothing does, try finding a starting point in one of these:

- ✔ If you just jumped into the front row of home theater enthusiasts, start in Chapter 1. It gives you a good overview of how a home theater works, what it takes, and what to do next.

- ✔ Curious about the content — the movies and shows appearing in your theater? Part II delves into DVD and VHS, plus satellite, broadcast, and cable TV. It even peers into the promising realm of personal video recorders, like the TiVo and ReplayTV, and PC-driven content.

- ✔ For an in-depth look at the sound and video presentation side of your entertainment empire, visit the chapters of Part III.

With that, leap into the world of home theater. Lights, camera, action — welcome to your adventure!

Part I

Welcome to the World of Home Theater

In this part . . .

1t's important to start your adventure with some solid basics — what's a home theater, why do you want one, what do all the various terms mean?

Part I lays a solid foundation for talking about home theater. An understanding of all your options not only helps you on the showroom floor, but also helps you when the time comes to install your gear and tune it so that it does what it was intended to do. Indeed, a lot of home theater is about making sure that your system is configured correctly for your environment, and to do that, you need to know what it's supposed to be doing in the first place. (We're sure there's some pithy phrase, like "cart before the horse," to throw in here now, but we never use those correctly. So think of a phrase of your choice here.)

We then follow up with some high-level basics about your home theater and its environment. We discuss things like where to put a home theater in your house and how to control it. We also delve into that hot topic — "Okay, how much is this going to cost me."

Then we walk you through all the things that make up the home theater at a high level — sources, outputs, PCs, cables, broadband, and so on.

And finally, we go a little deeper into the key terms, standards, and technologies that we use throughout the book. Here's where we talk about a lot of the things that probably got you to buy this book in the first place — the alphabet soup of home theater.

After you finish this part, you'll know enough to be dangerous in your local electronics store. (So be sure to read the rest of the book, too, so that you know how to control your now dangerous mind.)

Chapter 1

The Zen of Home Theater

*W*hen you hear the term *home theater,* you probably think of big screens, cool sound, DVDs, CDs, and lots of remote controls sitting around your living room. We're sure that football games, beer, and other fun images sneak into that image as well.

Home theater is truly for everyone — regardless of the size of your house or apartment, your economic wealth, or your taste in movies. And home theater is bound to mean something different to everyone. It's not just about boxes, cables, and remotes, or about discs, records, and cassettes: A home theater can be a real adventure.

Appreciating the Art of the Home Theater

Before you start on your home theater adventure, it's critical to understand what the makers of the equipment, movies, standards, audio CDs, and so on, mean when they say that they are supporting home theater.

To the companies that produce the equipment and media, home theater is all about trying to re-create the experience of watching a film in a movie theater, hearing the cheers of the crowd in a football stadium, or feeling the reverberations of music in an open air concert, in your home. Many of the people who devote themselves to creating atmosphere and mood using this medium consider what they do to be an art form. These are usually the people who are listed in the credits at the end of a movie.

When you take all the sensations of a movie theater and insert them in your living room, nothing changes. All the improvements in sound compression, surround sound, digital screen imaging, and so on, have been done not to sell more equipment at Circuit City or Wal-Mart, but to try to perfect the ability to suck you into another world where you can experience a piece of work.

So a lot of this book is about explaining to you the technologies and ideas behind that home theater that you are going to put together, because it's not just about seven speakers hooked into your stereo or a big honking TV screen. It's about how to make sure everything is put in its proper place to maximize your home theater out-of-body experience — the way the media creators intended.

Fitting Home Theater's Many Faces into All Kinds of Spaces

You've probably watched enough TV shows and movies about Hollywood and the rich and famous to know that, for some people, home theaters are as common as a kitchen or a bedroom. Indeed, home theaters were spawned out of the necessity of those working on the films to preview footage, screen tests, and full movies. They gradually grew to be a status symbol among actors, too, and spread out from there.

In those early days, a home theater was pretty much literally that, with Peerless Magnarc carbon-arc lamphouses and theater seating. They were often extensive and elaborate affairs — to match the surrounding house.

Today, you too can get into the act, and you're lucky enough to have available a broad range of projectors, screens, displays, seating, and equipment — heck, even popcorn machines — to create your own home theater.

Probably the first big decision you have to make is where you want to put your home theater. It was one thing to figure out where to put your 19-inch TV set; it's another thing to think about where to put a big-screen TV with six speakers and associated A/V gear. Few people are prepared for how overpowering a full home theater setup can be in a small home, so it's especially important to plan ahead if you have limited space.

Defining your home theater space is a necessary first step. If the only place to put a TV is on the mantle above the fireplace, then you're looking at a plasma screen TV and not much else. If you have to fit the whole system into the corner of the living room, then that narrows the search as well. Remember, you don't want to try to buy a home theater that just won't fit into your home and your lifestyle. A home theater is all about creating a surround atmosphere; so pick your spaces, and work from there.

You can most certainly put a home theater in your present living room, in your bedroom, or in a room devoted just to using your theater. In the end, what matters is not so much the size, but the way you establish its ability to coax you into its sound field and video experience.

Budgeting for Home Theater

We believe in setting expectations. We don't want to get you salivating over a 42-inch plasma and a nice Harmon Kardon system, and then smack you over the head with an unrealistic price. Unfortunately, a quick stroll through any consumer electronics store could lead you to believe that you can get an entry-level whole home theater in a box (without the video display, of course) for just $299. However, that $299 system will be right for some people and not for others.

Exploring equipment and prices

So what does it cost to get into a home theater system? Table 1-1 gives you an idea of what you can spend. We've broken this table down by the roles that each group of Audio/Video (A/V) components plays in your home theater. Audio sources are devices that provide music-only playback in your system, whereas video sources provide movies or TV content. The A/V system provides the control for your home theater (meaning it lets you select what you want to watch or listen to), and does all the heavy lifting in terms of sending surround sound signals to your speaker system. The video display, of course, is what you watch (think TV). We've also included some optional components — gaming systems and home theater PCs (which let you use a PC as a high-quality audio and/or video source device).

Table 1-1	Home Theater Budget Guide	
Role	*Device*	*Price Expectations*
Audio sources	Tape cassette player*	$100 to $800
	CD player/recorder*	$60 to $600+
	Turntable*	$100 to $5,000+ (really!)
	AM/FM tuner*	$200 to $1,000
Video sources	DVD player	$50 to $1,200+
	VCR*	$50 to $1,000
	Personal video recorder*	$200 to $1,000
	Satellite system*	$100 to $800
Computer/gaming	Gaming console*	$150 to $200
	Home Theater PC*	$1,800+
A/V system**	All-in-one systems	$200 to $3,000+
	A/V receiver	$100 to $4,000
	Controller/decoder	$800 to $5,000+
	Power amplifier	$500+
Speakers	Center, left, right, and surround speakers	$150+
	Rear surround sound speakers*	$100+
	Subwoofer speakers	$150+
Video display***	27- to 38-inch direct-view tube TV	$200 to $3,000
	Up to 65-inch rear-projection TV	$1,200 to $5,000
	Up to 120-inch front-projection TV	$3,500+
	32- to 60-inch plasma screen TV	$3,000 to $15,000+

*Optional
** You don't need all of these parts, just an all-in-one system, an A/V receiver, or a controller/decoder and power amplifier combo
*** You only need one of these displays

Certainly, you don't need all the gear in Table 1-1. You can buy a nice all-in-one Home Theater system and a relatively big-screen, direct-view (picture tube) TV for not much more than $500. Of course, you can spend a lot more money, too. One thing is for sure: Pricing is competitive and changing all the time. Two years ago, a lot of the gear listed in Table 1-1 cost twice as much as it does currently. As we go to print, the first plasma screen TVs for under $3,000 are hitting the market.

To get a quick grasp on pricing, go to a few Web sites, such as www.circuitcity.com and www.plasmatvbuyingguide.com to just get a sense of the going rate for different items. Compare that with Table 1-1, and get a sense of how much pricing has dropped just in the time that it took for this book to hit the shelves.

Buying on a budget

Given that you are probably working within a budget, here are some ideas about what you can expect to buy and install for different total budget ranges:

- ✔ **$0 to $500:** Definitely the entry-level package for home theater, a system in the $0–$500 range basically uses your existing TV (or includes an inexpensive TV in the 27-inch range) and an entry level all-in-one home theater system package (which comes with speakers and a receiver/DVD player combo). You can probably throw in a $50 VCR if you don't already have one, but even the lowest level all-in-one home theater sets have DVD players included. (Gotta have DVD!)

- ✔ **$500 to $2,000:** By spending a little more, you can go up a range in a number of the components. You can get up to 36-inch model TVs for about $400 more than the average price 27-inch versions. You could even get into a rear-projection TV, as they start around $1,200 for a 40- to 52-inch TV. There are a range of options for better surround sound systems in this price range, with packaged options available for your five surround sound speakers plus your subwoofer. And you can buy a fairly good A/V receiver to drive the system.

- ✔ **$2,000 to $5,000:** At this level, you start to create serious options for a very decent home theater system. The lowest-cost plasma screens are under $3,000, and accompanying midrange all-in-one systems can be in the $2,000 area. High-definition-ready, rear-projection TVs can be had for a bit more than $1,500. At this price level, you can also start to get serious with separate components, getting a very good A/V receiver, DVD/CD player/recorder, personal video recorder, gaming system, surround sound speakers, and potentially even more. At this price range, the average person can get a mighty fine system.

- ✔ **$5,000 to $10,000:** When you top $5,000 as your budget, you now can start expanding in some wonderful ways, by adding more throughout the house through multizone capabilities, whole-home audio, and universal remote control capability, or you can continue to go up the ladder in terms of higher-quality separates. We swear by audio servers that store all your CDs in one box. Front projection becomes a viable option here, as good projectors start around $4,000. High-definition TV (HDTV) units would fall in this budget range, too. Or, you can start to get fancy with furniture and chairs. Good home theater seats start around $350 each. A high-quality, universal remote control costs about $500.

- ✔ **$10,000+:** Above $10,000, the sky is truly the limit. For $10,000 to $20,000, you get to enjoy a lot of the next generation of home theater. Your TV and VCR should be HDTV-capable. Your DVD player should be top of the line. You probably want some extra amplifier equipment in the system, and you may also want to boost your controls, perhaps with a nice Crestron wireless touch screen control. If you get above $20,000, you are into high-end, audiophile type stuff, all the way. Whole-home audio and video, integration with home automation systems, consultants — the works. Believe it or not, it is not unusual for people to spend $1 million or more on a home theater. At that point, we think a lot of money is being paid for custom interior design, top-of-the-line projectors, and so on. Nothing is held back. To us, given more modest expectations, a $25,000 system is stunning in almost all senses of the word.

Getting Your Money's Worth

In deciding how much to spend overall, we can only give you this advice: Your home entertainment system is probably one of the most used parts of your home. It helps define your family, social life, business relationships, and so on. It's important, but spend within your means. You also want to save something to do for the future. Building and growing a home theater is fun, too.

One of the great things about home theater is that it is very modular, so you don't have to buy the whole thing all at once. If you really want a great TV display, get it, and go cheaper on the other components. And when you are ready to trade up, figure out what you want next. The better stereo stores have a trade up policy that gives you credit toward getting something better. And then there's always eBay (www.ebay.com) or similar auction sites, where you can get all sorts of gear in great condition — everyone is always trading in stuff to move to higher levels, so don't feel total pressure to do it all at once.

Realize that, even if you are installing home theater wiring and speakers into the walls and such, you're not likely to 'get that money back' when you sell the house. People are leery of other people's home-grown solutions — even the professional ones — and equipment becomes outdated quickly in this industry. So if you are going to do some remodeling and spend some money, recognize you are doing it for yourself first, everyone else second, and by all means not for the money.

Indeed, a lot of this book is about getting your money's worth out of whatever you buy. If you get an all-in-one home theater system for $299 from Radio Shack, or a high-end system with, say, a $60,000 Madrigal projector, $18,000 worth of MartinLogan Prodigy speakers, a $4,000 B&K Receiver, and other similarly priced (but well worth it) components, you're still going to need to figure out how to get the most out of the system. So stay tuned to find out how to get more per kHz, or disc, or channel, or whatever you track your home theater fun by.

Chapter 2

Defining Your Home-
Theatered Home

Consumer electronics have played a major role throughout the years in defining a home. The radio, then black-and-white TV, then color TV, and then all the various adjuncts to the TV and radio — VCRs, gaming consoles, tape decks, and so on — have all helped define who we are and how we interact with each other. Radio and TV shows that had a social impact are renown for crossing various barriers — the first on-screen interracial kiss, the first portrayal of a woman president, the first portrayal of a black president, and so on.

The home has grown around these devices, so when it comes time to put these together on a pedestal and proclaim them a home theater, this act seems to acknowledge the role that home electronics have grown to play in our lifestyles.

The Basic Home Theater

So what's in a home theater then? Well, a home theater is largely what you make of it, but we think that at least three major things constitute the core of a home theater:

> ✔ **A large screen display:** Note that we do not say *television*, because more and more, the receiver aspect of a television is being divorced from the display aspect, in the form of set-top boxes, external TV tuners, computers, and other source

devices. Appropriately, the display is being optimized for what its main purpose is — displaying the wide range of video output from a home theater system. These displays can be huge. We're talking greater than 120 inches diagonally, which is 10 feet for those of you who didn't do the math!

✔ **A digital video source:** Although you could say that a digital satellite or cable service is a digital video source, we're going to mandate a DVD capability. DVD is the focal point for all digital video innovation that will drive your home theater.

✔ **A surround sound capability:** You find out about the details of surround sound in a few pages, but you need to have surround sound to take advantage of all the audio power stored in your DVD content. With surround sound, you are truly starting to mimic the theater experience.

If you're lacking any of these, you really don't have a home theater. Without the display and surround sound, you lose the impact of the visual and audio experience, and without a digital video source, you just have a loud and big TV system. You really need all three. Figure 2-1 shows these elements in their native environment — your home.

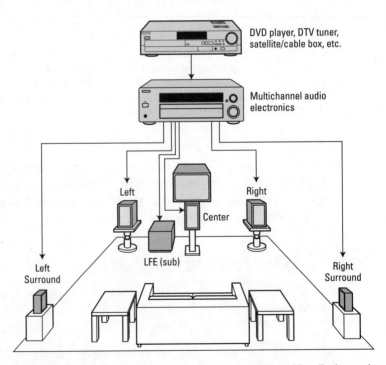

DVD player, DTV tuner, satellite/cable box, etc.

Multichannel audio electronics

Left

Right

Center

LFE (sub)

Left Surround

Right Surround

Figure 2-1: A home theater with a surround sound system, a video display, and a digital video source.

But you need not stop there. There are all sorts of other great sources to add to your system, as well as great devices you can add to enhance your overall experience. The rest of this chapter is devoted to really fleshing out the boundaries of your home theater realm.

The Complete Home Theater

In our discussion of budgets in Chapter 1, we give you a peek at what a really fleshed out home theater might contain. Here's a fairly comprehensive list of what you typically put in your home theater (we leave out the all-in-one units because they merely integrate various combinations of these devices into one unit):

✔ **Sources:** These provide the content you watch or listen to.

- Tape cassette player/recorder
- CD player/recorder/MP3 player/audio server
- Turntable
- AM/FM tuner
- DVD player
- VCR
- Personal video recorder
- Camcorder
- Satellite or cable set-top box
- Gaming console
- Home theater PC or Windows XP Media Center PC (a specific Microsoft software product)

✔ **Receivers/controllers:** The heart of the system, these feed content to your displays and speakers.

- A/V receiver
- Controller/decoder
- Power amplifier

✔ **Displays:** This is what you watch.

- Direct-view, rear-projection, or flat-panel TV display
- Front-projection with separate display screen

✔ **Speakers:** These are what you listen to.

- Two front speakers
- One front center speaker
- Two side speakers
- Two or four rear speakers
- Subwoofer

✔ **Connections:** These are connections to content coming from outside your home.

- Over-the-air antenna
- Satellite or cable video feed
- Internet connectivity — preferably broadband, such as DSL or cable modem

Naturally, as you extend your home theater to other points in your home, you can add to the quantities mentioned here, but most of the components are the same. You also might choose different qualities and (in the case of displays) sizes of these things, but the basic formula remains the same, too.

Using Your Existing Gear

A question that comes across most people's minds when they look to upgrade to a home theater is whether any of their existing A/V gear can be used in their new home theater.

The answer usually is, "Well you probably can, but you lose a lot by doing so (unless the gear is less than two years old)." If you are thinking about using existing equipment, consider the following:

✔ **TVs:** If it is less than 27 inches large, we'd say why bother. Home theater needs a big-screen display for maximum effect. Plus newer sets have things such as component video inputs, picture-in-picture displays, and even HDTV capabilities.

✔ **Receivers:** Chances are your receiver is an audio (stereo) receiver, which probably doesn't have surround sound processing capability, inputs for video gear, or built-in amplifiers for your surround sound speakers. You can use an audio-only receiver as an amplifier to drive some speakers, but if you want to listen to the latest surround sound capabilities, which are encoded on most DVDs, then you're going to need a new audio/video receiver, period.

- **VCRs:** As long as your VCR is a VHS HiFi VCR, it's just fine. But it won't replace a DVD player, which has about twice the picture resolution as a VCR (meaning the picture is about twice as sharp and detailed).

- **CD players:** Your CD player will probably work fine. Depending on your space constraints, however, you might just use your DVD player to play your CDs because the two are compatible. Over time, CD players will disappear from your system in favor of a combined disc playing/recording unit.

- **Speakers:** Chances are these are not going to be very useful, because you really want a *set* of speakers, not ones that are pieced together. Speakers work in tandem and therefore should have a similar foundation of performance. If you have a pair of stereo speakers that you can match into a complete set of surround sound speakers from the same manufacturer, you might be able to use what you have (we recommend that you choose additional speakers that are *timbre matched* with your existing speakers).

- **Other stuff:** Most other stuff can work with your system. Turntables, cassette decks, laser disc players, and so on can plug in and play their part without any problems.

- **Internet connection:** Okay, your connection isn't gear in the traditional sense, but still, if you're using a dialup connection, you should seriously consider upgrading to broadband if you want your home theater to take advantage of the Internet. As present and future consumer devices become increasingly reliant on the Internet for accessing information and content, you'll need a broadband connection to download this content.

Choosing a Room

As you go to build your home theater, all roads lead back to optimizing that illusion of participation, and where you put your system plays a big part. Here's a checklist to help you determine the right place for your home theater, because there are definitely wrong places to put your home theater:

- **Think about lighting:** The amount of ambient light in a room, day or night, can substantially affect the experience. A nice dark room actually makes the room itself disappear when watching a film, enabling that suspension of disbelief we keep aspiring to. Think about how lights from other rooms or street lighting might affect the experience.

✔ **Think about dimensions:** You tend to get more awkward sound patterns in perfectly square rooms. The best place to put the centerpiece of your system — the TV display — is along the short wall of a rectangular room, preferably a wall without windows or doors on it. Fully enclosed rooms are best for sound. You can pull heavy curtains across an open wall when you are watching films in your home theater.

✔ **Thing about sound:** Although people typically place a couch up against a wall, with a home theater, you want enough space behind you so that the sound can get in back of you and truly surround you. So the ideal position for the seating is more central to the room.

✔ **Think about the picture:** Sit close enough to your display to maximize the perceived size of the picture, but not so close that you see a somewhat grainy picture because you can see the lines on the TV set (that's too close). The bigger your display, the farther back you need to be to not see the lines. Also think about angle of viewing — all displays have a preferred angle of viewing to stay within.

✔ **Think about walls:** A rather muted color or wall covering — book cases are ideal — absorbs stray light. A dark grey or black room is best, or one with heavy, colored drapes. (Now you know why you see all those drapes and carpeted walls in theaters!) The last thing you want is a brightly colored gloss paint that reflects light, creating light ghosts to the sides of the screen. Think also about mirrors and picture frames; they do the same thing.

Take note of the front and rear wall surfaces, because in general you want to control the way your sound reflects off these surfaces. Typically, you want the back wall to be a little reflective, to help build a more general soundfield behind your seating area.

✔ **Think about floors:** Yup, the floors too. Bare tile or wood causes acoustical reflections that mess up your sound field. A good rug can absorb stray sounds that can affect the crispness of your signal.

✔ **Think about stray noise:** Listen closely to your room for regular interfering sounds, such as a clock ticking or a fish tank pump. Consider moving these devices if you can. And if the sound is coming externally, like from the dryer or washer, consider some cheap absorptive wall coverings to muffle it.

We talk about creating a home theater environment in more detail in Chapter 19.

Organizing Your Gear

The most obvious and easy place for all your home theater gear is where you historically have placed it — right next to the TV. And indeed, there's nothing inherently wrong with this approach. As we point out in Chapters 22 and 23, you can hide and manage your gear in all sorts of ways.

However, we ask you to look ahead for a moment and think about the investment you'll make in your home theater, and how you'd like to take advantage of that throughout your home. To do this, you need to think of ways your home theater's components can be used in a whole-home network. This whole-home planning can make your home theater itself better, too, because it facilitates connections between the home theater and other networks that might feed into it, such as your cable connection or your Internet connection.

Setting up a central wiring panel

Think about designating a space in your house as a *central wiring panel* where you can centrally house a lot of your whole-home infrastructure equipment (devices that let you connect the home theater to the rest of the house).

Remember that most of your commonly used, ultra-sensitive electronics gear will probably go right next to your home theater. You are better off relegating the gear that you just "plug and forget" (like video distribution panels that send your cable TV throughout the home) to a panel in an out-of-the-way place. Some of the devices that you might connect on a wiring panel include the following:

- ✔ Home cable interconnections with your cable company

- ✔ Home phone interconnections with your telephone company

- ✔ A centralized distribution point for your satellite dish wiring, if you have one

- ✔ Cable, DSL, or ISDN modems and routers, if you have them

- ✔ Ethernet hubs or switches for your Internet connection

You can also put items such as home servers and some of your central media equipment on the wiring panel if you don't need to get to it and need the extra space. Multizone amplifiers or MP3 servers are examples of such equipment.

Appreciating the advantages of a central wiring panel

By designating a central wiring panel, you gain some huge benefits:

- ✔ **Hiding wires:** Your home theater gear has a lot of cables, and can have a lot of gear you rarely touch. A well integrated home theater setup has a lot of cables hidden in the walls or running out of sight. We're not just talking component wiring (such as the wires between your DVD player and your A/V receiver), but also connections to your phone network (required by a satellite dish), to your Internet connection (could be wireless, but wireline is better long term), to your IR remote control network (more on this in Chapter 14), and other connections. Think of your wiring panel as a place where everything can connect to everything else, in the easiest fashion.

- ✔ **Hiding hardware:** Much of the hardware that facilitates home theater and whole-home networking (things such as power amps, video modulators, distribution panels, punchdown blocks, and the like) is designed with function in mind rather than form. A central wiring panel can put this hardware out of view. And that means less clutter for where you have the stuff that you get at the most, like your VCR or your DVD player.

- ✔ **Connecting at a single point:** Having a central connection point makes it easier to get networks like cable or your Internet-connected computer LAN (or Local Area Network) into the home theater. It also makes it easier for you to get movies and music *out* of your home theater, and share them throughout the home.

- ✔ **Providing easy access:** When you want to change the capabilities of your networks or troubleshoot a problem, having everything neatly arranged and easily accessible can eliminate a source of frustration.

The wiring panel should be in a place that is out of sight but is also easily accessible. It needs to have plenty of space and adequate power to run a great deal of equipment. Then, whatever you need to bring up to the media hub in the home theater, you can, through a range of easily connected wiring plates that make it look neat and more accessible at the same time.

Locating your wiring panel's home

In the best-case scenario (like when you've struck it rich and are building a custom-designed home), you can create a dedicated room for your home theater and associated equipment — a central wiring panel just like modern offices and other commercial buildings have.

If we were starting a home from scratch this way, we'd try to design the wiring panel

- ✔ On the main floor of the house

- ✔ Near an outside wall for easy interconnection to incoming service feeds

- ✔ Above an accessible part of the basement (if you have a basement)

- ✔ With adequate lighting, ventilation, and climate protection (not in the garage, in other words)

- ✔ With adequate AC power line receptacles to power devices, such as video amplifiers, Ethernet hubs, and phone systems

Such a panel needn't be too large. Most home theater equipment takes up one rack at the most.

Of course, the vast majority of homeowners or remodelers simply don't have the luxury of adding a dedicated space for a wiring panel. In these cases, you have to try to make some part of the house do double duty as your wiring panel. A first stop is the place where your cable, telephone, and electrical connections currently come into the house. You can mount some plywood on the wall on which to mount your gear. Here are some other places to consider locating your wiring panel:

- ✔ **The utility or laundry room:** The biggest disadvantage of this location is the potential for high humidity, so make sure your clothes dryer is well ventilated to the outdoors. Good ventilation also keeps all the dust and lint from your dryer out of your sensitive electronics.

- ✔ **A protected garage:** The potential for dust and extreme temperatures may make this location less than optimal for some homes, but the garage can be a useful location.

- ✔ **The basement:** Many people choose the basement for a central wiring node because it's easy to run wires through a drop ceiling. The basement can be a very good location, but keep in mind that basements can be both dusty and damp.

- ✔ **A weather-protected outdoor panel:** We recommend this location only as a last resort, but it could be acceptable in a place with a mild climate. We wouldn't recommend putting any active electronics, such as Ethernet hubs or phone systems, out here.

Who can help if you need it?

There are all sorts of people who can help you if you need advice.

✔ **Architect:** If you are building or renovating, an architect is probably involved. Home theater design usually isn't an architect's strong suit, but he or she can help you lay out the initial plans for your home and coordinate with other designers to get their respective visions on paper.

✔ **Audio/video consultant:** Your audio/video (A/V) consultant helps you select the right mix of components for your sight and sound systems and then integrate all those components. Your A/V consultant makes sure that the appropriate wiring is run to support your installations and then installs the gear when you're ready. If you're installing a dedicated home theater, expect your A/V consultant to get involved with the architect early on, too, making recommendations for room sizes, building materials, and so on. The A/V consultant may also hand you off to a specialized home-theater consultant if the job is too complex for his or her comfort. (Home-theater consultants get into additional details, such as sound-proofing, seating, lighting, and the room's shape and construction.)

✔ **Contractor/builder:** The general contractor/builder's role is to direct the other specialty contractors and make sure that they carry out the intent of the designers. Passing correct information from one contractor (such as the home-theater consultant) to the people doing the work (such as the cabinetmaker who builds the home-theater cabinetry) is crucial. The details are what count here, such as cutting out the right size cubbyhole for the kitchen media center.

✔ **Computer-systems contractor:** If you work at home or have complex computer-networking needs, bringing in a computer-systems contractor to network your computer hardware and interface it to the appropriate systems can be a great timesaver.

✔ **Electrical contractor:** Your home theater may require additional or different electrical wiring (for example, running dedicated electrical wiring to your media center).

✔ **Interior designer:** This person is responsible for making sure that your home theater technology doesn't stick out like a sore thumb. Installing a state-of-the-art home-entertainment center in the living room is one thing, and making it fit with the overall scheme of your home is another.

✔ **Lighting consultant:** Often an overlooked task on a to-do list, lighting design has an important effect on the ambiance of your home theater, so consider specialized lighting in key accent areas.

Whew! Did we leave anyone out? Depending on the amount of money you want to spend, you may indeed have this many people making your home theater a reality. A more modest project has a more modest number of people stomping around your house. Also, many of the previously mentioned professionals — A/V designers, for example — include their services when you purchase their equipment.

An important thing to keep in mind is that the natural enemies of electrical and electronic equipment are moisture, dust, and temperature extremes. So locations that may work for someone in Florida or California may not make as much sense for your house in Maine.

Setting up a hub

Your home's wiring panel provides a centralized place for all sorts of whole-home networks that connect into your home theater (and elsewhere). Within your home theater, you also need a centralized connection point — a *hub,* to use a techie term — for all that A/V gear we discuss in Chapter 1.

For most people, this hub comes in the form of an A/V receiver. An important thing to consider up front is the capability of this receiver to act as your home theater hub. An A/V receiver should be capable of accepting the connections from just about every single piece of A/V gear in your home theater (with the exception, perhaps, of an HDTV tuner/set-top box) and providing a central connection and control point.

 With the right pieces and parts and the right approach to making connections, your A/V receiver (or surround sound decoder/controller, if you go with separate components) should be the primary connection point in a home theater. With a small number of exceptions (mainly related to HDTV), you shouldn't be connecting components directly to the TV or display unit. All your audio and video should be routed through the A/V receiver, which then distributes these signals to your speakers and display. We discuss receivers in more detail in Chapter 10.

Note: Some folks feel that sending *any* video through the receiver's video switching circuitry slightly degrades the quality of this video. We think that, unless you're talking about a really high-end HDTV system, you probably won't see the difference. If you're worried about your receiver degrading your video quality, try it both ways (with the source device connected through the receiver and connected directly to your display) and see which looks better to your eyes.

Getting all this whole-home wiring (and "local" cables within your home theater) discreetly located in your home theater can be a bit problematic and messy. Your home theater room, unlike your wiring panel, is meant to be a public space in your house, not a place where you can hide away unsightly bundles of wire and racks of equipment. So your aesthetic requirements will be a bit higher.

The best solution to this problem is to design the room so that you have an enclosed equipment-and-connection area where you can put the equipment that you don't need to physically access to watch a program or listen to something — such as special equipment needed for whole-home audio and video systems. Your equipment and connection area could be a well-ventilated closet, if one is available. We've even seen really sophisticated setups with a false wall behind the TV and equipment racks to allow access to the backs of all of the gear (or that have pull-out shelves that give you easy access to the back, as well). If you have space for a rack, you can probably store a lot of your active componentry there, too.

If you can't find a separate space for your gear, you can at least make your environment neater and more professional-looking by hiding some of the wiring in the walls or in fake molding, and making the local connections available via wall outlets. You can use short cables to connect these outlets to the equipment itself. In this fashion, you don't have lumpy wires traveling under the rugs and wires that little children can easily grab.

Zoning inside your home

When most people think about a home theater, they think within a pretty confined box — the place where the home theater is going to be. And certainly, that's the predominant focus of this book.

However, a major theme that we'll hammer at (until you agree with us) is that you should spend a little extra money and be a little smarter in your planning so that you can access this great asset elsewhere around the house.

Creating *zones* around your house is a great way to extend your audio asset. When you go to buy your receiver or amplifier, the concept of *multizone* is going to come up. A multizone system allows you to access different sources and send them to independent outputs simultaneously. For example, your kids could be watching *Rugrats* in the living room, and you could be listening to *Dunne Roman* (www.dunneroman.com) in the kitchen. How cool is that!

We don't go into a lot of detail on this here; we cover it extensively in Chapter 17. But we want to mention it up front for the following reasons:

✔ This is a good reason why you are going to need to think out-side just your home theater (and another reason why a wiring panel makes a good idea).

✔ This is something you need to plan and budget for. Multizone means extra wiring and cables, extra speakers, possibly an extra amplifier, possibly extra controls, and some extra cost. (But it's well worth it.)

Doing It Yourself versus Hiring the Pros

A lot of home theater you can do yourself. However, if you want it done right, you may want to bring in some experts to comple-ment your work. If you don't have the right electrical outlets at your desired electronic station, for instance, you might call in an electrical contractor to put in dedicated home run electrical cables (so you're not on the same circuit as the dishwasher and have spikes hitting your system all the time). Also, setting up front pro-jection is an art and better left to professionals. And there's noth-ing like having your system fine-tuned by a professional who really can tell if your sound is just right. Still, you can do all of this your-self, with some patience (and respect for the live conductors in your electrical system).

If you want a professional to set up your entire system, you proba-bly need to be shopping in the high-end price range. We rarely see anyone brought in to help on systems sub-$10,000, and almost always it takes a $25,000+ system to get most contractors excited. So if you are on the low end of the equation, you'll probably do a lot yourself or rely heavily on the local installation services of the store from which you buy your equipment. Even if your dealer doesn't want to do the entire installation for you, we suggest you see if they can do a system calibration for you. If you buy online, expect to do most of the work yourself.

Home Theater For Dummies does not presume you are going to hire anyone. You should be able to plan, design, and install a very pro-fessional sounding (and looking) home theater system after read-ing this book. We just want you to know your alternatives, in case you get halfway through and need some help. Check out the earlier sidebar, "Who can help if you need it?" for some ideas.

The people involved in your project is dependent on the size of your project and whether you are building a new home, renovating an old one, or simply making do with that spare room in the basement. In the end, it will vary according to what you're trying to accomplish. If you plan to put a major home theater in your home — complete with theater seats, a popcorn and candy stand, and screen curtains — you may want to bring a home-theater consultant into the process. However, we've seen some very imaginative do-it-yourself (DIY) home theaters that trade love and patience for consultants and big bills, and the results are truly amazing.

Want some confidence that you can do this (and get some neat ideas for your own installation)? Check out all the DIY home theater projects at www.hometheatertalk.com and www.hometheaterforum.com.

If you do bring in some help, make sure that you choose advisors who share your vision of an ideal home theater. The people you choose should have experience with a broad range of home theaters, not just expensive or cheap ones. Find your home theater personality and match it with your contractors, and you'll have a winning combination.

You might have a hard time finding some of these contractors. For the more traditional groups of professionals (such as architects), we tend to rely on word-of-mouth, recommendations from in-the-know friends, and a thorough review of the contractor's references. For contractors who will be installing your home's electronics and wiring infrastructure, we do these same things, as well as check their credentials. The Custom Electronics Design & Installation Association, or CEDIA, has a rigorous training and qualification program for people who do nothing but build and install home theater systems for a living. There is a CEDIA Finder Service at www.cedia.net/homeowners/finder.php.

Chapter 3

The ABCs of Home Theater Audio

. . . .

. . . .

*I*n the early days of corporate video conferencing, system designers struggled to balance the audio and video needs for a video conference, with the cost for the transmission to carry the signals (which was really expensive). So there was a lot of focus on compressing the audio and video to low sizes and figuring out the right mix between the two.

One trend became clear quickly: When test subjects were presented with all the different variants and permutations possible for different transmission speeds, they always preferred to have better audio at the price of video, than vice versa. In other words, they preferred to accept crappy video rather than deal with bad audio.

Although you'd like to have the best of all possible worlds in all aspects of your home theater, we think you'll probably focus on audio first (at least we'd recommend it) for three reasons:

  ✔ The videoconferencing effect we just noted.

  ✔ The fact that your home theater also doubles as a home concert hall, so you want your audio CDs to sound perfect, too.

  ✔ Video display prices are dropping faster than any other device in a home theater, so if you are going to put off one purchase, putting of the video display makes a lot of sense.

For these reasons, we start our discussion of home theater technologies with audio first.

Surrounding Yourself with Sound

Unless you plan on installing a 360-degree Cinema-in-the-Round screen in your home, just like you'd see at Disney World, video plays a rather confined (but still big) role in creating the home theater illusion of "being" in the movie. The real job of surrounding yourself in the scene falls to your multichannel surround sound audio system.

Imagine on the screen are the soon-to-be victims of a firing squad, and from behind you, you hear the clicks of the rifles as they chamber a round. That sensation is brought to you by your rear channel-driven surround sound system. It simply does not carry the same weight for the sound to be coming from in front of you, when you can't see the firing squad.

Two-channel sound versus multi-channel surround sound

Most of us are used to age-old *two-channel* sound — that is, the stereo sound that gives us a left and a right speaker effect. *Multi-channel surround sound* builds on this by adding a front center speaker between the front left and right speakers, and adding two surround speakers. More recent versions of surround sound add two more rear speakers and side surround speakers to really enhance your surround soundfield. A subwoofer is part of all home theater setups, but as we discuss later in this chapter, a subwoofer is actually more a part of the bass management of the collective speakers than part of the surround sound system itself. Nonetheless, something needs to shake the room when the dinosaur's feet stomp the jeep in *Jurassic Park*!

To understand the impact of the concept of surround sound on your home theater, you need to understand a bit about *encoding* and *decoding* sound. When the master mixers at the movie studios create the audio track to go with the movie, they encode the music in some very specific ways. They designate which *channel* (you can read *speaker* into that if you like) the specific sound goes through. The goal is to decode those signals onto the right channels to replicate the studio's intent.

So let's say that a squadron of jets in a scene from *Top Gun* is doing a fly-by of the carrier command bridge. If we were in the command bridge, we would hear the jets coming in from the left, sweeping across in front of us, and then disappearing to the right and the rear as they turn off to the starboard side of the ship. If you are sitting in a well-tuned home theater, you should hear no differently. And in fact, as the bridge shakes, your subwoofers (and bass shakers, which we talk about in Chapter 21) provide you with the vibrations to make you feel you were actually there. Now we're talking surround sound!

To get you to this point, the encoders have to designate on the DVD track the specific sounds that, at specific times, are to be sent to specific channels in your system. Your speakers, connected to those channels, are given those signals by your surround sound-equipped A/V receiver, which properly decodes those tracks from the DVD. A home theater audio system needs to have it all correct from beginning to end.

In a 2-channel system, you might hear some of that effect, in that it might get the left and right part right. A 2-channel system can't help with the front to back movement, however, and that's the critical part of a surround sound system — it surrounds you!

Understanding surround sound lingo

For the most part, the entertainment industry boils down a lot of the surround sound terminology into numbers, such as 2.0, 5.1, and 7.1. Sometimes these refer to the playback system's speaker configuration, and sometimes these refer to the audio signal format being delivered. The lingo can be confusing especially when the speakers do not match the audio signals, but it's all perfectly normal for that to occur. In these numbers, the first number represents the number of speakers or main audio channels involved, and the 1 or 0 after the decimal point indicates whether or not the system has a subwoofer or supports a low frequency effects channel. Systems that end in 1 have a subwoofer or an effects channel.

Here's a rundown of the different numbers you'll probably encounter and what they mean:

- ✔ **2.0:** Normal stereo, which has a left and a right channel, is 2.0 in surround sound speak.

- ✔ **5.1:** This is the primary format for creating and delivering surround sound. It is in wide use in movie theaters, digital television, DVD-Video and Audio, and even the latest game consoles. Source signals have the five main channels and one LFE bass effects channel. Playback systems usually have five main speakers and one subwoofer.

- ✔ **5.1-channel ready:** Such an audio system has six discrete inputs to accept a 5.1 signal from a signal source such as a

5.1-channel DVD player. It does not necessarily mean these products can actually decode signals to a 5.1-channel output. The best way to ferret out true 5.1 systems is by reading reviews of the devices before you buy (we recommend many places to find these reviews in Chapter 24).

- ✔ **6.1:** 6.1-channel systems have an additional surround channel called the *back surround channel*. This drives a speaker (or preferably two) situated right behind the viewers, which in essence provides the same smooth flow in the back soundfield that the center speaker enables in the front speaker group. Dozens of DVDs are encoded with extra back surround information for this back surround speaker, and these DVDs also play perfectly well on regular 5.1 systems.

- ✔ **7.1:** Not to be outdone, some have taken the 5.1 or 6.1 channel encoding on a DVD and used some computer horsepower to create two, independent back surround speakers for even more surround sound, making it 7.1. Note that 7.1 is not a true surround sound format (there are no DVDs on the market with 7.1 channels of sound), but instead it refers to manufacturers' own systems used to derive two back surround channels from existing stereo or 5.1-channel sources.

- ✔ **8.1 and beyond:** You'll probably hear about even higher designations, 8.1, 9.1, 10.2, and so on. These are truly in the realm of the home theaterphile, and if you're evaluating such gear, a home theater consultant is probably standing next to you, so just follow his or her recommendations.

Bass management

Bass management is how your home theater manages the low frequency sounds. Better A/V receivers and other controller devices will have several options for how you want to handle the bass sounds in your system. If you have nice tall speakers that have a very effective bass range of their own (often called *full range speakers*), you might pass all bass frequencies to them. If you want smaller speakers that can sit on a shelf, then the bass frequencies might fall to the subwoofer, which is a speaker designed to play low-frequency sounds. One area that causes a lot of confusion is the difference between the *Low Frequency Effect channel* (LFE) and the subwoofer channel. The LFE channel is encoded in the soundtrack of a DVD or other surround sound source; the subwoofer channel is the connection on the back of your A/V receiver that provides amplified low frequency sound signals to your subwoofer. The LFE channel is encoded in surround sound material — it's the ".1" in 5.1 and other surround sound formats. This low frequency sound is often sent to the subwoofer channel in your surround sound system, but it doesn't necessarily have to be sent exclusively to your subwoofer. For example, some people send these low frequency sounds to both the subwoofer and to the front left and right speakers. The bass management system within your A/V receiver (or A/V controller) lets you customize these settings to best fit your A/V system (we discuss how to set this up in Chapter 18).

You don't have to have a subwoofer to take advantage of the LFE channel, because many normal left/right speakers can take these cues from your receiver and play the sound accordingly. But having a subwoofer gives you that stomach-rattling, vibrating-room effect at just the right times — an effect we're sure you'll want to take advantage of.

Dolby Galore

Here's where surround sound gets complicated, unfortunately. There are a host of different terms and brand names applied to everything we just described, and these terms can get downright confusing.

When you go to optimize your home theater, however, you need to understand these terms. Because you probably have some older gear in your home audio and video system already, and because some older movies use older encoding schemes, we mention older terms, too, so that you can have the big picture.

We start with Dolby (`www.dolby.com`). You've probably seen Dolby on your cassette tape deck for years and seen advertisements for Dolby Digital at the beginning of movies. But you've probably never known exactly what Dolby does. Well stand by, because we're going to make you look smart on your next date at the movies.

Dolby surround sound

You have to go back a few years to get to where we are today. Although Dolby has been enhancing sound for decades, the true mother of all surround sound encoding schemes is Dolby Surround (introduced in 1982), which encodes four analog audio channels into two channels for storage and/or transmission. If you play Dolby Surround on a normal stereo, you get two channels. If you play it on a Dolby Surround-enabled decoder device, the device separates the full four channels for playback. Over 40 million consumer products have been shipped with Dolby Surround Pro Logic decoding on-board. That's a lot.

With Dolby Surround, the four channels encode front left, front center, front right, and monophonic surround as their channels. The left, center, and right channels are *full-range* channels, meaning that they carry the full range (20 Hz to 20 kHz) of audio frequencies. The fourth surround sound channel is a *limited bandwidth channel,* meaning that it carries only a subset of the frequency range (not the real low frequency stuff).

At first, consumer audio/video receivers with Dolby Surround decoders could only separate the left, right, and monophonic surround speaker channels. However, with the advent of Dolby Pro Logic in 1987, receivers could decode the center channel as well. The consumer devices just took awhile to develop the same processing power that the more expensive movie theaters had onboard.

Dolby Pro Logic is what's called a *matrixed* multichannel system, meaning that some channels are actually derived from other channels. In this case, the center channel and surround channels are created from the existing left and right channels — the two channels we mention earlier, which are used to transport the encoded signals.

So with Dolby Pro Logic, you have four channels and five speakers, with the two surround speakers playing essentially the same monophonic sound. You often see a subwoofer channel on Pro Logic receivers as well; note that this is not a separate channel, but is derived from the low frequency information from the front channels.

One problem with the dual monophonic surround sound channels is that, in some ways, they defeat the purpose of having surround sound. You can't send information specifically to one speaker, as is done with a left or right front speaker. And because they have the same signal, they tend to create a localized sound field between the speakers — and that goes against surround sound's goal of creating a large diffuse background soundfield. Proper placement of the surround speakers on the side walls aiming across the listening area helps achieve the optimal results. (In Chapter 11, we discuss dipole speakers and how they can help with this.)

A newer version of Pro Logic, Dolby Pro Logic II, came out in 2001. The biggest new feature that Pro Logic II offers is a fuller sound experience for two-channel stereo sources that were being played over 5.1 channel systems. Pro Logic II does extra processing and extends the Pro Logic work substantially. Importantly, Pro Logic II decodes the surround sound speakers in full bandwidth stereo, and therefore provides a more complete rear soundfield.

Dolby Digital arrives on the scene

It was the advent of Dolby Digital in 1997 that really started to make things interesting. As you would surmise, Dolby Digital is all digital, so it's available only for digital content. DVD and HDTV content use Dolby Digital (DVDs may also contain some other system, such as DTS). To give you an idea of scope, by the beginning of 2003, more than 290 million consumer devices had shipped with Dolby Digital on-board, and more than 4,500 films are encoded in Dolby Digital. It's the scheme you want your equipment to support.

You probably need to buy a new receiver to take advantage of the latest in encoding technologies — in other words, Dolby Digital. Dolby Digital represents the current minimum level of performance that you should require from your system. Any receiver with Dolby Digital decoding can also decode Pro Logic.

What's so great about Dolby Digital is that it encodes six discrete audio channels. (*Discrete* means that the sound signal contained in each of the six available channels is distinct and independent from each of the others.) Remember that the older Dolby Surround encoded four channels onto 2-channel soundtracks, and that often resulted in all sorts of bleed-overs between channels and less than clear demarcations in the sound levels.

Because Dolby Digital has six clean channels, your receivers and controllers can precisely control the different elements of your sound mix. Importantly, the rear surround speakers are each fed by their own independent channels, enabling true spatial separation for that rear soundfield. With this setup, when you hear that bullet whiz by or that starship warp overhead, the sound moving across your entire speaker system is smooth and controlled — and in digital. This is the home theater your momma always warned you about!

Dolby's ability to encode and decode information is only as strong as its source data. If it is working with a 2-channel stereo movie, then you may see something like Dolby Digital 2.0 on the package, designating that it is a stereo signal being encoded and decoded using Dolby Digital. But it's still a stereo signal.

You may hear some people talk about Dolby Digital and Dolby Pro Logic as a choice between more expensive and less expensive technology, and these people may start discussing whether you really need Digital at all. What a pile of bunk. Tell them the Earth is flat and to go for a good long row on the ocean. The future of home theater is digital. All content and components are moving digital. If you have a Dolby Surround or Pro Logic receiver, you can rest comfortably knowing that more than 14,000 films are encoded with these technologies and so you've got a way to go before they become obsolete. But if buying new, go Dolby Digital, and make sure you have Pro Logic II on-board to make the best use of all those stereo movie and music recordings.

We talk more about how your DVD, HDTV, and other gear supports Dolby Digital and how to make sure it is all set correctly, in later chapters, notably, Chapter 6. For now, know that this is the baseline upon which you grow.

Dolby Digital Surround EX

Back surround speakers are a relatively new development made possible by an additional surround channel that drives the center back surround speaker. This is 6.1 in industry parlance. Dolby avoids 6.1 and calls it Dolby Digital Surround EX.

The back Surround EX channel does not have its own encoded channel. Instead, its signal is matrixed in (intermixed) with the left and right surround channels, just like Dolby Pro Logic has the center speaker information encoded in the left and right front speakers.

The first consumer devices with Surround EX were based on licenses from Lucasfilm THX (www.thx.com), so you'll probably see it called THX Surround EX in stores and online when you're doing some shopping.

THX isn't a surround sound format itself, but rather a *certification and testing* program for home (and movie) theater equipment and movies. So equipment like A/V receivers and speakers may be THX certified, as may DVDs themselves. THX's main mission in life is to create a set of standards for surround sound playback, and to then certify that equipment or DVDs meet those standards. A big part of these standards revolves around THX's criteria for the levels and equalization of the sound sent to the surround speakers.

Many newer DVDs are encoded for Dolby Digital EX and have that extra channel of surround information on-board. Also, if you're playing a regular Dolby Digital 5.1-channel DVD, a THX Ultra 2 decoder can simulate 6.1- or 7.1-channel surround by processing the audio information in the regular surround channels and sending the information to your back surround speaker.

If you're playing a movie (say on a DVD) that's been encoded using Dolby Digital EX, and you have only a regular Dolby Digital decoder in your A/V receiver, you won't have any problems. You still get the full 5.1 surround sound you expect. You just won't get that extra surround channel behind you.

DTS: Bring It On!

Dolby is not the only game in town, although it clearly has the lead in the marketplace. Digital Theater Systems (DTS) has invented a competing lineup of surround sound encoding schemes. The first movie to use DTS was *Jurassic Park.*

As with Dolby Digital, DTS Digital Surround provides 5.1 channels of digital audio. However, DTS uses less compression (higher data rate) than Dolby Digital. Where Dolby Digital encodes six channels with 384,000 or 448,000 bits per second, DTS, in its master quality mode, encodes 1,536,000 bits per second, which many audiophiles believe delivers a better sound quality. Of course, that means that the DTS encoding takes up more space on a DVD, so the DVD doesn't have as much room for extra features, such as foreign languages, commentaries, and multiple versions of the movie.

The DVD powers that be require all DVDs to carry either a Dolby Digital or a PCM soundtrack to ensure compatibility with all DVD players. Because DTS is an optional feature of DVD, DTS has an uphill battle getting studios on board, because the space on DVDs is limited. (For these space reasons, most DVDs containing a DTS soundtrack are encoded at half the 1.536Mbps rate mentioned above in order to retain the Dolby version and other content.) Today, a few hundred DVDs are issued with master quality DTS Digital Surround.

You might hear of some other DTS innovations:

- ✔ **DTS-ES:** DTS-ES uses existing digital multichannel technology to deliver the 5.1 channels of regular DTS. It also adds a discrete (meaning each channel is individually encoded, instead of being combined with others), full-bandwidth back surround channel. That additional channel may be played through one or two speakers.

- ✔ **DTS-Neo:6:** DTS Neo:6 Music and Neo:6 Cinema are decoding techniques for stereo or Dolby Surround-encoded, 2-channel sources. Neo:6 Music keeps the front left and right channels intact while synthesizing the center and surround channels from the 2-channel source. Neo:6 Cinema can create a 6.1-channel signal from 2-channel movie sources.

The bottom line on DTS is that the DTS folks have some innovative algorithms, but the sheer prevalence of the Dolby solutions clearly makes it the solution for the masses. Most higher-end A/V receivers offer both DTS and Dolby Digital options, so you can try them both and set your receiver to your preference.

Other Key Audio Standards

In the realm of "music only" (and yes, we play a lot of music in our systems, in addition to movies and college basketball games and other video content), you might hear about a few other audio standards. We don't spend a ton of time beating these into your head — mainly because you don't need to do a lot to your system to accommodate them. With the exception of MP3 (which might take some special gear), these are things that you just plug in, and they work.

I want my MP3

MP3 is great for online music trading and downloading because it uses a compression scheme to make the files small enough to be easily downloaded. You don't find any MP3 music encoded in movies on DVD, nor will you (typically) find MP3 encoded music in stores. MP3 comes into play when you start getting involved in online music downloading or when you want to move your CD collection to a computer hard drive. We talk about these activities in more detail in Chapter 5.

MP3 is designed to be an efficient encoding system for taking big fat PCM music files and moving them into download-friendly computer files. MP3 trades a little sound quality for a lot of room (it's another of those *lossy* compression systems, which means that the system removes some information). So MP3 files are typically ten times smaller than the corresponding PCM files on a compact disc.

PCM is perfect

PCM (or pulse code modulation) is not really perfect — nothing is. But it's pretty darn close. PCM is an older (but still vital) system for encoding and compressing analog music (such as the sound from a guitar amplifier) into a digital format that can be saved on a computer disk or "burned" onto a CD.

We say that PCM is nearly perfect because it's a *lossless* coding system, which means that what goes in comes out exactly the same, bit for bit. In a PCM world, none of the sound is thrown away. If you have sharp ears and a good system, PCM-based files sound better than MP3s, for example. Traditional CDs are based on PCM, as are the sound files on many computers, such as .wav files on a Windows computer.

PCM isn't the only lossless system out there. Another one is MLP, or Meridian Lossless Packing, which is used by the new DVD-Audio format and discussed in Chapter 5. Another new audio format is the SACD, which we also discuss in Chapter 5. It uses its own coding format called DSD (or direct stream digital).

The bottom line here is that for the utmost in digital audio reproduction, lossless is the way to go.

Chapter 4

The (ABC) DEFs of Home Theater

*W*e call the video portion of a home theater a *display*. Your display can be a direct-view television, a rear-projected television, a front-projected screen, a plasma or LCD screen, or even a properly painted wall (as long as you combine it with a projector).

Whatever its form factor, the video aspect of your home theater tends to be the main focus of many people. Let's face it — a big-screen display simply overpowers mere A/V source equipment and controllers. Big screens are just plain cool!

There's a lot to know about video formats, though, and in this section, we lay the groundwork for more a detailed discussion of specific video options in Part III.

Learning to Talk Videoese

Before we talk about the different kinds of analog and digital video, it's worthwhile to find out how to talk about video. Like any other technology, video has its own set of arcane terms and other jargon that makes casual listeners just want to give up. We promise not to lay too much on you here, but a few key concepts are essential:

✔ **Resolution:** At a high level, resolution is basically the level of detail that your eyes (or a good pair of eyes, if yours have gotten a little blurry from too much time in front of the computer) can *resolve* (or see) on the screen. In the PC world, this is measured according to the number of *pixels* (the individual points of light and color) on your monitor. For example, smaller home-PC displays are set to show 800 x 600 pixels. Video systems are typically measured by the vertical number (the smaller of the two) — usually by measuring the *scan lines* that move across your screen and by counting up the number of these lines stacked on top of each other. Video systems typically display 480; 720; or 1,080 of these lines.

✔ **Fields and frames:** This is a hangover from the film world, where each individual picture on a reel of film is called a frame (and 24 of them flash by the projector bulb each second). When TV was first developed, the technology of the day wouldn't allow full frames to be displayed at the rate at which TV signals worked, so each frame was divided into two *fields,* each of which contained half the scan lines we discuss in the preceding bullet (all the odd lines in one field, and all the evens in the other). Traditional TV systems display 60 fields every second — 30 frames per second.

✔ **Scanning method:** Up until very recently, just about all video systems (all the common ones, at least) used something called *interlaced* scanning, which we actually describe in the preceding bullet. In an interlaced system, half the lines are drawn on the screen in one cycle of the video system, and in the next cycle, the other half are drawn (not the top and the bottom, but weaving — or interlacing — every other line). Because this happens really fast (each set of lines is drawn 30 times per second), your eye can't really tell that things are being drawn this way — unless you stop to think about the flickering you see and the way some vertical and diagonal lines on your TV screen appear jagged. *Progressive scan* systems draw all the lines (a whole frame) at the same time and can help reduce these characteristics. The effect is a picture that is more like film, which is what we're shooting for in a home theater.

Switching from Analog to Digital

Television is undergoing some radical changes — and we're not talking about programming. Like most other devices before it, the television is beginning to make the leap from the analog to the digital world. Unlike many of those devices, however, TV is making the leap in a series of agonizingly slow steps. In this section, we discuss how this transition might affect your choices in the video world. We talk also about the various kinds of TVs you can buy.

The conversion from analog to digital and old-style TV to next-generation TV comes into play in many places:

✔ The encoding of the programming signal itself — whether it goes onto a DVD or over a cable to get to your home theater

✔ The transmission (or production) path that the signal takes in getting to your house

✔ The receiver — internal or external — that receives and decodes the signal for display

In the progression of standards and technical development, change is taking place along all three of these paths.

Understanding the current standard: The analog signal

The vast majority of television signals coming into homes are still analog. Analog TV signals reach homes through over-the-air broadcast TV, by traditional cable TV systems, and by satellite.

In North America, an analog system known as NTSC (National Television Standards Committee) has been in place for decades. In fact, it hasn't been changed or updated since the advent of color television in the 1960s. Although this system is capable of producing a surprisingly good picture under ideal circumstances, its analog nature makes it susceptible to various kinds of interference and signal degradation. Consequently, the picture can be downright awful by the time it actually gets to your television, which is why the TV world is slowly turning digital.

 Analog television displays a maximum of 480 scan lines (525 total, but you can't see them all because some are used for things such as closed captioning), displays 30 frames (60 fields) per second, and is an interlaced system. See "Learning to Talk Videoese," earlier in this chapter, for explanations of these specs.

Just as the NTSC standard is common in North America (and Japan), a couple of other standards — known as PAL and SECAM — are common in other parts of the world. Unless you have a special TV designed for the purpose, you can't watch PAL with an NTSC TV, and so on. This is one reason why you can't buy videotapes in many parts of the world and use them at home.

Making film into video

As if resolution and scan rates were not complex enough, you may run into something called 3:2 pulldown removal, or simply 3:2 pulldown. This is a process that deals with the fact that an extra field (screen) image appears when the 24-frames-per-second films are transferred to 30 frames per second for TV (or 60 fields). See, when you take 24 frames and make them fill a 60-field space, your system will copy each field two or three times, in alternating sequence, to fill the 60 fields required. This creates motion artifacts that appear like jerky movements on the screen when you look closely.

What 3:2 pulldown does is remove that extra third field, so the original balance between frames is restored. You want a progressive scan DVD player with great 3:2 pulldown removal. You can tell how good it is by looking at sharp lines on the screen, such as telephone wires or porch railings. Some fancier TVs have their own 3:2 pull-down systems built in, as well, in case your DVD player can't do this for you.

Anticipating the rise of digital TV

The move from analog to digital is well afoot. Millions of homes have some form of digital TV, but the conversion from analog to digital is still an evolving process. The key concept behind any kind of digital TV is that the audio and video programming is converted from an analog signal into a series of digital bits (a whole lot of ones and zeros that make up a video picture). The primary technology behind any kind of digital TV (at least in the United States and Canada — other countries have their own variant of digital TV) is something called *MPEG* (Motion Picture Experts Group).

Several video and audio compression and digitization standards are based on MPEG. Most are named by adding a number to the end of the word *MPEG*. The MPEG-2 standard is by far the most common in the video world, with MPEG-4 coming on strong.

The digital television (cable or satellite) and DVDs that most people receive today use MPEG-2 as their encoding to digitally transport or store standard, analog NTSC signals. This is an important fact to repeat: Typically, when you use a digital TV system (such as a DSS satellite system) or a prerecorded digital source (such as a DVD), you get an analog signal that has been transmitted or stored digitally. The signal itself, the program that goes into your TV, is still analog. Digital over digital is our nirvana and is coming soon, as we discuss shortly.

Even though the video signal coming out of a DVD player is NTSC (an interlaced format, as we mentioned above), some DVD players can convert this into a progressive scan version of NTSC, if you have a progressive scan TV.

When this digitized signal gets to your house (over a digital cable system, a DBS satellite system, or on a DVD), a set-top box or DVD player converts the signal back to analog NTSC TV, which your TV understands and can display. This digital transmission signal coming into your house usually looks and sounds better than an analog one because the digital transmission path is cleaner and isn't susceptible to the interference that usually messes up analog signals. The same is true of DVD versus analog sources, such as laser discs and VCR tapes. Digital is always better.

You can get better-quality analog content on DVD, and higher-quality DVDs are on the way. For instance, you might run across Superbit DVD, which is a Sony standard for super-encoding (using more digital bits and bytes to store) DVD content. Superbit DVD follows the existing DVD format, so you don't need a special player to play a Superbit DVD. Simply, these discs use storage space that's normally taken up by fancy on-screen menus and extra features (such as movie trailers and outtakes), and the discs use that space to store more encoding (about double the bits) for the movie signal itself. The result is a much more stunning picture.

Looking toward the next generation of digital TV

Today's digital television isn't all it can be. Several years ago, the FCC (the controlling regulatory authority for broadcasters, cable companies, and telephone companies in the United States) brought together a big bunch of television industry folks. After a long, painful, and contentious process, the group came up with a new generation of digital TV. This new system goes by the catchy name ATSC (Advanced Television Standards Committee), and follows a bunch of new, higher-definition television standards.

Introducing ATSC

Specifically, ATSC uses digital-video signals (not analog ones) that are transmitted using digital technologies and are played on TVs set up to display these digital signals. Even the connection to the TV itself is digital. "It's digital all the way, baby," as sportscaster Dick Vitale would say. (Did we mention we're Duke Blue Devils fans, too!)

ATSC TVs and DVDs

Hollywood has been concerned about making digitized versions of its content available to the masses for fear of mass duplication by film pirates. So while there are digital (DVI or FireWire) connections for ATSC systems (and for D-VHS player/recorders, which we discuss in Chapter 6), you won't find a digital video connection on any DVD player. You can connect a DVD player to an ATSC (and get a superb picture), but you can't do it digitally. We discuss this in more detail in Chapter 6. Just know for now that it'll be a while before you can take a DVD and connect it in a fully digital fashion to your HDTV.

And, as we already mentioned, although DVD is a digital format, it outputs an analog NTSC video signal, not ATSC.

Many people call ATSC *digital TV* or *DTV*. We do, too, sometimes, but we're going to stick with the name ATSC in this discussion to help keep the difference between ATSC and other digital television services (like digital cable or digital satellite TV) distinct. Aren't we user-friendly?

Even though ATSC is all digital, TVs that are designed for ATSC can also connect to good old analog NTSC systems as well. And some of the stuff coming in over an ATSC system is NTSC. For example, commercials will probably continue to be taped using NTSC systems for quite some time (though this NTSC signal will be carried digitally over the ATSC system).

ATSC television standards are different than the digital cable or satellite TV we discuss in the preceding section. To view them in all their glory (and we've seen enough of high-definition television to tell you that it is indeed glorious), you need to buy the newer, fancier, better, more expensive TV.

Exploring HDTV

When we talk about new ATSC-based televisions, we're talking a whole new ballgame (or at least a whole new way to watch a ballgame). It takes only a glance to see the striking difference between older NTSC displays and the new ATSC ones.

ATSC signals can be divided into different groups, depending on the resolution and the scanning method (which we discuss in the beginning of this chapter). They are further divided into

✔ **SDTV (standard-definition television):** These signals are about the same or a little bit better than NTSC.

✔ **HDTV (high-definition television):** HDTV has truly spectacular, filmlike, picture quality.

Within the ATSC standard there are 18 SDTV and HDTV variations, but you're most likely to see just four, as shown in Table 4-1.

Table 4-1	Common Digital-TV Variants		
Name	*Lines of Resolution*	*Scanning Method*	*Quality*
480i	480	Interlaced	Standard definition (same as NTSC)
480p	480	Progressive	Standard definition
720p	720	Progressive	High definition
1080i	1080	Interlaced	High definition

Theoretically, a progressive scan system has a better picture than an interlaced one, but in our minds, resolution is more important (not everyone agrees). We'd rather have 1080i than 720p if given the choice. But we'd take either kind of HDTV over anything else. It's just awesome to see HDTV in action.

To take advantage of all the benefits of digital TV, you'll eventually have to replace your televisions. Today's televisions don't have the internal circuitry to decode digital TV signals, and they generally don't have screens that can display high-definition ATSC pictures in all their glory. (And HDTV is the big deal in this story — we focus our discussion on HDTV rather than SDTV.)

Traditional TVs aren't even the right shape. The *aspect ratio* (the ratio of screen width to height) of HDTV signals is wider than that of NTSC signals. NTSC is 4:3; HDTV is 16:9. Figure 4-1 shows the difference in aspect ratios. The HDTV screen has an aspect ratio like the elongated screens in movie theaters. (You may have already been exposed to this aspect ratio because many movie DVDs today allow for this sort of viewing as an option. See the sidebar, "Wide, wider, widest: Aspect ratios," later in this chapter.

4:3 / 1.33:1 Standard TV and older movies	16:9 / 1.78:1 US Digital TV (HDTV)	1.85:1 Standard Widescreen	2.35:1 Anamorphic Widescreen (Panavision or Cinemascope)

Figure 4-1: An HDTV screen is much wider than today's NTSC screen.

HDTV-capable TV sets, which became available at the end of 1998, are more expensive than traditional sets. However, prices have come down significantly. Just three or four years ago, HDTVs were often more than $6,000, but now you can get one for $1,000 or less. We talk a lot more about HDTVs in Chapters 12 and 13.

After the switch to digital TV is complete, you don't have to pitch your old TVs. Special, separate digital TV tuners (such set-top boxes used for older TVs on cable networks) enable you to watch DTV programming on older TVs. Of course, the picture quality and resolution won't be as high as it would be with a new digital set, and you might not have a widescreen (16:9) aspect ratio. But you can see (at today's resolutions and quality) the programming coming in over tomorrow's digital networks.

Wide, wider, widest: Aspect ratios

Aspect ratios are one of the more confusing parts of video, although they used to be simple. That's because television and movie content was all about the same size, 4:3 (also known as 1.33:1, meaning that the picture was 1.33 times as long as it was high). The Academy (as in, "I'd like to thank the Academy") Standard before 1952 was 1.37:1, so there was virtually no problem showing movies on TV.

However, as TV began to cut into Hollywood's take at the theater, the quest was on to differentiate theater offerings in ways that could not be seen on TV. Thus, innovations such as widescreen film, Technicolor, and even 3-D were born.

Widescreen film was one of the innovations that survived and has since dominated the cinema. Today, you tend to find films in one of two widescreen aspect ratios:

✔ Academy Standard (or "Flat"), which has an aspect ratio of 1.85:1.

✔ Anamorphic Scope (or "Scope"), which has an aspect ratio of 2.35:1. Scope is also called Panavision or CinemaScope.

HDTV is specified at a 16:9 or 1.78:1 aspect ratio.

If your television isn't widescreen, and you want to watch a widescreen film, you've got a problem. And the industry powers that be have come up with two solutions (other than "go out and buy a widescreen display").

The most common approach in the past has been what's called Pan and Scan. For each frame of a film, a decision is made as to what constitutes the action area. That part of the film frame is retained, and the rest is lost. What's left is usually a fraction of the main frame, sometimes as little as 65 percent of it, and this can often leave out the best parts of a picture. Wow. Imagine some of the scenes from Gunfight at OK Corral with the two gunslingers at each end of the picture. One of the gunfighters would have to go off the screen in Pan and Scan.

The second (and growing more popular) approach is to display the original full image on the TV set without filling the whole screen. When watching content formatted for a widescreen TV (1.85:1, 2.35:1, and so on), you see black bars at the top and bottom of the image. This technique is known as letterboxing (after the effect of seeing an image through an open mail slot in a door). Conversely, when watching content formatted for TV (4:3) on a widescreen TV, you see black bars on the left and right of the images. This is known as windowboxing.

An obvious problem with viewing widescreen images on a normal 4:3 TV is that the image does not use all 480 scanning lines of the screen. Some of those 480 lines get used just to draw black bars, instead of drawing video you actually watch. (Some 4:3 TVs use a technique called anamorphic squeeze to eliminate this issue.) This yields lower resolution, something that anamorphic formats attempt to resolve. Also known as 16:9 Enhanced, Widescreen Enhanced, or Enhanced for 16:9 Televisions, anamorphic presentation squeezes the image horizontally until the full 4:3 frame is filled. If you were to look at an anamorphic picture on a 4:3 screen, the picture appears somewhat distorted because everything is compressed, the full 480 lines of content are retained. Luckily, when you tell your DVD player you have a 4:3 screen, it puts the anamorphic image back into a letterbox. When played through a 16:9 player, the original width is presented, while maintaining the full 480 vertical lines of resolution.

Most DVDs have both a Pan and Scan and a widescreen format (either letterboxed or anamorphic) on a DVD. Because including both versions creates an added expense to the studios, some DVDs ship with just one format on-board, and some titles actually have different formats on different discs. Be sure to check before you buy a disc, if this is important to you.

Look Ma, It Can Do Audio, Too!

The DVD format was enhanced in the late 1990s to enable high-quality audio storage, too. Dubbed DVD-Audio, or DVD-A, it can store much greater sound quality for the same musical selection as a CD. A DVD-A disc can store both two-channel stereo as well as 6-channel surround sound for any given musical selection. You decide which you want to play. (We talk about DVD players in Chapter 6.)

A couple of things distinguish DVD-A from CDs:

- ✔ **Sampling rate:** A CD samples the music input at 44.1 kHz. A DVD-A can record from 44.1 kHz up to 192 kHz. The higher the sampling rate, the better the sound quality stored.

- ✔ **Sample word length:** The quality of a sample depends in part on the number of bits that are created during each sampling period. A CD sampling process uses 16-bit words, where the DVD-A format stores words of up to 24 bits. The greater the number of bits in the sample, the better the sound quality stored.

- ✔ **Lossless compression:** The DVD-A format uses Meridian Lossless Packing (MLP Packing) to store its data. This means that bit-for-bit, nothing is lost in the compression and decompression of the stored information. This makes DVD-A highly superior to systems such as Dolby Digital and DTS, which use *lossy compression* (a type of compression in which information is lost and quality is sacrificed for smaller file sizes).

The closest competitor to DVD-A is the SACD (discussed in Chapter 5). Both are extremely high-quality audio sources, and both have their benefits and disadvantages. If you were to pin us down, we honestly couldn't tell you which sounds better. They both sound great to us.

Part II

What Are You Going to Watch?: Source Devices

The 5th Wave   By Rich Tennant

"It's amazing how they always fell asleep during 'Matlock', but this is their third hour watching the live Marilyn Manson concert on MTV."

In this part . . .

*P*art II builds upon the basics with more detailed coverage of all the things that you might want to drive
your home theater — the *source devices* that feed audio
and video into your system.

We start at the, er, source of twentieth-century entertainment — audio sources. These range from the venerable
AM/FM tuners up to the fanciest of MP3 players. After
that, it's on to the video realm, where we talk about things
like DVDs, VCRs, and PVRs (personal video recorders) —
and even how you can bore your neighbors with home
movies on your home theater. Yawn!

Then we discuss sources from outside your home — cable,
broadcast TV, satellite, and even new services that offer
you video on demand and other network-based content.

PCs are on tap next, where we help you understand how
to really take advantage of all audio and video sources
that the Internet has to offer, and how to get them into
your home theater system. We help you understand how
to download movies (legally) off the Internet to watch
whenever you want to and how to record those episodes
of *The Sopranos* that you keep missing.

We close this part with the really fun component in your
home theater — the gaming systems. Whether your heart is
in Xbox, Nintendo, Sony, Sega, or some other system, you'll
want to know how to set these up — even if you don't have
kids. (Pat doesn't, by the way; he needs to have this chapter in the book so he can convince his wife that he really
needs to do research on his Xbox.)

Chapter 5

Treating Your Ears to Music

- -

In This Chapter

▶ Playing that old standby, the CD

▶ Getting into high-resolution audio

▶ Moving MP3s off your computer

▶ Tuning in to the radio world

- -

A home theater is about more than just movies and TV. Most people spend as much money on the audio side of their home theaters as they do on their video equipment.

In this chapter, we discuss the components you might add to a home theater system for listening to prerecorded music and audio broadcasts (what we used to call *radio,* back in the old days — but it's more than just AM/FM now).

Checking Out Your CD Player Options

Since the CD format debuted in the 1980s, over 11 billion CDs have been pressed. So it goes without saying that you need a CD player in your home theater, right? Well, actually, that was a trick question.

Although you *definitely* want your home theater to have a device that can play CDs, you may not need (or want) a traditional CD player in your system. Your DVD player, which we think you absolutely need to have in your home theater, can do double duty as your system's CD player. You can also play CDs on the game consoles we talk about in Chapter 9, or you can use a home theater-ready PC, which we discuss in Chapter 8.

Despite this, you might want a standalone CD player (instead of using another device to play your CDs) for the following reasons:

✔ **You are shooting for the highest quality CD reproduction:** If you're a real audiophile, you might want to spend a considerable chunk of cash on a fancy, no-holds-barred, top-of-the-line CD player that can eek that last little bit of musical fidelity out of a disc. If so, check out companies such as Arcam, Naim, or Rega, which make fancy and expensive ($1,000 and up) CD players.

✔ **You want special CD features:** Some people buy jukebox CD players that can hold hundreds of CDs (so you never need to load a new disc after the hours-long initial setup). Others want a CD player that can also burn (create your own) CDs. Keep in mind that these features are percolating over into the DVD world as well, but for now, the CD versions of these devices are much cheaper.

✔ **You are creating a multizone system:** In a multizone system (which we discuss in Chapter 10), you can listen to different source components in different rooms. For example, you can watch a movie on the DVD player in the home theater, while the kids listen to a CD in the kitchen. Can't do that if the DVD player is your only CD player.

These three reasons are all perfectly valid — for some people. Don't let them scare you into buying a CD player. Today's DVD players do a great job at playing back CDs, so skipping over the standalone CD player is a good way to save a few bucks.

Choosing a CD Player

So you know you want a standalone CD player, but which one? If you've already got a CD player, go ahead and use it. The following list highlights some things you might want to look for if you choose to buy a CD player (or aren't sure about the one you have):

✔ **Digital outputs:** You can often get better sound out of a CD player if you connect it to your receiver via a digital connection instead of an analog one. On the back of a CD player, you can find one (or both) of two kinds of digital outputs — optical and coaxial, which are equal in quality. (We discuss these in Chapter 15.) The key thing to consider, however, is what kind of inputs you have on your receiver, and to buy your CD player accordingly.

✔ **The ability to play CD-Rs, CD-RWs, and MP3s:** If you're into burning your own CDs or like to listen to others' homemade CDs, make sure the player you buy has these buzzwords on the box. Otherwise, you won't be able to listen to those home-made discs.

✔ **Multidisc capability:** If you like to load up the CD player with a bunch of CDs, consider a CD changer, which usually holds five to ten discs, or a CD jukebox that can hold hundreds of discs.

✔ **Remote control:** Many manufacturers have special connect-ors that can go between their components (like a CD player and a receiver) to facilitate controlling everything from a single remote control. For example, with Sony's S-Link, a Sony receiver and remote can control a whole bunch of different Sony devices. As you shop for a CD player, keep your receiver in mind, but if you're set on, say, a Sony CD player and a Pioneer receiver, don't let the remote options hold you back. It's very easy to get a universal remote control that can oper-ate gear from different vendors.

In addition, always look for some basic quality measures when you're choosing gear. For example, does the CD tray open and close smoothly? Can you read the display from across the room? Before you buy, always try to test drive gear in the showroom or your home (if you're shopping at the high end).

The New Kids on the Block — SACD and DVD-A

The CD is overwhelmingly the most common source of prere-corded music in a disc format, but around the turn of the millen-nium, two new formats hit the streets — SACD (Super Audio Compact Disc) and the DVD-Audio disc.

Both formats are designed to sound better than a CD while maintain-ing that familiar, 12 cm (quick — grab that metric converter) disc format. Although you may remember the marketing tag line, "Perfect sound, forever," when CDs debuted, here's how SACD and DVD-Audio have managed to improve upon the now old-fashioned CD:

✔ **Sampling:** SACD uses very small sample sizes but records them 64 times more often than with regular CDs. The DVD-Audio system uses a lower sampling rate (still two or more times faster than CD), but a much bigger sized sample (20 bits or more, compared to 16 with CDs). Either way, you get higher audio frequencies with less noise and thus greater *dynamic range* (the difference between the quietest and loudest musical passages on the disc).

✔ **Multichannel format:** Because the discs can hold more data than the older CD format, record companies can release DVD-Audio and SACD discs in both traditional 2-channel (stereo) and home-theater-friendly 5.1-channel formats (with five channels of surround sound and a subwoofer channel). Some folks don't particularly like the surround sound for music; they say it makes sense only for movies, where things are happening all around you. But lots of others, us included, like surround sound for at least some of the music we listen to.

Some of the early SACD players didn't support the multichannel format, though all the current models we know of do. Also, not all SACD or DVD-Audio discs are recorded in surround sound format.

Both the SACD and the DVD-Audio have been tested by the experts, measured by the measurers, and reviewed by the reviewers, and the consensus is that both sound better than CD. How much better is a matter of great debate, but in a high-quality system, with a good recording, you'll probably be happy to have one of these systems. Before you buy, though, keep in mind three things:

✔ **You can't find much material in either of these formats, yet.** Chances are, you can't buy all your favorites on these formats.

✔ **You might have a hard time finding a single player that can play both formats.** As we write, a few players (usually in the $1,000+ price range) are "universal" players that can play CD, DVD, SACD, and DVD-Audio. But generally speaking, most manufacturers have chosen one camp or the other.

Most SACD players and DVD-Audio players *do* play regular CDs and regular DVDs, which is nice. Look for ones that can play MP3s, CD-Rs, and CD-RWs, as well, so that you can play homemade CDs, too.

✔ **Because of copy-protection concerns, you can't connect your DVD-Audio or SACD player to your receiver *digitally.*** This means that all that high-resolution audio must travel to your receiver in the analog domain, making the audio more susceptible to picking up noises or generally degrading during its trip to your ears. To make matters worse, multichannel systems require six of these analog cables. Ugh. Luckily a few manufacturers have begun, as we write, to come out with matched A/V receivers and DVD-Audio players that let you use a single digital connector to connect these devices — but only if you buy both from that manufacturer.

If you're not sure what to do with DVD-Audio and SACD, we suggest you consider waiting. There's still an ugly war going on in the marketplace between these two formats, and no one knows which one will end up becoming the dominant, new, high-quality audio format (or if either of them will). If both formats hang in there and don't go the way of the 8 track, we suspect that universal players will start becoming more common.

If you want to hear some really great tunes on your new SACD player, ABKO Records just re-released all of the 1960s Rolling Stones CDs in newly remastered editions that are *dual layer*. This means that there is a layer of CD data *and* a layer of SACD data on the same disc. This means you can play the same disc in your car and in your home theater SACD player. Can't do that with a DVD-Audio disc today — at least not until someone comes up with dual-layer DVD-A discs. Plus these new Stones records sound better than they ever have before.

Moving MP3 into Your Home Theater

MP3 is the most common format for digitally storing music and other audio files on a computer or computer-like device. A few other formats, such as Microsoft's Windows Media, are popular, but none is really close to MP3 in terms of market share as we write.

MP3 mania has exploded worldwide over the past couple of years, initially because online services such as Napster (now dead and gone) and Kazza (www.kazza.com) have enabled people to share and download songs converted from CDs to the MP3 format. MP3 has retained its popularity because its small file size has made it a very attractive system for carrying music around on computer-like portable audio players, such as our current favorite, Apple's iPod (www.apple.com/ipod), or SONICblue's RioRiot (www.sonicblue.com).

Lots of people are moving their MP3 files beyond the PC and the portable player these days, and beginning to find ways to incorporate MP3 music into the home theater. This makes a lot of sense to us — why not listen to all your MP3s on the highest quality audio system in the house?

Getting your hands on MP3s

We bet you've heard a lot about MP3 music, but where do all these MP3s come from, anyway? Is there an MP3 fairy out there somewhere who magically dumps them on the hard drives of good girls and boys?

Well, in fact, there used to be something pretty similar. Napster (which is now gone, due to legal actions) and other file-sharing services allowed people to put their music collections online and share them with the world. Of course, record companies weren't all that supportive of this grassroots music revolution, so most of these services got sued out of existence soon after starting.

Today, you can get your own MP3 files (and notice we call them files, because they're just that — computer data files on a hard drive) in two legal ways:

✔ **Rip your own:** You can convert your CDs to MP3s on your PC (this process is called *ripping*).To do this, you need a PC with a CD or DVD drive (which we bet you already have) and an MP3 program. Our favorite programs are MUSIC-MATCH Jukebox for Windows (www.musicmatch.com) and iTunes for the Mac (www.apple.com/itunes).

✔ **Download legally:** Although it's still harder than it should be (in our opinion) to find legal places to download the most popular music on MP3, even if you want to pay for it (those darn record companies!), you can find lots of cool music on sites such as www.mp3.com and www.emusic.com.

Using a media server

The best way to get your MP3s into the home theater is to use a computer-like device called a *media server*. These devices (our favorite is the AudioReQuest — www.request.com) contain a few common features:

✔ A big (usually 20GB or larger) computer hard drive for storing your MP3 files

✔ Computer chips that can decode your MP3 files (convert them into an analog audio signal)

✔ The ability to convert songs on a CD into MP3 files (just put a CD in the drawer, press a button, and the server saves your CD on the hard drive as an MP3 file)

✔ A display system that lets you view information about your stored MP3s (artist, title, length, and so on) on a built-in LCD screen, or (on fancier models) on your television screen

High-end MP3 servers, such as AudioReQuest, also include networking connections so that you can hook one up to a computer LAN and even synchronize your MP3s with another AudioReQuest. Danny has one in his house in Connecticut and another in his vacation home in Maine and does this all the time.

Using cheaper methods

If you aren't ready to invest in a fancy system, like the AudioReQuest (which starts off at around $2,500), or in a less expensive system, like SONICblue's Rio Central (which costs about $1,150), you can still enjoy the convenience of MP3 in your home theater. Our three favorite ways of getting MP3s into the home theater "on the cheap" (but without killing sound quality) are the following:

- **Connect a PC to your home theater:** We talk about Home Theater PCs in detail in Chapter 8, and one of the great things about these PCs is that they already have all the parts of a standalone MP3 server. A PC with a big hard drive and a good sound card can do a great job supplying MP3 music to your home theater.

- **Make your portable MP3 player do double duty:** With a simple adapter cable (which we discuss in Chapter 15), you can use the headphone output of your portable MP3 player to connect to your home theater's A/V receiver. You can also buy some neat radio devices (such as the iRock Wireless Music Adapter — www.myirock.com) that plug into your portable MP3 and send the music out over an unused radio station frequency. Just tune the radio tuner in your receiver to the right station and listen to your MP3s without wires.

- **You can burn your own CDs containing MP3 files:** If you have a PC with a CD burner (and most new PCs have one), you can create your own MP3 CDs containing hundreds of songs, and play them back on an appropriate CD or DVD player.

Old School Jams — Turntables

For most of the world, the LP has unfortunately gone the way of the dodo, but although LPs are far from the public eye, they've never really gone away. Many artists still release LP versions of their new records, and a handful of small manufacturers (and a few big ones) continue to crank out turntables.

In fact, the turntable has become hip again in some circles. And many audiophiles have long felt that LPs (at least when played on super high-quality turntables) sound better than CDs.

Buying a turntable isn't as simple as buying a CD, DVD-Audio, or SACD player. It's a much more subjective process. In the digital world, it's easy to keep a checklist of features in mind, such as digital output, or MP3 CD support. But when you start shopping for turntables, you're really getting into a whole different world. There's some really esoteric stuff out there, such as vacuum hold down systems (which suck the record flat on the platter to alleviate warps), and there are what we call "religious wars" between proponents of different turntable design philosophies. Having said that, here are a few things to consider when buying a turntable:

- **Belt drive or direct drive:** The platter (the thing that the record sits and spins around on) can be spun in two ways. There are pros and cons for each.

  - **Belt drive:** In this setup, the motor is separated from the platter and spindle and turned by a rubber belt that runs around the outside of the platter. A belt drive tends to isolate the rest of the turntable from any vibrations coming from the motor (vibrations which the stylus or needle could pick up and transmit to the receiver and to your ears).

  - **Direct drive:** An electric motor is directly attached to the spindle (the small cylinder that the platter rests upon). Direct drive turntables tend to be a bit more constant in their speed, so the turntable is more likely to turn 33⅓ times per minute without any speed variations (which tend to make your music sound warbly).

- **Suspended or unsuspended:** Vibrations are a big deal with a turntable, because the stylus dragging through the grooves of the LP can pick up extraneous vibrations (like those caused by your feet walking across the floor) and transmit them along with your music. Some turntables have elaborate suspension systems designed to isolate the platter (and therefore the record) from these vibrations, whereas others rely on the user to isolate the *entire* turntable (by placing the whole thing on a very sturdy rack, for example).

- **Automatic, semiautomatic, or manual:** An automatic turntable lets you put a record on the platter, push a button, and listen. The turntable itself moves the tone arm over the record, drops

it down before the first song, and then lifts it up and returns it
to the resting position when the side of the record is done.
High-end audiophiles *hate* these, because they — well, we
don't know why they hate them so much, though we guess
they just love to drop that needle down. Manual turntables
require you to manually move the tone arm over the record
and then lower it onto and off the record. Semiautomatics do
half your work for you — when the record side is finished playing, they lift the tone arm and stylus up off the record so you
don't have to hear that repeating *fpppt fpppt fpppt* sound as the
stylus does an endless loop at the end of the record.

In our opinion, good turntables can have any of the attributes
we just mentioned. We've heard good automatic turntables and
good manuals, good belt drives and good direct drives, and so on.
If you're buying a turntable, think about what your needs are. Do
you have a lot of records that you're going to play all the time? If
so, invest $500 to $1,000 dollars in a nice turntable from a company
such as Rega (www.rega.co.uk) or Pro-Ject. Have just a couple of
old favorites you can't get on CD? Check out some of the $150 to
$200 models from Sony or Denon. Want to be a DJ (and do some
scratching like the late, great Jam Master Jay)? Check out
Panasonic's Technics brand of DJ turntables.

Whatever you do, don't leave a turntable out of the equation if
you've got a few boxes of records in the closet.

Because LP records are much less popular than they used to be,
many new A/V receivers don't have the proper inputs on the back
to connect a turntable. So before you plunk down some cash on a
new turntable, check to see if your receiver even has a turntable
connection (usually labeled "phono"). If it doesn't, you can use an
external *phone preamp,* which connects between the turntable and
the receiver. You simply plug the cables from the turntable into the
phone preamp, and then use a standard audio cable to connect the
preamp to any open audio inputs on the receiver (most people use
the ones labeled "aux"). Recoton (www.recoton.com) makes an
inexpensive phono preamp for about $50, but you can buy more
expensive (and better) preamps from some of the turntable manufacturers that we mention in this section. You can also build your
own phono stage from kits available online at such places as
www.bottlehead.com.

Tuning In to Radio

Sometimes, we just can't be bothered to put in a CD or SACD, or cue up an MP3 (not to mention pull out and clean off and play a record). You know that couch potato lethargy we're talking about? If you're a music lover (and we bet you are), then nothing allows you to enjoy music with absolutely no involvement like turning on your favorite radio station and vegging out.

Local radio

In the home theater, there's usually not much you need to think about when it comes to radio. Unless you're buying separate components, you have a radio tuner built in to your A/V receiver.

If you *do* buy separate components instead of an A/V receiver (sneak over to Chapter 10 if you don't know what we're talking about), you probably will have to buy a radio tuner and plug it in to your system as an audio source device, just as you plug a CD or DVD-Audio player into your system. AM/FM radio tuners usually range in price from about $150 to $500 (though like any A/V component, you can buy high-end versions that cost ten times the average). Things to look for include:

- ✔ **AM and FM sensitivity:** Measured in the oh-so familiar decibel ferrowat (dBf), this is a measurement of how well the tuner can pick up signals. The lower this number is (it's usually in the range of 9 to 11 dBf), the better.

- ✔ **Adjustable selectivity:** Some tuners come with a switch on the front (or on the remote control) that let you choose between wide or narrow selectivity. The wide mode gives you better reception and sound quality on powerful stations, whereas the narrow mode can be used to tune in weak signals from distant stations (while avoiding interference from stations on adjacent frequencies).

- ✔ **Antenna diversity:** Not a necessity, but some fancier tuners have *two* antenna inputs that you can manually or automatically have the tuner choose between when you're trying to pull in a radio station.

If you're lucky enough to live in an area with some good radio stations, you might want to invest in a high-quality tuner near the top of your price range.

Catching up with cassettes

If you need a cassette deck because you have a ton of tapes filling shoeboxes in your closet, or because you want to make tapes for playing back in the car or in a portable headset, there are a few things you should look for:

- **Single or dual well:** If you think you might end up dubbing (or making copies of) a lot of cassettes, you need a *dual well* tape deck that has this capability. If you plan to record only the radio or your own CDs, you can save money by getting yourself a single well deck.

- **Noise reduction:** Before Dolby Labs became famous for its surround sound standards (like Dolby Digital), millions of audiophiles knew the company for its Cassette Noise Reduction standards. These standards (which go by the names Dolby B, C, and S) are electronic processes that are designed to increase the sound quality of cassettes by decreasing noise (like tape hiss — the sound you can hear when quiet passages are playing). The general rule for these systems is that the higher the name of the system, alphabetically, the better (so S is best, then C, then B). The key thing to keep in mind is that you must have the same system that you record the tape with on the tape deck you use for playback. If you record with Dolby C, you need to play your tape on a Dolby-C deck. Dolby S is a slight exception to this rule, as tapes recorded with this system can be played back on Dolby B decks with at least some of the benefits of S intact.

- **Number of heads:** Most tape decks have two heads (the heads are the electromagnetic devices that read and write audio signals onto the tape itself). The two-head design uses the same head for both playing back recorded music and for recording music on the tape (the other head is used for erasing the tape when you are recording). Fancier tape decks have a three-head design, which has separate playback and record heads. Because each head is used for only one function, each head can be designed for optimal functionality for its purpose.

- **Number of motors:** A tape is moved over the heads by means of a pair of spindles (which fit in the little wheels on the cassette) and — more importantly — by a pair of devices called a *capstan* and *pinch roller*. The capstan and pinch roller are the essential devices that keep the tape moving over the heads at the correct speed, without any speed fluctuations. Inexpensive tape decks use a single electric motor and a belt (like a radiator fan belt in a car) for this function, while higher quality decks have a motor for each of the spindles and a third for the capstan/pinch roller combo.

Satellite radio

If you're like us, however, you live somewhere where there isn't a whole lot of programming you really want to listen to. In that case, you might check out satellite radio, which offers a huge number of stations (over 100 each) beamed to your house or car from a handful of geostationary satellites hovering above the equator. We find that there's just a ton more diversity and just plain interesting stuff coming across these space-based airwaves than we find on our local radio today. Satellite radio services, from startups such as XM Radio or Sirius, require you to — gasp — *pay* for your radio (about $10 to $12 a month).

If you want to get into satellite radio, first of all you need to check out the Web sites of the two providers, www.xmradio.com and www.sirius.com, to see which one has programming that you prefer. Then, you need to get your hands on a satellite radio tuner (you can find a bunch of different models listed on each company's Web page). The majority of these satellite tuners are designed for in-car use (because people tend to listen to the radio most while they're driving), but XM Radio offers some really cool tuners (from Sony and Delco) that can do double duty. You can put these tuners in your car, and when you get home, pull them out and plug them into your A/V receiver. As we write, Sirius does not yet offer a receiver for in-home use, but we expect that they will shortly.

These satellites are down by the equator, so no matter where you live in the United States, you need to be able to put the antenna in a south-facing window to pick up a good signal in your home.

Internet radio

If you set up a home theater PC in your A/V system, you can get lots of great radio programming from Internet radio broadcasts. Using an MP3 player, such as MUSICMATCH Jukebox or iTunes, or a streaming media player, such as Windows Media Player or Real Player (www.real.com), you can tune in literally thousands of radio stations from around the world. With a broadband DSL or cable modem Internet connection, the quality is pretty decent, too.

So if you're like Pat, and you find that San Diego is out of range of the great PBS station in Santa Monica (www.kcrw.org), you can just tune in on the Net. Pretty cool, and it doesn't cost you an extra penny. This is also a great way to get the radio broadcasts of your favorite college sports team. Neither of us ever misses a Duke basketball game, even if we're on the road, because we can tune in on our laptops. Go Blue Devils!

Chapter 6

Feeding Video into Your Theater

. . . .

. . . .

*I*f you're like us, watching movies is the main reason you decided to get a home theater in the first place. High-quality music reproduction and high-impact video gaming are just (awesome) side benefits. You can get movies (and TV shows and other video content) into your home theater system in many ways — such as plugging into a cable or satellite TV system. For most folks, however, watching a movie means watching a *prerecorded* movie (typically a movie on DVD that you've bought or rented from the local video store).

In this chapter, we talk about the key sources of prerecorded video in your home theater. We spend most of our time discussing the source that's most important to us and most likely to you as well — the DVD. We also talk about the VCR, the personal video recorder (or PVR), and some other nonbroadcast sources of video.

DVD Rules the Roost

The DVD is a high-quality centerpiece to a home theater. Keep in mind the cardinal rule of any A/V system: Garbage in equals garbage out. Or the corollary of this, which states that no matter how good your video display and audio system are, if you put a junky, low fidelity signal into them, you're going to see and hear junky, low fidelity home theater. That's why DVD is so important — it's a cheap, easy-to-use, high-quality system for movies and movie soundtracks.

In this section, we spend a little time taking about the DVDs themselves and what they can do. We do this because we want to convince you that, if you don't have DVD in your home theater, you're really missing out. Now maybe in five or ten years, there will be a better, higher-quality source for home theater. But today, DVD is essential.

Getting to know DVDs

The DVD is a 12 cm optical disc (by the way, *optical* means that the data on the disc is read by a laser). From a distance, a DVD looks just like a CD. The big difference between the DVD and the CD is the format that each uses for burning those little digital pits into the disc (pits that turn into digital 1s and 0s when the laser reads them). Because the DVD uses a more complex formatting scheme, the DVD has the capacity to store a lot more data than a CD. A DVD can hold a minimum of 4.7GB of data, whereas a CD's limit is about 650MB (so a DVD can hold more than seven times as much data).

A DVD's extra capacity is crucial to home theater, because it lets the DVD store about two hours of high-quality digital video *and* digital audio signals using Dolby Digital or DTS (see Chapter 3 if you don't know what these are) *and* an analog 2-channel stereo signal as well. A CD, well, it can't hold more than a few dozen minutes of this kind of home theater data.

 You'll also hear, as you begin getting deeper into the home theater world, about *dual layer* and *double sided* DVDs. These discs (which work just fine in any DVD player) hold even more data for long movies and cool extras, such as deleted scenes or director commentary. The additional space is made possible by putting the extra data on either — no surprise here — a different layer of the DVD or on the other side (so you just have to flip the disc, like an LP).

Like a CD, the DVD stores its information in a digital format (you probably guessed that from the name) and, for video, uses the MPEG format that we discuss in Chapter 4. The DVD can also hold the audio soundtracks that correspond to this video in a variety of Dolby and DTS formats, as well as cool extra features, such as additional foreign language soundtracks, subtitles, scene indexes (which let you skip to different scenes in a movie, just like you can skip to different songs on a CD), and more.

The DVD can also do something that most other home theater source devices (we talk about a few others later in this chapter) can't do. It can display *true* widescreen video.

Not all DVDs (the discs themselves, not the DVD player) give you a true widescreen anamorphic picture. Many DVDs have been formatted in the standard 4:3 aspect ratio instead. If you want widescreen, you need to pick DVDs with labels that say "anamorphic" or "widescreen DVD" or something similar. Many movie companies put both versions on a single disc (using the dual layer technology we just mentioned), or release both widescreen and Pan and Scan (frames cropped to fit a traditional television screen) DVDs of an individual movie. See Chapter 4 for the details about widescreen viewing.

Choosing a DVD player

Well, we've talked a lot about why we think DVD players are so important in a home theater. Now comes the fun part — picking one out. There's some really good news here, especially if your budget is like ours (and most people's), which is to say, limited.

DVD technology has advanced incredibly in the few years that DVD players have been on the market, and the price drops have been stupendous. For example, Pat bought a DVD player for his parents for Christmas as we were writing this book (the end of 2002), and he was able to get a highly rated DVD player for just $129. (If you see his parents, don't tell them how little it cost — they were impressed by his generosity!) So if you're still sitting on the DVD fence, get off it!

Like every single piece of A/V gear we discuss in this book, you can spend a fortune on a DVD player if you want to. And you may want to if you're building a really fancy, no-holds-barred, high-end home theater. Although you can get a great picture from that $129 model, if you have a high-end video projector and a top-of-the-line surround sound audio system, you might want to buy a fancier model. Such a system yearns for higher-quality electronic components and more powerful chips to convert the digital data on the DVD disc into video and sound. Just to give you an idea of the range of prices, as we write, the current prices of a single company (Denon) range from $300 to $3,500.

So what should you look for? We think the following items are the key things to put on your mental checklist as you start shopping:

> ✔ **Connections on the back:** We talk in detail about the "hierarchy of connections" in Chapter 15. For video, the best connection for DVD players is the component video connection, and not all DVD players have these (nor do all TVs). If you have a TV that can accept these connections, make sure you get a

DVD player that can also use them. On the audio side of things, you'll find two kinds of digital connectors (for Dolby Digital and DTS digital surround sound) — the coaxial and optical (or Toslink) connections. The key thing here is to make sure that the connectors on your DVD player match up with those on your A/V receiver.

✔ **Single or multidisc capability:** DVD players come in single and multiple disc models. For just watching movies, a single disc player is fine, but if you plan to use your DVD player as your only CD player, you might want to pay a bit more for a multidisc player that lets you provide hours of background music during, for example, a party.

✔ **Progressive or interlaced:** Progressive scan is becoming a really big deal because the video industry is gradually moving from interlaced video towards a progressive video future. We discuss progressive and interlaced scans in more detail in Chapter 4, so we don't bother you with that here. Bottom line: If you have an HDTV or other progressive scan monitor, you want a DVD player that offers progressive scan capabilities. Although most progressive scan TVs have a built-in deinterlacer for playing interlaced material (DVDs are still interlaced), the deinterlacers in most progressive scan DVD players (not all, but most) are better. Even if you don't have a progressive scan TV but might someday, consider a progressive scan DVD player, as well, especially because prices on these DVD players have dropped so much that they're hardly more expensive than a regular DVD player.

✔ **Adjustability:** To get the best out of a home theater, you need to do more than just plug everything in properly. You also need to spend some time tweaking the audio and video settings to get the best picture in your room. Most of these adjustments are done on the TV or projector itself, not on the DVD player. But some DVD players allow you to adjust things such as brightness (or black level) in the DVD player.

✔ **Surround sound decoder:** If you are starting your home theater from scratch, we recommend that you buy a home theater receiver (or separate components decoder) that is capable of decoding (at a minimum) Dolby Digital 5.1 and DTS Digital surround sound signals. If, however, you are adding a DVD player into an existing home theater with an older receiver that doesn't support digital surround sound, you can buy a DVD player with a built-in surround sound decoder. The downside of this is that you need to use *six* analog audio cables to connect the DVD player to your receiver, instead of a single digital interconnect. Some of the older receivers were marketed as "Digital ready" with six preamp jacks on the back for just this purpose; if your receiver doesn't have these six inputs (or its own Dolby Digital decoder), you can't play back digital 5.1 channel surround sound with it!

✔ **Audio disc support:** All DVD players can play back store-bought, prerecorded CDs. Not all, however, can play back homemade CD-R or CD-RW discs, nor can many DVD players play back CDs containing MP3 music files. If these features are important to you (and you don't have a CD player that can handle this for you), make sure your DVD player can handle all these formats before you buy.

✔ **Recording capability:** Just as the CD has moved from a factory produced, read-only CD to a "make your own" medium (such as CD-Rs and CD-RWs), so has DVD recording started to become a truly consumer-friendly technology. We discuss the pitfalls of DVD recording (and there are pitfalls, due to some incompatible industry standards) in the sidebar, "Recording your own DVDs," later in this chapter.

✔ **Remote control:** Most people have too many remote controls when they get into home theater. To avoid remote overload, look at how other systems in your home theater can control your DVD player. For example, many A/V equipment vendors have special "system link" cables that let the receiver control the DVD player and other components. The downside of such systems is that you must buy all your equipment from the same vendor to take advantage of them. The alternative (which we discuss in Chapter 14) is to use a *universal remote control* to control everything. If you're going down this route, ask your dealer if there are any special codes or other things you need to consider before buying a specific DVD player.

✔ **DVD extras:** Many DVDs include extra features that you'd never get on a VHS tape, laserdisc or other (older) video source. For example, some DVDs have alternate camera angles — so you can click a button on the remote control and see the film from a different character's perspective. Most DVD players support this feature, but not all do. You can also find DVD players that have special features, such as a digital zoom that lets you enlarge part of the picture on your screen, or a frame-by-frame fast forward, so that you can watch that starship explode in excruciating detail. You can even buy DVD players that will display pictures on your TV from Kodak's PictureCDs or your own homemade CD-R with standard PC or Mac JPEG picture files.

✔ **All-in-one functionality:** The DVD players with built-in surround sound decoding are a first step in this direction, but if space is limited in your home theater you might want to take the full leap — DVD players and A/V receivers all in one slim chassis. Lots of these models are part of lower-priced "home theater in a box" systems, but you can also find very high-quality (and expensive) all-in-ones. For example, the Scottish high-end A/V manufacturer, Linn (www.linn.co.uk), has a very cool all-in-one system called the Classik Movie System.

If you're buying an inexpensive DVD player, it's probably okay to choose one based on features and reviews (we list a bunch of places to find these reviews in Chapter 24). But if you plan to spend $1,000 or more on a DVD player and are lucky enough to have a good home theater shop or dealer nearby, take the time to get a good audition of the DVD player. Do this in the showrooms of the dealer, at a minimum, and at home with a demo model, if possible. You're the one who's going to be watching movies on this machine, so make sure your eyes like what they see.

Playing DVDs on an HDTV

Many folks hear "widescreen" and "digital" and think "HDTV" (or High Definition TV). Well, DVD is not HDTV. DVD is digital. It provides a great picture. But it isn't a true high-definition video source. Although DVD looks better than ever before when you play it back on an HDTV (using a progressive scan DVD player we mention earlier in this chapter), DVD doesn't give you the same quality of picture that a full-on HDTV signal (coming in over a broadcast TV signal, or from your cable or satellite provider) can give.

Why don't DVDs "do" HDTV? Well, for one reason, HDTV wasn't fully finalized and on the market when the DVD was developed, so DVD was designed to work with the TVs of the time (which are still the majority of TVs today). More importantly, HDTV requires a ton (literally, we measured) of digital data. Using the traditional NTSC signal, you can fit a two-hour movie comfortably onto a DVD, but you wouldn't be able to fit more than a fraction of that movie onto a DVD if it were encoded as an HDTV signal.

VCRs Ain't (Quite) Dead Yet

We spend a lot of time talking about DVD players, because we love them so much. But we realize that some movies just aren't available on DVD yet (or ever, in some cases). And you probably want to record TV shows that you won't be home for or watch home movies you've recorded with your camcorder. Or you've got a zillion VHS tapes that you're stuck with in a DVD age, like Danny. These are all areas in which a videocassette recorder (or VCR) comes in super handy.

What's the region thing all about?

Region codes, which you may see in catalogs or on DVDs themselves, enable movie studios to control who can watch DVDs (the studios are like that about a lot of things). The codes are both embedded in the DVD itself and also coded into the circuitry of the DVD player primarily so that movie studios can release movies and DVDs at different times, in different places. So a movie may be released theatrically in the United States first, and then, several months later, it is released theatrically in Europe and also released on DVD in North America. What the region code does is prevent North American retailers from selling the DVD to European customers while the movie is still in theaters there.

If you dig around on the Internet, you can find region-free programs for the PC or modified, universal, region-free DVD players. We're generally supportive of this concept (especially when we find some foreign movie that we *really* want on DVD isn't available in our North American region code), but we're going to leave you to your own devices when it comes to region-free players. The movie studios are really down on this concept, and often aggressively pursue legal actions (including jail time) against people who try to crack the region codes. In fact, we're not going to say any more on the subject — jailhouse uniforms don't really fit either of our senses of fashion and style.

By the way, here are the regions:

✔ Region 1: North America

✔ Region 2: Western Europe, Middle East, Japan, and South Africa

✔ Region 3: South Korea, Taiwan, Hong Kong, and Southeast Asia

✔ Region 4: Australia, New Zealand, and Latin America

✔ Region 5: Eastern Europe, Africa, and India

✔ Region 6: China

✔ Region 7: Reserved (For the moon maybe? We're not too sure.)

✔ Region 8: Special international venues (such as cruise ships and airplanes)

You can buy three kinds of VCRs today:

> ✔ **VHS VCRs:** These are your standard, garden-variety VCRs that have been around for 30 years or so. They use VHS videocassettes and record a low-resolution TV signal (only about 240 lines of resolution). Most of these VHS VCRs are cheap (less than $100) and most include stereo audio capabilities (if so, they're labeled HiFi) and analog Dolby surround sound capabilities.

- ✔ **S-VHS VCRs:** The S-VHS (or Super VHS) VCR uses a special S-VHS tape to provide a higher-quality, higher-resolution (400 lines, instead of 240) picture. Regular VHS tapes work on these decks, but S-VHS videocassettes don't work on most regular VHS decks. (If you plan on trading tapes with someone or using a regular VHS VCR you have elsewhere, keep that in mind.) S-VHS VCRs start off at around $130.

- ✔ **D-VHS VCRs:** The latest and greatest in the VCR world, these are high-definition VCRs. D-VHS VCRs can play and record standard VHS and S-VHS videotapes. More importantly, D-VHS VCRs can also record all the HDTV formats (discussed in Chapter 12). To record and play back HDTV, the D-VHS system needs an i.LINK (also called IEEE 1394 or FireWire) connector to connect to an HDTV TV or a standalone HDTV tuner. Many HDTVs and HDTV tuners don't have this connection, however, because broadcasters and movie studios don't want you to be able to record HDTV programs. So check carefully before you invest in one of these D-VHS VCRs. You can get a limited number of movies on prerecorded D-VHS videocassettes, but it's a small number compared to what you can get on DVD. You can buy a D-VHS VCR for about $800.

When buying a VCR of any kind, look for the following things:

- ✔ **HiFi capability:** All the D-VHS and S-VHS VCRs have this, and most regular VHS decks have this feature as well. If you buy a model without it, you won't even get stereo sound — just crummy mono (1-channel) sound.

- ✔ **VCR Plus+:** This system enables the average human being to record a certain show at a certain time more easily. With this system, all you have to do is punch in a special code that is listed next to the show you want to record in your paper's TV listings (or in *TV Guide*). More advanced versions of VCR Plus+ (called Silver and Gold) allow you to localize your VCR Plus+ settings for your area.

- ✔ **All-in-one units:** Some VCRs are incorporated into a single chassis with a DVD player or with a MiniDV or other camcorder tape player. These all-in-one units take up less room on your equipment rack, if space is a concern. And the VCR/camcorder tape combo units make it easy to make VCR copies of your home movies.

Putting the HD in DVD

Several A/V equipment manufacturers are developing HD (high definition) DVDs. A lot of the development revolves around new variants of the DVD that can hold more data. To play back these DVDs, DVD players need a different kind of laser, a blue laser, which is much harder to build than the red lasers used today. Other companies are designing high-definition DVD systems that use a more efficient compression system (MPEG-4, instead of the MPEG-2 used by today's DVDs) to fit the high-definition data onto a standard DVD.

This development is happening at a fast and furious pace, but two things are holding it back:

✔ The movie companies (paranoid as they tend to be) are hesitant to offer any content (such as, movies) in an HDTV format unless they can be convinced that exceptionally strong copy protection systems will be built in.

✔ The manufacturers have not agreed among themselves (or in their industry group, the DVD forum) on a single standard for HD DVD. Instead, they're all pushing their own formats — which guarantees a ton (we measured this, too) of confusion and frustration for customers.

We're not sure where this will all end. Some vendors have promised to have HD DVD players on the market in 2003. We are sure of one thing: Unless all the manufacturers get together and decide on a single standard, we're not going to be the first on our blocks to buy an HD DVD. We don't want a digital age Betamax on our hands!

Even if your VCR is in the same chassis as a DVD player, you can't make tapes of your favorite DVD movies. A copy protection system called Macrovision keeps you from doing this, and it's built in to all DVDs and all VCRs. Even if you want to copy your favorite movie from DVD to VHS to play back on a VCR in your vacation home or somewhere else, you're just plain out of luck.

We're not all that enthusiastic about the VCR these days (although we think the D-VHS would be pretty cool, if many people weren't restricted from using it for its intended purpose — recording HDTV shows for later playback). Even big movie rental places, such as Blockbuster, are phasing out the VHS in favor of DVD. But we do think it's worthwhile to have an inexpensive VCR in your home theater, just to have the capability of playing older movies that you can't find on DVD. We recommend you get an inexpensive S-VHS model — and don't spend too much money on it.

PVRs Rock!

One reason we're not all that interested in VCRs these days is because we've found the PVR, or personal video recorder, which offers a much better way to tape our favorite shows. PVRs are basically purpose-built computers that record video onto a standard computer hard drive. Think of it as a computer-based VCR. There are no tapes to wear out, break, or jam — just a fast, reliable computer hard drive.

Actually, the metaphor of a PVR being like a computer-based VCR really sells the PVR short. Using a PVR is soooo much better than using a VCR that it's actually hard to begin to describe the benefits of the PVR. Don't just take our word for it, look at these things you can do with a PVR (and not with a VCR!):

✔ You can play back one recorded show while simultaneously recording another.

✔ You can pause live TV (if you're recording it on your PVR).

✔ You can skip the commercials with the click of a button if you are recording the show, and start watching a couple minutes past the start time. (Broadcasters *hate* this feature and are suing some PVR vendors.)

✔ You can let the PVR automatically record your favorite show every time it's on. (All PVRs connect to a program service, usually via a telephone line, that has a complete program guide for weeks at a time, customized for your area.)

✔ You can use the program service to help you find shows.

✔ You can connect some PVRs to a computer network (some models even have built-in wireless network connections) and the Internet so you can share recordings with your friends or send copies of shows you've recorded to your PVR at your vacation home (if you have one).

Most PVRs are sold as standalone boxes — generally the size and shape of a cable set-top box, a DVD player, or any other A/V component. These units start off at around $299 for a unit that has enough hard drive space to record 40 hours of programming, and go up in price for larger capacity units. You also need to pay a monthly fee (around $10 per month, though you can pay $250 for a lifetime subscription) to get the necessary programming guide service.

Recording your own DVDs

PVR hard drives, no matter how big, eventually run out of space, and home movies take up a lot of digital space, too. Eventually, you have to store your video some-where — both to archive it so that you can use the hard drive or camcorder tape for new stuff, and also so that you can share your content with others. The best way to do this, in our minds, is by making your own DVDs.

Just as you can create your own CDs using a CD *burner* (or recorder), you can now easily make your own DVDs using a DVD recorder. There are two ways you can do this:

 ✔ **Buy a DVD recorder:** This is an A/V component, like a DVD player that has a built-in mechanism for recording DVDs as well.

 ✔ **Use a PC with a built-in DVD recorder:** Apple, Sony, and a few other PC vendors sell computers with built-in DVD recorders. You can also buy an internal (inside the PC) or external (connected with a USB or FireWire cable) DVD burner for your existing PC.

In either case, you have a somewhat difficult decision to make, because the makers of DVD recorders have decided that cooperating (for the sake of the consumer) is simply not something they have in them. So there are three *completely incompatible* systems out there for DVD recording: DVD-R/RW, DVD-RAM, and DVD+R/RW. Ugh — acronym soup. Although it's really ugly and very confusing to the consumer (look at the plus and minus signs closely), here's a little help.

DVD-R/RW systems are generally considered the most compatible with existing DVD *players* — so you have the best shot at having your homemade DVDs play back on your Mom's or friend's or whomever's DVD player (though even with this stan-dard, it only works on about 80 percent of DVD players). DVD-RAM is the least com-patible; you basically need another DVD-RAM recorder or player to play back these discs. DVD+R/RW is somewhere in the middle.

If you're only making DVDs for yourself, these distinctions might not be too impor-tant. You can play back your DVDs on the machine that made them no matter what. If you have sharing in mind, then we suggest the DVD-R/RW recorders.

In the future, we expect PVRs to be incorporated into other devices, instead of being standalone units. For example, you can now buy PVRs that have been incorporated into satellite TV receivers, and in some areas, you can get a digital cable set-top box that has a built-in PVR. We've also seen announcements for future PVRs that can record and play back HDTV content.

You can also use a PC as a PVR. We talk about this more in Chapter 8.

Homegrown Video Programming

You don't have to limit your home theater viewing to prerecorded DVDs and television broadcasts. You can also incorporate video from your own sources. Many folks like to make their own video programming — home movies and the like. We think that these videos deserve a proper playback system — and we think that the home theater is the right place. There's also another source of video in the home that a lot of people don't think of when designing their home theater: in-house closed circuit or surveillance video.

Camcorders

Although the topic of camcorders is beyond the scope of this book, we do want to put in a few words about fitting a camcorder into your home theater. (See *Digital Video For Dummies,* 2nd Edition, by Martin Doucette, published by Wiley Publishing, Inc., for details about camcorders.)

First off, we think that digital camcorders are the way to go (look for formats like Mini DV, MICROMV, or Digital 8 instead of an analog Hi8 format), for two reasons. First of all, these digital formats can take higher-quality, better looking, higher resolution video and digital audio (which will look and sound much better in your bigscreen home theater). Second, digital camcorders can connect to your PC using a standard FireWire cable (also known as i.LINK or IEEE 1394) and transfer video to your computer's hard drive for editing. Editing is a key thing — no one wants to watch your "raw" video footage, they want to see a nice finished product, without any mistakes, and possibly with a soundtrack.

Connecting your camcorder to your home theater is really a simple process. All these digital camcorders use standard S-Video (which we discuss in Chapter 15).

If you use a camcorder in your home theater, we recommend you choose an A/V receiver with a set of inputs for the camcorder on the front. With this setup, you don't have to monkey around behind the equipment rack when you want to plug in your camcorder.

Video surveillance

Surveillance is kind of a scary word. We hesitate to use it, because it sounds kind of paranoid and big-brotherish. But it's an accurate word for what we're talking about — video cameras mounted in and around your home that let you keep an eye on what's going on from the comfort of your home theater (or any room with a television).

Surveillance video is not high-quality, surround sound video. In fact, most surveillance video (often called closed circuit TV or CCTV) is pretty awful to look at. But if you want to know who's ringing the doorbell or keep an eye on the baby asleep in her room while you watch a movie in the home theater, then you probably don't need a high-quality picture. Heck, you might not even want a color picture, or sound. You just want to see what's going on.

There are a couple of ways to get this home surveillance video into your system:

- ✔ **You can use a wireless system like those offered by X10 (you know, the company with all those pop-under Internet ads that show up on your screen when you surf the Web).** These systems (which start at around $80 on www.x10.com) use a 2.4 GHz radio signal (like those used by many cordless phones) to send video from a remote location to a small receiver that plugs into your home theater receiver or directly into your TV. You might put one of these cameras by your front door, or use Danny's favorite, X10.com's FloodCam, which is built in to a set of motion-sensitive floodlights on the side of your house.

- ✔ **You can use networked cameras that connect to your home's computer network.** These systems, from companies like Panasonic and D-Link, are a bit more expensive (starting at around $400 per camera) but much more capable. Using a standard (wired) Ethernet network or a wireless computer network (802.11b or Wi-Fi), you can feed the video from these cameras into your home theater PC, and you can even view them from outside the home theater (if you've got a broadband Internet connection) using the built-in Web server on these cameras.

- ✔ **You can use a traditional "wired" CCTV system.** These cameras are connected to your home's coaxial video cabling (the cable that brings antenna and cable TV connections to your home theater, as we discuss in Chapter 15), and use devices called *modulators* that let you turn this video into an in-house TV station. To view a modulated CCTV channel, you just need to tune your TV to the right channel. If you've got a picture-in-picture system in your TV, you can even keep an eye on things in a small window while you watch something else on the rest of the screen.

These cameras are not only good for viewing, but for recording as well. Danny likes the FloodCam because it records when motion sets it off, day or night. You never know when you might need that.

Chapter 7

Feeding Your Home Theater from Outside Your Home

In This Chapter

▶ Aiming your home theater at the stars

▶ Connecting to cable

▶ Tuning your antennas

▶ Watching new network-based services

*I*n the previous two chapters, we talk about a bunch of different audio and video sources that let you enjoy prerecorded content (like movies on DVD or music on CD) or content that you've created yourself (like home movies and recordings you've made of broadcast TV). For most people, this kind of content is just part of the overall home theater experience. You may also want to use your cool A/V equipment to do standard couch potato stuff — watching the big game or the sitcoms on TV. In this chapter, we discuss the different ways you can bring these "outside the house" sources into your home theater.

 We talk about three primary ways you can get television into your home — satellite, cable, and broadcast. We don't think these three things need to be mutually exclusive. You might, for example, get a satellite TV system but also have an antenna to pick up local stations. Or you might get digital cable to pick up those mythical 500 stations but still hook up an antenna to pick up the local HDTV broadcasts. So keep an open mind as you plan your theater.

Digital Satellite Does It All

For many home theater enthusiasts, TV means one thing: satellite TV. DSS (Digital Satellite Service) is the way people do satellite today (many people also call it DBS, Direct Broadcast Satellite). If you wanted satellite TV ten or so years ago, you were stuck with something called C-Band (named after the radio frequency on which these satellites operate), which required you to put a *huge* (9 foot or so) satellite dish in your backyard.

DSS is a much more user- and landscape-friendly version of satellite TV. DSS dishes can be as small as 18 inches across and are much easier to integrate into the average backyard. Despite this more compact size, DSS has all the advantages that drew people to those big dishes back in the '80s — tons of channels and interesting programming you can't get from your local broadcast channels.

If your cable company offers a digital cable service (which we discuss in the next section), you can probably get just as many channels on that service as you can on a satellite service.

Signing up for digital satellite

In the United States, the two main providers of DSS services are DirecTV and Echostar (Echostar's service is called DISH Network), and they are pretty similar. Both services offer digital transmission of their video content using MPEG-2 (discussed in Chapter 4). This digital transmission has advantages for both the satellite companies (because it lets them fit more TV channels into the radio waves over which their satellites broadcast) and the customer (because it eliminates the distortions which often occur in nondigital transmissions).

We like both services. To decide between the two, shop for pricing and channels that are best for you. You can look at channel lineups and prices online at `www.directv.com` and `www.dishnetwork.com`.

Although DSS systems broadcast all their content using digital technology, the majority of the programming sent out over these systems is analog TV, or NTSC, which we discuss in Chapter 4. However, DSS systems still carry a relatively large number of HDTV stations, which is why many home theater owners choose DSS as their primary source of television. (The total number carried is still only a handful of the hundreds of stations carried by these systems, but in many areas, that's more than are available by cable or broadcast.)

Some of the key features of both DSS systems include

✔ Hundreds of channels, including movie, sports, and sometimes even local broadcast channels

✔ On-screen program guides that include all the current and upcoming (for a week or so) programming scheduled on the system

✔ Dozens of digital audio channels

✔ High-definition TV

Understanding the drawbacks

DSS services are pretty awesome, we think, but they're not all good. If you decide to go the DSS route, keep a few things in mind:

✔ **You might not get local stations:** In some parts of the country, you can get a local package that includes most if not all of your local broadcast stations. In some smaller cities and more rural areas, you still need to get cable or set up a broadcast antenna to pick up local stations.

✔ **You need a special satellite receiver:** You can't just plug the cable from your satellite dish into a TV; you need a special satellite receiver. You can share this receiver with other TVs in your house, but if you want to watch different programs on different TVs, you need a receiver for each TV.

✔ **You need to hook into a phone line:** Your satellite receiver has to "talk" back to the service provider to maintain your pay-per-view account and to check for software upgrades. The receivers usually do this in the middle of the night, so they don't interfere with phone calls. If you never use pay-per-view or some of the premium sports channels, you may be able to skip the phone line entirely. Check with the provider before you buy in on this, if getting a phone line in your home theater is an issue.

✔ **Your satellite dish antenna must be able to "see" the satellites:** It must have a clear line of sight to the satellites, which hover over the equator. Some folks in northern areas (or in Hawaii) might not be able to pick up all the satellites, so they get only some of the channels, not all. Even if you're in the right spot, geographically speaking, you still need to have a clear view to the south, without hills and trees in the way.

✔ **You have to install the system:** This isn't a really big deal for most folks, particularly when free installation deals are constantly being advertised. If you don't own your home, however, installation could be a deal breaker. So check with your landlord first (unless you just don't care what she or he says).

One more thing: You may run into some resistance from home-owner's associations, neighborhood covenants, and the like. Don't take this lying down. The FCC ruled in 2001 that these laws can't be used to prevent you from installing a DSS dish. The only big exceptions are DSS safety (for example, you can't be too close to a power line) and for homes in historic districts. Otherwise, no one can keep you from using a dish if you want to. Know your rights! Check out www.fcc.gov/mb/facts/otard.html for the actual, long-winded text of this ruling.

Getting the dish on the dish

On your roof (or on the side of your house, or on top of a big rock in your backyard — you can stick these things just about anywhere) goes an 18- to 21-inch round or oval satellite dish. This dish is your main link to those satellites floating around in space, so it has to be aimed properly to pick up the signals. (By the way, this aiming is really the hardest part of the whole installation — but despite the existence of self-install kits, we think aiming is sufficiently hard that it warrants a professional installation.)

Don't buy the round dish if you're getting a new DirecTV system. Only the slightly larger oval dish picks up the HDTV signals available on that service. For DISH Network, you need a second dish for HDTV, so this caveat doesn't apply.

Within this dish assembly are devices called *LNBs* or *Low Noise Blockers* — the horn shaped dinguses that sit in front of the actual parabola of the dish. These devices sift the high-frequency satellite signals out from other radio signals and block out the extraneous signals. Dishes can have one or more LNBs, depending on what you want to do with them. (Dishes with more than one LNB are referred to as *dual* or even *triple* LNB dishes.)

Deciding how many LNBs and what shape of antenna you want can be really confusing. It depends on where you live, what service you are subscribing to, and how many TVs you want your satellite to feed into. There's no simple formula because there are multiple variables (and we really hated that multiple variable stuff back when we were in school).

One key factor to remember is that single LNB dishes can only feed a single DSS receiver. If you want to watch different programs on different TVs simultaneously, you need at least a dual LNB dish. We recommend that you get at least a dual LNB dish; it's a false economy to get the marginally cheaper single LNB dish.

If you subscribe to DirecTV, you may have to consider a triple LNB dish if you want HDTV, or local channels in some parts of the country. DISH Network uses a second dish for HDTV, so you won't ever run into a triple LNB dish for that service.

Choosing a receiver

The television signals feeding in from a dish (or dishes) and through an LNB (or LNBs!) are in a format that basically no TV can decode and display. So between the dish/LNB and your TV, you need to install a DSS receiver.

Although many things about DirecTV and DISH Network are similar, the receiver is one area in which they diverge. DISH Network maintains a tight control on the receiver business and sells its own brand of receivers directly to its customers (you can choose from several models in different price ranges). DirecTV has a more open outlook on the receiver business, so you can buy your receivers from a range of companies, such as Sony, Samsung, and RCA.

Regardless of how you get the receiver, you have a few decisions to make before you buy a receive that's

- ✔ **HDTV-capable:** If you have an HDTV or an HDTV-ready monitor, you can get the awesome high-definition programming through your DSS system. If you don't have one of these HDTV capable TVs, you gain nothing from an HDTV-capable DSS receiver. You may still want to buy one if a TV upgrade is in your near future, but if you don't plan to upgrade for several years, we suggest you wait. Receiver prices are always dropping, and you'll probably get a much better deal in two years, even if you have to get rid of your existing receiver.

- ✔ **Home-theater-capable:** Any DSS receiver can be used in a home theater, but some of the cheaper receivers don't have the proper chips inside and connectors on the back to provide the highest quality home theater experience that DSS can offer. We highly recommend that you make sure your DSS receiver has at least an S-Video connector on the back (we talk about video connectors in Chapter 15), as well as a digital audio connector (coaxial or optical) for Dolby Digital surround sound (which some, but not all, DSS programs include).

- ✔ **PVR-equipped:** Some DSS receivers now come with a built-in hard-drive-based PVR (personal video recorder). Although you can certainly add your own PVR to a DSS-fed home theater, the integration of these units is kind of nice because the program guide that lets you select what show you want to watch live is well-integrated into the PVR's recording scheduling system. See Chapter 6 for a discussion for PVRs.

You might also want to choose between DSS receivers for more prosaic features. For example, some receivers have better (and easier to use) parental "lockout" controls that keep the kids from watching stuff you don't want them to watch. Others have remote controls based on RF (radio frequencies) instead of IR (infrared), so you can control them without a direct line of sight to the receiver. It always pays to check out the little details when you're making these investments. (By the way, the investment isn't too steep. You can find complete dish and 2-receiver packages for under $200, but the price can rise to $500 or more for each HDTV-capable receiver.)

A handful of TVs on the market don't need an external receiver to connect to a DSS dish. Several manufacturers, most notably Thompson, make HDTVs with built-in DSS receivers for DirecTV. (So far, DISH Network still requires a separate receiver.) We're not sure this setup is a good thing, because it limits your upgrade path and gives you twice as much to break down in a single device. It does save room, however, if you're tight on space.

Cable Cornucopia

The biggest competitor to the DSS companies comes from local cable companies, such as Time Warner, AT&T Comcast, and Cox Communications. Until recently, most home theater buffs didn't really consider cable TV to be much of a competitor to DSS — old fashioned *analog* cable systems didn't offer nearly as many channels (particularly when it came to movie channels) as the satellites did. That fact has changed however, with the advent of *digital* cable systems. These systems use MPEG-2 compression technology to carry analog (NTSC) programming into your house, and many provide you with Dolby Digital signals for at least some of the programming.

Lots of people confuse digital cable with HDTV, but in the *vast majority* of cases, digital cable is not HDTV. A few cable companies offer a few channels of HDTV over their digital cable systems (for example, Pat's cable company offers him five HDTV channels, out of about 500 total channels). But the rest is just digitally compressed and transmitted *analog* NTSC TV.

Functionally, DSS and digital cable are very similar. Both offer hundreds of channels, including tons of movie channels, pay-per-view movies, and every iteration of the Discovery channel you can imagine (Discovery Brain Surgery channel anyone?). Like DSS, digital cable includes a pretty on-screen interface that lets you browse through TV listings, set reminder timers, and the like.

The way that digital cable connects to your A/V system is even very similar to DSS. Digital cable requires a set-top box (equivalent to the DSS receiver) that converts these digitally compressed MPEG-2 channels into analog NTSC signals for your TV. And like DSS, if you want to get HDTV signals over digital cable (if your cable company offers them), you need a special set-top box with HDTV capabilities and HDTV connectors on the back, such as DVI or wideband component video.

The big difference between DSS and digital cable, in our minds, is the fact that DSS gives you a choice of receivers (that you have to pay for), whereas digital cable gives you no choice. You rent the digital cable set-top box as part of your monthly service fee, and you get what the cable company gives you. The advantage of this approach is that the cable company has to fix or replace your set-top box if it stops working, but the disadvantage is that you really can't pick a set-top box that has the features you want. Like Model Ts, they come in any color you want, as long as it's black.

The other big difference between DSS and digital cable is one that we can't measure ourselves (we'd need to invest much of our book royalties on the test gear), but which we've heard many industry experts tell us: Many cable companies *compress* the analog NTSC signals carried over digital cable more than the DSS providers do. Because MPEG-2 is what's known as a *lossy* compression technology (meaning that, when MPEG-2 files are uncompressed for viewing, some of the original data is lost), this extra compression means your picture is less sharp and detailed than it would be at a lower compression level.

It's not all bad news, however. There are two big advantages to going with digital cable over DSS:

✔ **Digital cable systems always carry all your local channels (they're required to by law).** You might even get local cable-only channels that you'd never get over DSS or with a broadcast TV antenna.

✔ **Digital cable systems are two-way systems, communicating back to the cable company over the same line that carries your cable TV to you.** So you don't need a phone line (like you do with DSS), and you can actually do neat interactive TV stuff with digital cable. In many areas, you can actually do video-on-demand (or VOD) over a digital cable system. (We talk about VOD in more detail at the end of this chapter.)

Making a decision between DSS and digital cable is really tough. In some parts of the country, it won't be tough at all. Digital cable may not be available, or it may be in a primitive state (for example, no HDTV channels, no VOD, and fewer channels than DSS). In these cases, it helps to have either a good dealer or a lot of friends with home theaters so that you can judge different systems with your own eyes.

Antennas Make a Comeback

Remember the good old days? Yeah, neither do we, but we can remember a day (not so long ago) when all the homes in our neighborhoods were dotted with rooftop TV antennas. Sorta like many homes in our neighborhoods are now dotted with rooftop DSS antennas. For most of us, the rooftop TV antenna (and its close ally, the back-of-the-set rabbit ears) went the way of black and white TVs and dodos a long time ago. Tuning in to broadcast TV was just too much of a pain in the butt compared to the "plug and play" of cable (or the "have a professional aim and then play" of DSS).

But a funny thing happened on the way to obsolescence. Antennas became hip again. HDTV is the reason (it's always the reason for us, but we're like that).

Moving everyone to ATSC and HDTV

HDTV is the reason because our good buddies at the FCC (the Federal Communications Commission) came up with a ruling a few years back that made a huge deal with every single TV broadcaster in the nation. The deal was this: We'll give you an extra chunk of the airwaves for a second TV channel absolutely free, but you've got to use it to broadcast HDTV (and eventually you've got to give us back your old channel so we can use it for other purposes like wireless Internet connections).

Now this deal was supposed to be totally complete by 2006. And when we say totally, we mean that by 2006, every single station in America was supposed to be broadcasting all its programming digitally, using one of the many different digital TV (ATSC) formats. So 2006 was really the cutoff date when all the old analog stations were turned off and the airwaves were turned back over to the FCC. There's a good (and important) story about where this whole transition has gone, but let's leave that aside for one second. (We'll get back to it shortly — we promise.)

What about analog cable?

Most cable companies now offer digital cable service. They have to if they want to compete with the DSS guys, and they can if they've upgraded their cable plants to two-way in order to offer cable modem Internet access (which most cable companies have done). In some areas, however, you're still stuck with analog cable. There's nothing inherently wrong with analog cable. It was good enough for the cable TV industry to convince about 70 percent of Americans to buy their service in the first place, but it's not a particularly sexy service. If you need or want to get analog cable into your home theater, there's not a lot that needs to be done.

Any TV purchased in the past five to ten years (and certainly any TV you may shop for when building a home theater) is cable ready, with one big exception: Some high-end TVs (such as plasmas and front-projection models) ship as monitors without any kind of TV tuner built in. Besides this small group, any modern TV should be able to plug directly into an analog cable system and work, without any extra pieces and parts. In a few cable systems, you need a set-top converter box (the analog equivalent to digital set-top boxes) in order to get pay-per-view or certain movie channels — often called *premium channels.*

Although most home theater builders will move up to digital cable or DSS, there's still a place for analog cable. For example, a basic analog cable package (which might cost less than $20 a month) is a good way to add all the local channels you want to receive to your DSS-based home theater system — particularly if you live in an area where over-the-air broadcast is spotty, and you can't get your local channels via DSS. If Pat ever switches to DSS, he's going to keep his basic analog cable service for two reasons: he has a cable modem that he can't live without, and he gets all the Padres games on cable and can't get them anywhere else.

This transition has caused a revitalization of the TV antenna industry. DSS and (some) digital cable systems carry a few HDTV stations, but they each have severe limitations to how many they can fit on their systems, because HDTV is a bandwidth hog. It uses a lot more bandwidth than NTSC programming does (especially when the NTSC has been compressed using MPEG-2), and bandwidth is a limited commodity on cable and DSS systems. To give more to HDTV means taking some away from something else. It's a zero sum game.

Because broadcasters got a free chunk of bandwidth to do HDTV, this limitation didn't affect them (we're getting back to our story now). Unfortunately, it's 2003, and broadcasters are nowhere close to making this transition in time to meet the 2006 deadline. Constant battles are breaking out, and fingers are being pointed in

Congress, in the FCC, at conventions, anywhere people get together and discuss this transition. The bottom line: 2006 ain't gonna happen, though we're still cautiously optimistic that broadcasters will eventually switch over to ATSC and HDTV.

The government is helping the transition along. In the summer of 2002, the FCC made a ruling that every TV sold in America must have a receiver that can get ATSC broadcasts by 2007. Keep in mind, this doesn't mean that these TVs will be able to display HDTV (for example, they may not have a high enough resolution, or they may not be able to display widescreen content properly), but they will be able to receive it and display it at lower resolutions and at a 4:3 aspect ratio. Eventually, when enough of these TVs are in people's homes, analog TV as we know it will go away, replaced by ATSC and HDTV.

Sorry for the long background discussion, but we really felt it was important to understand what's happening before we discuss what you can do today.

Picking up ATSC with an antenna

Today, if you live in or around a large city, you can pick up ATSC programming (much, but definitely not all of it) by hooking up an antenna and tuning it into your local broadcasters. If you live in a smaller town, you just may have to wait it out for a while. The costs of putting in the new transmission and other broadcast station equipment to do ATSC are pretty expensive, and small stations are going to need frequent and persistent applications of something like an electric cattle prod to their posteriors to get it done.

Before you start investing in an antenna, check with your local broadcasters and see who actually has their ATSC channels up and running. You can also look online at www.hdtvpub.com. Just type in your zip code and find out who's broadcasting in your area.

The law requires these TV stations to broadcast in ATSC, not HDTV. HDTV is a subset of ATSC (check back in Chapter 4 if you missed this distinction). Generally speaking, of the 18 formats allowed under ATSC, we consider only two, 720p and 1080i, to be HDTV.

We focus on antennas for ATSC here, and not older NTSC antennas, but the same general characteristics apply to each.

You can choose from both indoor and outdoor antennas. Indoor antennas work just fine if you are lucky enough to live in an area

with great signals coming over the air, but most people get better
results with outdoor antennas. Outdoor antennas are further cate-
gorized by three features:

- ✔ **Size:** We won't spend too much time explaining the concept of
  size to you, but ATSC antennas fit into small, medium, and
  large groups.

- ✔ **Directionality:** Some antennas (multidirectional) can pick up
  signals coming from any point of the compass, whereas others
  (directional) need to be aimed towards the incoming signal.

- ✔ **Amplification:** Most antennas are unamplified (meaning they
  don't have an electronic signal booster), but for weak signals,
  some antennas use a small *preamplifier* to boost the signals
  and help your TV tuner decode it.

Tuning in over-the-air HDTV can be a tricky business. The good
news is that digital broadcasts are free of the snow, fade, and other
things that made broadcast analog TV so frustrating. The bad news
is that in place of these distortions, digital broadcasts tend to be,
well, digital. In other words, they're either on (working) or off
(nothing, nada, zip). It's not even a matter of just being too far from
the broadcast tower either. We've heard of people being too close,
or people being in the right range, but behind a hill.

The Consumer Electronics Association (CEA) has developed a great
system to help you figure out which kind of antenna you need to get
ATSC signals in your home. Go to its Web site at www.antennaweb.
org, type in some basic address information, and its database spits
out an antenna recommendation for you. The CEA even has a color
coding system that participating antenna manufacturers put on the
outside of their boxes so you can choose the right one at the store.
Very handy.

Neat Network-Based Services

As service providers (such as cable companies) have spent their
billions of dollars building out broadband networks for Internet
access and digital cable, they've come across one big issue: They
need to make money to pay back this investment. So they are constantly looking for new services that take advantage of these high-
speed networks — services they can charge users for.

Well, we're often leery when service providers try to charge us
more (well, not really, our day job is helping them figure out what
these services might be!), but we definitely think that these new
services are a case where the customer also wins. These companies

are looking at offering lots of different entertainment services (including neat stuff such as video games on demand), but the two most interesting (in our minds) are the following:

- ✔ **Video-on-demand (VOD):** Like to watch movies, but hate to go to the video rental shop? One alternative is to join a service that does movie rentals online (and via the U.S. mail) like Netflix (www.netflix.com). Another very cool way to watch movies is to use a VOD service (now being offered by many cable companies as a part of digital cable services). VOD is kinda like pay-per-view (PPV). You pay for individual movies, and you watch them on your cable-connected TV. But the similarities end there, because VOD movies aren't run as scheduled broadcasts (like every hour on the hour). Instead, VOD movies are stored on big computers (video servers) as MPEG-2 files. When you want to watch one, you simply select it on your on-screen guide, and press Play on your remote. The movie gets streamed to your set-top box (just like movies you watch on the Internet, but at a much higher quality), and played back on your TV. You have complete control of the stream, so like a VCR or DVD player, you can start, stop, pause, fast forward, and rewind — the works — all for the same cost as regular PPV. One other neat VOD service is called SVOD (subscription VOD), which allows you to subscribe to a certain channel or show, such as HBO, and get VOD access to all the episodes of a favorite show (such as *The Sopranos*).

- ✔ **Networked PVRs:** This is a more futuristic service, but it's on the verge of appearing on the market. Networked PVR is a cross between regular personal video recorders (PVRs), such as ReplayTVs, and VOD. Like a PVR, a networked PVR records the shows you want to save on a big computer hard drive. But like VOD, this big computer hard drive is located in the service provider's office, not your home theater. So you tell the system what you want to save, and it saves it in a centralized location. When you want to watch, you just click a button on your remote, and the programming is streamed to your TV over the cable company's broadband network. You can still do all the fast forward and pause type stuff you do on a regular PVR, but you've got no extra boxes in your home theater and nothing to buy (you will have to pay a monthly fee for this, of course).

You might even see your phone company (believe it or not) get into these services. Phone companies are investigating new high-speed technologies (such as faster versions of the DSL Internet service they offer now, and even faster fiber optic-based services) that will allow them to compete with the cable companies. We can't wait for some competition!

Chapter 8

Introducing the Home Theater PC

....

In This Chapter

▶ Saying hello to the home theater PC

▶ Going with Windows

▶ PVRing away on your PC

▶ Getting music, movies, and more from the Internet

....

*F*or years now, there has been a huge digital divide between the PC world and the consumer electronics world. You have no doubt been exposed to the concept of multimedia in a PC in the form of animations, video games, MP3 audio, and maybe even short movie clips. Indeed, the ability to play these forms of media is a basic requirement of a multimedia PC.

Similarly, consumer electronics devices have been enabling much of the same (video games, audio, video, and so on), but within its domain, the home entertainment center or home theater.

What most people have been waiting for is a sensible, economical, standardized, and indeed mass market way to link the two. Well, wait no more — the era of the home theater PC is here and now.

In this chapter, we talk about what a home theater PC is, what kinds of pieces and parts you need to create a home theater PC out of your present PC, and also how you can buy a home theater PC right off the shelf (or off a Web page). We also talk a little about the kinds of *content* (audio and video) that your home theater PC can feed into the rest of your A/V gear in your home theater (and vice versa).

Meet the Home Theater PC

You should think of a home theater PC (or *HTPC*, as all the cool kids refer to them), as a high-quality source device attached to your A/V system, just as you think of a DVD player as a high quality source. In fact, if you go relatively high end, you can create an HTPC that funnels audio and video into your system at a higher quality level than many moderately priced, standalone components. HTPC can be that good.

 Building an HTPC is not something you can expect to do without a fair amount of knowledge about PCs, including some skills at opening up a PC and installing new cards and drives and being able to install and troubleshoot *drivers* (the software that integrates hardware devices with the operating system of a PC) and other software. We simply don't have room in this book to give you all the nitty gritty details. You *can* however, buy a ready-to-go version of the HTPC off the shelf (and we explain how later in this chapter).

Sizing up a home theater PC

Depending on your needs, a home theater PC should be able to do some or all of the following things:

- ✔ **Store audio (music) files.** No matter the file type, HTPCs need hard drive space and software for audio files.

- ✔ **Store video clips.** Homemade camcorder movies, downloaded movie trailers, or even downloaded full movies and shows belong on the HTPC. You need (again) hard drive space and software to make this happen.

- ✔ **Play CDs and DVDs.** This is an easy requirement, because most PCs can at least play back CDs, but DVD is also essential in a home theater environment.

- ✔ **Act as a PVR (personal video recorder).** This is an optional (but almost essential, we think) function that uses the HTPC's hard drive to record television shows like a ReplayTV or TiVo.

- ✔ **Let you play video games on the big screen.** With the right hardware, PCs are sometimes even better than gaming consoles (which we cover in Chapter 9) in terms of game-type stuff, such as frames per second (or things blown to bits per millisecond).

✔ **Tune in to online music and video content.** You can grab a lot of really awesome content on the Internet these days. If you pay for this content (and you do have to pay for the good stuff, legally speaking), why not enjoy it on the big screen, with the good audio equipment?

✔ **Provide a high-quality, progressive video signal to your display.** All PCs have a built-in video system that's designed to display on a PC monitor (which by the way is inherently progressive — check out Chapter 4 if you don't remember what this is). Most PCs, however, can't display on a TV, at least not at high quality. An HTPC needs special hardware, which doesn't cost too much money, to make this happen. (This investment also gives you better performance on your PC's monitor, which is never bad.)

✔ **Decode and send to your display HDTV content.** This is another optional function, but a really cool one. With the right hardware inside (an HDTV-capable video card and TV tuner card), HTPCs can provide a cheap way to decode over-the-air HDTV signals and send them to your home theater's display.

Building an HTPC

If the idea of putting together your own HTPC puts a twinkle in your eye, then this section is for you (and the HTPC we describe here really involves a building process — although there's an increasing number of small, specialty PC builders, like www. digitalconnection.com, who will put one together for you). So what do you need besides steady hands, nerves of steel, and a handy dandy TORX screwdriver or two? Well, let us tell you. The key pieces and parts to any HTPC are the following:

✔ **Fast processor:** Generally, you need a fast Pentium IV processor (preferably 1.6 GHz or faster), or an equivalent AMD processor. You can get away with less, but you might have performance issues (such as DVDs having *artifacts,* or leftover or poorly presented pixels, on the screen because the PC can't keep up decoding the DVD's MPEG content).

✔ **Sufficient RAM:** For an HTPC, you need at least 256MB of RAM, and 512MB or more is a good idea.

✔ **A big hard drive:** If you're not planning on saving a lot of video on your HTPC (meaning you won't be using it as a PVR), you can probably get by with a 20GB hard drive. If you are going to start doing the PVR thing (or if you're going to put a lot of MP3 files on the HTPC), we recommend a much bigger hard drive. You can buy a 250GB drive for about $450, and even go as big as 500GB for about $1,000 (that's huge!).

✔ **Powerful, high-quality video card, with an appropriate TV interface:** This is perhaps the most important feature. You need a graphics card that has TV outputs (at least an S-Video output, preferably component video outputs). If you're using a front-projection TV system (see Chapter 13), you might be able to use a different interface (like a VGA or DVI cable) that is more common to PC applications than home video (because many projectors can also be used as PC project-ors — in meeting rooms, for example). We like the graphics cards available from ATI (www.ati.com) and NVIDIA (www.nvidia.com). Some specific things to look for in a video card are the following:

- **Look for a card with a built-in *video processing engine* (or VPE).** These are specifically designed for video.

- **Don't look for a *gaming* card:** Super high-end graphics cards designed for the ultimate in PC gaming are typi-cally not optimized for video display. They work, but you can probably do better with a (cheaper) card designed for video.

- **Look for a card with a built-in TV tuner.** Some prod-ucts, like ATI's "All-in-Wonder" series of cards, have a built-in cable-ready TV tuner. So you can plug your cable TV or broadcast antenna directly into the card for TV viewing. Unfortunately, we don't know of any cards that can handle DSS or digital cable. Sorry.

- **Think about HDTV.** Most HTPC video cards do *not* have built-in TV tuners that are capable of capturing ATSC/HDTV over-the-air broadcasts. But these cards (at least the better ones) are certainly capable of sending video to your display at an HDTV resolution (such as 720p or 1080i). So if you want to feed HDTV into your HTPC (wow, acronyms galore — sorry!), you need to add in an HDTV tuner card (like AccessDTV's — www.accessdtv.com).

- **Check the resolutions of the card:** If you have a non-HDTV ready display unit (like a regular NTSC direct view TV), you need only a 480-line output (with progressive scan, if your TV can handle it). If you have a projection TV or a plasma flat panel TV, it may have a *native* resolution (which we discuss in Chapters 12 and 13). Make sure your card can display video at this resolution (you normally set the resolution of the card using supplied software).

✔ **High-end audio card:** Because you'll probably be playing surround sound formats on your HTPC, you'll want a video card that can support this. Audio cards may have either a coaxial or an optical output (make sure you get one that has the same kind as you have on the back of your receiver). Many sound card manufacturers call this an *S/PDIF* (Sony/Philips Digital Interface) interface.

✔ **CD/DVD-ROM drive:** This one is kind of a no-brainer — you're going to want to listen to CDs and watch DVDs. You might, however, also want to create your own CDs and DVDs, so consider a CD-RW/DVD combo drive, or even a DVD-RW drive (that can record DVDs). If you have a slower PC, you might consider adding in a hardware device called a *DVD decoder* — this device performs hardware-based decoding of the MPEG video on DVDs, leaving your computer's main processor free to do its thing (like running the operating system). You can get these from companies like Creative Labs or Sigma Designs (www.sigmadesigns.com).

✔ **An appropriate operating system:** We recommend that you use a modern operating system, such as Windows XP or Macintosh OS X. (If you use Linux, you're on your own.)

✔ **Software for playing or recording content:** At a minimum, you need some MP3 jukebox software to take care of your CD/MP3 playing, storage, and organization needs, and a similar DVD player program. For music, we like MUSICMATCH Jukebox (www.musicmatch.com), and for video, we like InterVideo WinDVD (www.intervideo.com). If you want to use your HTPC as a PVR, you need some software (and perhaps hardware) to make that work, which we talk about in the following section.

✔ **A remote control:** Now, very few PCs come out-of-the-box with a remote control, but many of the HTPC video and audio cards we've discussed do. The key attribute of any remote for an HTPC is that the accompanying software can control all your applications — MP3 jukebox, DVD player software, and so on. (All these remotes come with software that makes the PC recognize them.)

We focus mainly on the Windows side of things in this section, not because we hate Macs, but because we realize that something like 95 out of 100 PC owners have a Windows computer. You can make an HTPC with a Macintosh, too (and a lot of the recommendations above remain in force). The only issue is this (something we Mac

---

A mini office home theater

You can also use a lot of the advice about putting a PC into your home theater in this chapter to create a "personal" home theater in your home office or computer room. Substitute a (smaller) high-quality PC monitor, a set of smaller PC surround sound speakers, and (optionally) a PC-connected A/V receiver such as Yamaha's PET RU-100 (search on www.yamaha.com to see details), and you can enjoy the home theater experience right on your desktop. (Of course, no one ever really hears of 'chair potatoes' much; we much prefer the couch ourselves.)

---

users run into more than we like to admit): You've got a lot fewer hardware and software options with a Mac then you do with a Windows PC.

That's really all there is to say (at our high-level view) about HTPCs. In Chapter 17, we discuss what you need to do to get this beautiful, high-tech monster hooked into your home theater.

Getting an HTPC the easy way

What if you don't want to go through all this computer building? Well, your friends at Microsoft (really, they're your friends) got together with a handful of their closest PC hardware partners and came up with their own version of the HTPC called the Windows XP Media Center Edition (www.microsoft.com/windowsxp/mediacenter).

Media Center (we're just going to shorten the name to that) is both software (XP Media Center Edition operating system) and hardware (the Media Center PC). One big deal about Media Center is that it's like the old Frank Sinatra song, "Love and Marriage": You can't have one without the other. As of early 2003, you can get Media Center only by purchasing a brand new PC that has been outfitted specifically to be a Media Center PC. We expect that, over time, you'll be able to add the software to your own hardware.

You can't go to Microsoft.com and buy a "media center upgrade" to your existing Windows XP PC. You've gotta buy a new machine.

What do you get out of a Media Center PC? Well, the details (such as the exact model of graphics card) depend upon the vendor, but the basic features of a Media Center PC include the following:

✔ **A remote control:** All Media Center PCs come with an infrared remote control that lets you control the various A/V functions from across the room (including other devices such as cable boxes).

✔ **An "advanced" graphics card:** We put *advanced* in quotes, because that's Microsoft's official term for describing it. Can't argue with strong words like that! Most of the Media Center PCs we've seen use something like NVIDIA's GeForce4 Ti graphics card (which is a card you might purchase if you were building your own HTPC). These "advanced" cards must include a TV tuner function, and a TV output for connecting to your display.

✔ **A hardware encoder:** This turns video from your TV source (like cable TV) into MPEG digital video, and turns your Media Center PC into a PVR.

✔ **A digital audio output:** As we discuss in the preceding section, this lets you connect your PC to your A/V receiver for surround sound purposes.

✔ **Software that makes it all work:** This is the cool part (well the whole thing is cool, but this makes it even cooler). Software to play your MP3s, CDs, and DVDs, and to run your PVR is all included and well integrated. So you don't have to try to make it all work.

A Media Center PC acts just like a regular PC most of the time. You use it for e-mail, Web surfing, writing books, and whatever. But when you click the remote, the PC shifts over to Media Center mode, and your normal PC desktop is replaced by a simplified interface (designed to be read from across the room on either a PC display or a home theater display). You can perform all the HTPC functions we discuss earlier in the section, "Sizing up a home theater PC," and also play games, manage and display digital photographs, and more. Very cool.

There are about a half dozen Media Center PC vendors as we write (beginning of 2003), and more are coming. The coolest model we've seen so far is the Alienware Navigator Pro (www.alienware.com). Check it out; it's the coolest looking PC Pat's seen since he got his Titanium PowerBook. (He loves his Macs.)

Checking out PC PVRs

We mention earlier in the chapter the concept of using an HTPC as a PVR (personal video recorder). This is something that is a standard feature in a Media Center PC, and something we think you should consider adding to your home-built HTPC.

Coming soon: Media servers

While HTPCs and Windows XP Media Center Edition PCs are really just what their names say they are — PCs — there's a new generation of computer-*like* devices hitting the market that will do many of the same things, in a more consumer-friendly fashion. *Media servers* are what we call them (and what most people call them — we're not just making this stuff up). A media server is really just a souped up version of a standalone PVR (such as a TiVo) or a standalone MP3 server (such as an Audio ReQuest). The media server doesn't run a PC operating system and doesn't do normal PC stuff. It just serves up media (hence the name). We expect consumer electronics companies, such as Sony and Toshiba, to start selling media servers any day now. You'll be able to hook them into your PC network *and* into your home theater, and use them to store music, video, digital photographs, and more.

In fact, it's so useful that, even if this were the only thing you wanted to do with your HTPC, it would be worth it. You can simply install a PC PVR kit and skip a lot of the other stuff we listed earlier (such as the DVD player, decoder, and software).

The biggest limitation to any PVR system is the amount of space on your hard drive for storing video, so you might consider a hard drive upgrade regardless of your other HTPC intentions.

A couple of the PC PVR kits on the market include the following:

- **SnapStream Personal Video Station (PVS):** An inexpensive way into the PC PVR realm is the PVS, a software-based solution that works with a TV capture card (there's a list on the Web site, www.snapstream.com). PVS can control your DSS receiver or a cable set-top box, and it uses an online programming guide service. Saved videos on the PVS use the Microsoft Windows Media format (not MPEG), which limits the system to Windows PCs. The coolest feature of the PVS is that you can use it outside the home theater. For example, you can share files on a computer network or even view them (with a special extra bit of software) on a Pocket PC.

- **Pinnacle PCTV Deluxe:** An external box, the Pinnacle PCTV ($199, www.pinnaclesys.com) sits next to your HTPC and connects via a USB connection. The PCTV Deluxe has a built-in TV tuner that can connect to your antenna or cable system, and it records your shows as standard MPEG video. You need your own video card in the PC to display the recorded video on your TV or home theater display.

✔ **ATI All-In-Wonder 9700 Pro:** If you're after the real top-of-the-line in PC PVR (and HTPC video cards for that matter), you really need to check this baby out. For $449, you get the latest and greatest PC video card, DVD acceleration, a TV tuner, PVR software, an online programming guide, and HDTV support in one! As we write, this is the hottest HTPC/PC PVR device you can buy. We're sure the price will go down too!

Internet Content for Your HTPC

HTPCs are good as an alternative to other home theater source devices — for example, as a high-quality way to play back DVDs. But for most folks, they're not worth the trouble just for that purpose. What really makes an HTPC useful is its ability to provide a *portal* to all sorts of great Internet-based content. Now, if you're a real PC aficionado, you might build an HTPC just for fun. But if you're like us, you're only going to go down this road if there's something in it for you. There is!

In fact, a load of good content is on the Internet, just waiting for you to come around and get it. This is particularly true in the music realm, where legitimate (in other words, pay) music content has become a reality (after years of false starts). In the video world, the story isn't as bright yet. Movie studios have been really dragging their feet when it comes to getting content online. One movie source, Movielink, is out there now, but others have been squeezed out of business by the movie studios.

You're not getting much Internet content if your HTPC isn't connected to the Internet. So don't forget that a connection to your high speed Internet access (DSL or cable modem) is part of the overall equation.

Some of the most popular online content providers include:

✔ **Listen.com:** Listen.com's Rhapsody online music service (www.listen.com) is a great way to feed quality music into your home theater (via an HTPC). Listen.com has made deals with all five of the major record labels and many smaller independent labels, too, which gives them a library of over 20,000 albums. For $9.95 per month, you get unlimited, *on demand* access to all these songs, which means you can play back any of the songs in Listen.com's library at any time. There's also a radio service (for half as much) that doesn't give you the on-demand feature, but offers a bunch of differently themed radio stations. You can even pay a bit more and download music for creating your own CDs (99 cents each).

The Rhapsody player (the service uses its own proprietary player) is based on Windows Media Player, so it should work with just about any HPTV remote control. You can try out the service for free for a week. We recommend that you do.

✔ **MUSICMATCH MX:** Besides making our favorite Windows MP3 Jukebox, MUSICMATCH also offers an online service called MUSICMATCH MX. Like Listen.com, MUSICMATCH MX comes in two versions — a gold version ($2.95 per month) that gives you radio access, and a platinum version ($4.95 per month) that gives you on-demand access to the catalogs of over 8,000 artists. The nice thing about MX is that it's fully integrated into MUSICMATCH jukebox, so you've got a single interface to deal with.

✔ **Movielink:** If you want to start getting movies from the Net, check out Movielink (www.movielink.com). Formed by five huge movie studios, this site allows you to download and play current Hollywood movies (at about the same time as they make it to DVD). You pay about $3 per movie, and the system uses either the Windows Media Player software included with all versions of Windows or Real Networks' RealOne player (www.real.com). To use Movielink (on Windows PCs only), you simply "rent" the movie online, and it is downloaded to your PC. You have six days to watch it (and you pay even if you don't remember to watch it), and after you start playing it, you have to finish within 24 hours. We're not sure that the quality of Movielink is really up to a big screen playback, but we mention it because it's the first service of its kind. We hope more are to come!

Chapter 9

Gaming Galore

● ●

In This Chapter

▶ Plugging into the PlayStation

▶ Marking the spot with the Xbox

▶ Cubing your game fun with GameCube

▶ Using a game console as a DVD player and more

▶ Powering up your games with a PC

▶ Controlling your games

● ●

*T*oday's video gaming systems are crammed full of high-powered audio and graphics chips that can put your home theater through its paces. With DVD-based games, you get audio that can use all the speakers in your surround sound system, and video that can fill up your screen. Video games aren't just kids' toys any more; they can be an integral part of your home theater experience!

In this chapter, we talk about how video consoles can fit into your home theater system (and some folks they think they have no role at all — we disagree, as you'll see). We talk about the leading console systems as well as how you might bring PC gaming systems into your home theater. By the way, we think game consoles (such as the Xbox) are the best way to bring gaming to the big screen, but if you're handy with your PC, you can get a great gaming experience with a gaming PC as well.

Integrating Cool Consoles into Your Home Theater

If you have or are considering buying a modern gaming console, such as an Xbox or a PlayStation 2, you really need to be thinking of how to integrate it as a source device (in other words, a device that provides audio and video) in your home theater. Yeah, we know — some "high end" home theater folks might be cringing right now. Let 'em. We think video games fit into even top-of-the-line home theaters.

Game consoles are, of course, built for video games, but if you're not deep of pocket, you might even think about letting your game console do double duty as your DVD player (yep, they can do that), at least until you've saved up the money for a nice, new, progressive scan standalone DVD player (discussed in Chapter 6). Two of the consoles we discuss here can replace a DVD and/or CD player in your home theater, and more importantly, all of them can be a heck of a lot of fun. In the following sections, we give you an overview of the different consoles and how you can integrate them into your home theater.

Playing with PlayStation 2

The most popular gaming console to date has been Sony's PlayStation 2 (or PS2). This cool, black and purple box has a 300 MHz processor under the hood, which might not sound like much in PC terms, but this processor is especially designed for gaming and can really crank out the video. The processor includes secondary processors, called *floating point* processors, which help the PS2 do the math on all of a game's polygons (remember polygons from geometry?) at supercomputer speeds.

Besides this high-powered processor, the PS2 includes a bunch of additional features:

- **A powerful graphics chip:** Called the Graphics Synthesizer, this chip does the actual work of creating all the pixels (or colored dots) that show up on your TV screen as the game video. For you tech types out there, this is a 256-bit graphics chip.

- **32MB of RAMBUS:** RAMBUS is a high-speed type of RAM or computer memory, and it holds all the computer instructions and codes that make up the game.

- **A DVD-ROM drive:** This drive plays the optical discs containing the PS2 games and can also play PlayStation 1 games, movie DVDs, and CDs.

- **Lots of ports and connections:** You get the following:
  - Two gaming controller ports (The controllers are the physical interface between you and the game.)
  - Two USB ports (USB stands for Universal Serial Bus — like on a PC.)

- Two memory card slots (to store game data, such as your current level in a game), as well as an expansion bay that lets you install a computer hard drive for even more storage

- A single i.LINK port (Sony's name for IEEE 1394 or FireWire — a super high-speed connection used for all sorts of computer-related devices such as hard drives and digital video cameras) that lets you connect multiple PS2s together for head-to-head gaming. (We talk about these fancy connections in Chapter 15.)

You can also buy an online gaming connection kit for the PS2 that lets you connect your PS2 console to the Internet to play games against other people who aren't *anywhere* near your home theater. Neat. See the sidebar, "Playing games online."

You can find out more about the PS2 (and the hundreds of games available for it) online at www.playstation.com.

Xbox marks the spot

Until late 2001, PS2 was the king of the hill, the A#1, fastest game console you could wrap your mitts around. Nothing faster . . . anywhere.

In November 2001, however, Microsoft launched its own competing game console — the Xbox (www.xbox.com). If you've ever picked one up and tried to move it around, you probably already know that this is a serious chunk of hardware. But the Xbox isn't just a big lump of metal — it's a seriously fast gaming console, with faster-than-the-PS2 chips that have made it a serious contender to the PS2.

When we say a game console is fast, we're not talking about how many MHz the processor operates at or other computer-centric measures of speed (though these are very important). Rather, we're talking about how much information the console can push up onto the TV screen when it's playing a game (okay — when you're playing a game and the console is processing the game). Most experts use the number of polygons per second as a measurement for speed, and that's a pretty good measure, although some gaming experts use other graphics measurements.

When comparing the Xbox and the PS2, most gaming geeks have found that the Xbox is a *bit* faster and more powerful. Not a lot faster, but if you have a high-resolution display (such as an HDTV), and are playing the same game, you'll probably find the video on the Xbox to be a bit sharper.

Not surprisingly, because Microsoft is primarily a PC software company, the Xbox has a lot in common with a Windows PC. However, everything has been altered, modified, and tweaked for gaming, and you can't use an Xbox to write a book using Microsoft Word. Intel builds the main processor, which is a 733 MHz variant of the Pentium III PC processor. More PC hardware can be found in the Xbox in the form of the graphics processor, dubbed the X Chip, which NVIDIA builds and which is a variant of the company's GeForce 3 PC video cards.

Other cool features of the Xbox include:

- ✔ **A built-in 8GB hard drive (like a PC hard drive):** You can use the drive to save game data or to store audio tracks ripped from your own CDs, so that you can customize your game soundtracks with your own favorite music (*ripping* is the process of converting CD audio to files on the hard drive, like the creation of MP3 music files).

- ✔ **64MB of high-speed RAM:** This is good for holding the game data that the Pentium processor and NVIDIA chip are processing.

- ✔ **A built-in Ethernet port:** Ethernet is the high-speed (10 Mbps) networking system that most computer networks use. Ethernet is also the connection found on the majority of DSL and cable modems for home high-speed Internet, and this port lets you connect your Xbox to the Internet for online gaming (as we discuss in the sidebar, "Playing games online").

- ✔ **A DVD optical drive for games, CDs, and video DVDs:** Unlike the PS2, however, the Xbox can't play DVD movies out of the box — you need to pay about $30 for a remote control and adapter (which plugs into one of the controller ports) to make this work.

- ✔ **Ports and slots:** You get four USB-type game controller ports (two more than the PS2) for multi-player games, and a slot for an 8MB memory card.

What's really cool about the Xbox, from a home theater perspective, is the fact that the Xbox is the only console that can display its games on 1080i high definition TV. This means you can have some really awesome, high-resolution gaming going on in your theater. Keep in mind that not too many games on the market have been specially designed (as they must be) to really take advantage of HDTV, but more and more are being so designed. And even if games aren't 1080i games, they still work well with (and look good on) HDTVs.

Xbox is also the only game console to have full Dolby Digital audio designed into games. The other consoles have surround sound using Dolby Pro Logic, but they don't have the full, high-quality digital surround sound of the Xbox.

Not Rubik's Cube; it's GameCube

Not to be outdone by Sony and Microsoft, the granddaddy of game consoles, Nintendo, has its own new, high-powered, home theater-ready gaming console called the GameCube. This is by far the cutest of the three. It's positively tiny, especially compared with the huge hunk of metal that holds in the innards of the Xbox. The GameCube (or GC to the gaming cognoscenti) is no slouch, performance-wise, despite its diminutive dimensions (the GC is only 4 inches high).

Inside of the GC is a 485 MHz PowerPC processor — just like the ones inside of Apple Macs and PowerBooks. (IBM, the maker of PowerPC chips, and Nintendo have code-named this chip "Gekko.")

Other features of the GameCube include

- ✔ **A powerful graphics processor:** This one is code-named "Flipper," like the Dolphin (though you shouldn't get this Flipper wet). Built by ATI (who's a leader in the computer graphics chip market), Flipper can crank out up to 12 million polygons per second to fill your screen with gamey goodness.

- ✔ **40MB of system memory:** This includes 24MB of some super fast RAM called MoSys 1T-SRAM. (No we're not sure what that name stands for either, but it *is* faster than regular memory chips.)

- ✔ **Four ports for gaming controllers:** These are for multiplayer games.

- ✔ **Two memory card slots:** You can use these to save game information.

- ✔ **A proprietary optical disc that's smaller than traditional DVDs or CDs:** This smaller disc helps keep the size of the GC down to a minimum, but it does have the unfortunate draw-back of keeping the GC from doing double duty as your home DVD player.

The GameCube lags behind the other two consoles in some ways. Namely, its performance is slightly lower (though still excellent), and it can't play DVDs or CDs, which is why we mention it last. It does have some advantages though. Its small size makes it quite portable if you want to move your GC to the kids' bedroom (or take it out of the kids' bedroom!). Nintendo has a lot of incredibly popular games (think *Mario*) that you can only play on the GC. And finally, the GC costs less than the other consoles. (We haven't talked about prices too much yet, because they change all the time and because so many different packages are out there. But as we write this book, the basic console and one-controller package for a PS2 or an Xbox is $199, whereas the GameCube is only $149.)

If you or your kids have one of the handheld Nintendo GameBoy Advance units, you can buy a cable to hook it up to your GameCube to play head-to-head between the units, or to view your GameBoy games on the big screen.

Consoles aren't just for games

A game console isn't just fun — it can also be a multipurpose device that does more than just games. In fact, all of the manufacturers of game consoles have scores of engineers in white lab coats squirreled away at their headquarters, developing new ways that game consoles can be the centerpiece of a home's media room. So, although we're about to mention a few of the things that game consoles can do in the here and now, there's more to come.

Let's stay in the present for a moment, however, and look at what game consoles can do today:

- ✔ **Play DVD movies:** The Xbox and PS2 can both do this, although neither has progressive scan DVD functionality (see Chapter 6 if you're not sure what that means).

- ✔ **Play audio CDs:** Again, both the Xbox and the PS2 can play any of your audio CDs when connected to your home theater.

- ✔ **Surf the Web:** Not for novices, but if you have a PS2, you can buy Sony's Linux Kit for the PS2 for about $200. Linux, in case you aren't familiar with it, is a UNIX-based computer operating system favored by many techies, and this kit (which includes a hard drive, mouse, keyboard, and network adapter) lets you run all sorts of Linux applications on the PS2. Find out more at www.playstation.com.

This last item isn't exactly mainstream, but it gives you a good idea of where consoles are heading — right into the PC mainstream.

Playing games online

Playing a video game by yourself can be a lot of fun, but some games are just meant to be played head-to-head against a human opponent. It's really a lot more fun to blow up your friends than it is to bomb an artificial computer opponent. Unfortunately, your friends can't always come over to play — especially if, like Pat, you're in your 30s and find yourself trying to convince your friends to come over to play games. ("Uh, no, you can't bring your baby.")

Luckily, the broadband revolution that's given so many of us high-speed Internet access at home (using cable modems or DSL) has come to the video game world. All three of the gaming consoles we discuss in this chapter now have optional online gaming kits that enable you to connect your console not only to the home theater, but also to the Internet.

This connection opens up a world of new opportunities in game play. Play head to head against your buddy across town — or across the country. Join in on online games with complete strangers. Whatever floats your boat.

If the Xbox is your game console of choice, you'll need to check out Xbox *Live* (www.xbox.com/live). For $50, you get the components you need to get online and a year of gaming service. Microsoft *doesn't* provide the broadband service for Xbox *Live*, just the gaming service itself, and Xbox *Live* is broadband only. The gaming service eliminates the need to subscribe to one service for Game A and another for Game B.

If you use a PS2, you need to spend $40 on Sony's PlayStation 2 Network Adaptor, which enables you to connect via broadband or dialup connections. We think you really need broadband to do online gaming right (otherwise the play is just too choppy and lagged), but if you can't get broadband, it's nice to have the option of dialup. Regardless of how you connect, with a PS2 you'll need to sign up for a separate gaming service for each game you have (through the game software companies like Sega or EA).

The Nintendo GameCube can be connected to your online service using either a standard dialup Internet connection or a broadband connection. Nintendo sells two separate adapters — one for each type of connection, for about $69 each. As we write, there's only one game that you can play online — Phantasy Star Online, which requires an $8.95 per month subscription and works with most online services (but not, unfortunately, with the biggest one — AOL).

Remember that the cost of getting into online gaming is higher than just the price of the kit or service. You also need to account for the costs of new, online-ready games (we expect to see a ton of new ones hit the market) and gaming services. If you're not using an Xbox and Xbox *Live*, you'll also need to keep in mind that there may be costs associated with the online gaming services that let you connect with others online — meaning you may have to pay some additional fees to the game software companies.

Because video game consoles tend to display parts of their images in a *static* fashion — in other words, part of the picture never, or rarely, changes — you need to be careful when picking a television for your video game-enhanced home theater. Some projection televisions (mainly those that use CRT picture tubes) and some flat panel TVs (plasma screen TVs) can experience "burn in" when you use video games on them a lot. This means that the thin phosphor layers on these TVs that light up to show your picture become permanently etched with the images from your video game. Check with the TV manufacturer's instructions before you use a video game console with one of these TVs.

Integrating PC-based Gaming into Your Home Theater

Although most people think of console gaming as something you do in the living room (or home theater room), and PC gaming as something you do in the home office or at a desk somewhere, in fact PC-based games do have a role in the home theater. Speaking even more generally, we think PCs have a place in — or connected to — your home theater for a lot of functions (read Chapter 8 for more on this, if you've skipped it).

Gaming on the PC has evolved over the years to be as sophisticated, fast, and graphics-rich as console gaming. In fact, if you want the ultimate in gaming machines, the no-holds-barred, polygon-generating king of the hill, you need to look at a PC, not at a console. And PCs are inherently more networkable than a console; you have to try hard to find a PC these days without a modem, an Ethernet port, and a dozen other ways to connect to other devices and networks. So PC-based gaming can be a great alternative to the consoles we discuss earlier in this chapter. You're no longer limited to that Minesweeper game that comes loaded on all PCs.

We should mention right up front in this section that purpose-built gaming consoles make the most sense for most people in a home theater. They're ready to go out of the box; with Plug-and-Play, they're simple to connect, set up, and play. Most PCs, on the other hand, need some serious tweaking to do gaming in a home theater environment (and by that, we mean using the surround sound system and television/monitor of your home theater). So keep that in mind.

Upgrading to Windows XP Media Center

The easiest way to get your PC involved in your home theater is to go out and buy an entirely new PC — one that uses Microsoft's new Windows XP Media Center Edition operating system. You can find out a ton about this new evolution of Windows at Microsoft's "test drive" site: www.testdrivewinxpmediacenteredition.com.

Media Center is all about the convergence of the PC and the TV (and other home theater components). It's been designed from the ground up as an operating system *and* a set of PC hardware that lets you easily connect the PC to your home entertainment gear. For this reason, you can't (at least currently) just go out and buy a Media Center upgrade for your current PC. Instead, you need to buy a new PC that includes some hardware specifically designed around the new operating system that will facilitate this new PC-to-TV connection.

Media Center Edition PCs usually include the following extra (or enhanced) components compared to a regular PC:

- A graphics card (or controller) with a TV out connection that uses an S-video or composite video (RCA) plug to connect into your TV or home theater receiver. (Check out Chapter 15 for more details on what these connections are.)

- A sound board that can output surround sound using Dolby Digital 5.1 (see Chapter 4 for details on Dolby).

- A remote control that lets you sit on the couch and click away at your PC.

The only things you need to transform a Media Center PC into a full-fledged member of your home theater are the cables to plug things together and, of course, the games and controllers that you want to play with.

Roll your own gaming PC

You don't *need* to get an XP Media Center PC to get your PC games hooked into your home theater. Creating your own is a very valid approach — as long as you keep in mind that it might take a bit more PC expertise than just buying a new PC that's been specially designed for such use. We talked at length in Chapter 8 about how to choose PCs and PC components and accessories as source devices and video recorders for your home theater, and exactly the same rules that applied there apply to using your PC as a gaming machine in your home theater.

You need just a couple of things:

- A graphics card that can connect to a television and display properly on the television (meaning it can output the right resolution for your particular TV)

- A sound card that can connect to your home theater receiver using either analog (RCA) jacks or a digital connection, and that can provide the receiver with analog Dolby Pro Logic or (preferably) Dolby Digital signals

That's basically it. In Chapter 17, we talk more about setting up your PC with your home theater.

Adding Extra Game Controllers

Whatever game system you choose — console or PC, Xbox or PS2, whatever — you need to interface with it. That is the whole point of games: interactivity. Of course, by connecting your game system to your home theater, you've covered how your eyes and ears (and rear end, if you've got a big enough subwoofer) interface with the system. The other key interface is, of course, your hands (and sometimes feet), which connect to your games with a controller.

All game consoles come with one or two basic multipurpose controllers that usually have enough buttons and joysticks and four-way pointers to drive us adults crazy (though the kids seem to catch on to them right away). These controllers (sometimes called *gamepads*) allow you to play just about any game if you can twist your thumbs in the right direction and have the appropriate level of dexterity and coordination. You might, however, want to consider some specialized controllers if you have some certain games that you simply love to play again and again. (You might save yourself from repetitive stress injuries this way — and increase your score!)

Some of the controllers you can buy include:

- **Wireless controllers:** These are usually just like the general purpose controllers, but they connect using radio waves, not wires. If you have dogs, small kids, or are simply sick of tripping over wires, pick up a pair of these wireless wonders.

✔ **Wheel controllers:** The kids like *Mario,* but we like *Grand Turismo 3* (at least Pat does). In other words, we want to pretend that we're not stuck in traffic, that we're Colin McRae zipping through the World Rally Championship in our WRX. Thumb buttons don't cut it for this activity. Get a wheel controller that includes brake and accelerator pedals, a big fat racing wheel, and a nice short throw shift knob. Racers start your engines! Check out www.madcatz.com for our favorite wheels.

✔ **Joysticks:** Want to pretend you're "Cool Hand" Grafton's wing man in *Flight of the Intruder?* Well, then you need a joystick controller, with enough buttons to "pickle" your bombs on target. Check out www.thrustmaster.com for some cool joysticks.

There's literally a ton of controllers out there you can buy (really, we bought one of each and weighed them! — okay, that's a lie), including some really funky ones. There are skateboard-shaped controllers that you stand on for skating, surfing, or boarding games, and even one that consists of a mat for replicating dance moves you see on-screen. You can find something for everyone, and controllers are truly a way to maximize your home theater fun.

Part III

Watching and Listening: Display and Control Devices

The 5th Wave   By Rich Tennant

DAD ADDS MULTIMEDIA SOUND AND GRAPHICS TO THE TRADITIONAL CAMPFIRE GHOST STORY.

In this part . . .

*O*ur journey through Home Theater Land continues with a look at the heart of your system — the receiver and controller devices. We look at what's really important about these systems, in terms of interfaces, power levels, multizone capabilities, and so on. We also help you decide if you want an integrated box (a receiver) or separate components. We even talk some about power amplifiers (which is an area of conversation that makes lots of guys — yes, 99 percent guys, sorry — very excited).

Then we walk you though a discussion of everything you've ever wanted to know about speakers, building off the surround sound knowledge from Part I.

The next chapter delves into your TV display options. Your home theater's display often overwhelms the home theater with its presence, and with displays that can go to 120 inches and higher, the options can get really overwhelming. You can go in lots of directions, and we talk about HDTV, LCDs, plasma screens, and other display choices.

Then we get to the projectors. We talk about all the latest technologies and what the pros and cons are for each. CRT, LCD, DLP, LCoS — we've got all the hot acronyms here.

And then finally, we help you make your way through the myriad of options for remote controlling your system. Find out about the best solutions that are on the market today.

Chapter 10

The Heart of a Home Theater: The A/V Receiver

*T*he A/V receiver is the hub of your home theater. It's the device that has both the brains and the brawn to control and drive your home theater experience. A growing home theater market, intense competition, and computer industry-like efficiencies at making electronic components have all benefited the A/V receiver. It's no longer a rarified, esoteric piece of equipment. In fact, you can get a good one for quite a reasonable price. Picking through the lingo and marketing speak and choosing a good one can still be difficult, but that's why you bought this book!

In this chapter, we talk about the features and specifications that are important to keep in mind as you're evaluating A/V receivers. We also talk about a different approach to controlling your system — using separate A/V controllers and power amplifier systems.

Digging into the A/V Receiver

Think of the A/V receiver as the digital and electronic hub of your home theater. An A/V receiver does a bunch of things, all in one nice and relatively compact package. (It's sort of the Swiss army knife of the home theater, except you can't fit one in your pocket.) Among the tasks assigned to the A/V receiver are the following:

✓ **Connects and switches your audio sources:** Every audio source in your home theater should connect to your A/V receiver. The preamplifier section of the receiver allows you to easily switch to (or select) the audio source that you want to listen to.

✓ **Connects and switches your video sources:** With a few exceptions (which we discuss later), all your video source devices are also connected directly to the A/V receiver, which is in turn connected to your display device. This setup greatly simplifies the selection of video sources when you want to play a DVD, a show recorded on a PVR (like a TiVo), or anything else. In most cases, you select what you want to watch on the receiver's remote and don't have to adjust anything on the display.

✓ **Tunes in radio programming:** Part of the definition of a receiver is that it includes a radio tuner. So you can tune in PBS or Howard Stern (or whatever floats your boat between those two extremes).

✓ **Decodes surround sound formats:** The ability to decode analog and digital surround sound formats (we talk about these in Chapter 3) is one of two features that distinguish an A/V receiver from a more traditional stereo receiver (the plain old stereo you've had around for years).

✓ **Amplifies audio signals to drive multiple speakers:** Another distinguishing characteristic of an A/V receiver is the fact that it contains multiple channels of amplification (at least five) to drive (or provide power to) your surround sound speaker system.

✓ **Provides the user interface for your home theater:** The interface includes the receiver's remote control (or your own favorite remote, as we discuss in Chapter 14), the displays on the receiver's face, and (in many cases) an on-screen display on your television. All these elements enable you, the human (or your dog, if he's very talented), to command all the electronic components in your home theater.

In the following sections, we discuss each of these A/V receiver responsibilities in more detail.

Counting the inputs

Most people like to *ooh* and *ahh* at the bells and whistles — pretty design, big macho power ratings, and the like. When evaluating any A/V receiver, however, we think a good place to begin is by counting the inputs that let you connect source devices to the receiver.

After all, if you have a DVD player, a cassette deck, a satellite receiver, an SACD (super audio CD) player, a turntable, a PVR (personal video recorder), and a VCR, you want to hook all these devices into your home theater.

Well, to use all your components, you'd better have enough jacks on the back of your receiver. A receiver may have enough power to wake up people across town and a design so beautiful that your home theater skeptic spouse *begs* you to buy it. But that beauty won't do you much good if have to climb behind it and switch wires every time you want to switch sources. So before you buy anything, think about the components you have (and what you'll soon be getting) and make sure the receiver has enough inputs.

Most A/V receivers have enough inputs for most people. We don't want to scare you. In fact, most have enough jacks on the back to make your head swim. But many inexpensive receivers don't have enough of the *right kind* of jacks for some folks. This is particularly true for digital audio and video jacks, but can also be true for the analog audio inputs if you've decided to go down the SACD or DVD-Audio path, which we cover in Chapter 5.

Deciphering digital audio inputs

Digital audio inputs (we show examples of these in Chapter 15) on an A/V receiver let you connect the audio outputs of DVD players, CD players, game consoles, HDTV tuners, and some digital cable set-top boxes or DSS satellite receivers. Connecting these audio sources using digital inputs (instead of the traditional analog inputs) is always a good idea for sonic reasons, because the digital signals are much less prone to electrical interferences than analog signals. A more important consideration is that digital inputs are *required* to get digital surround sound formats, such as Dolby Digital and DTS, into your receiver. (The 2-channel analog outputs on DVD players and other devices move you down to the lesser Dolby Pro Logic surround sound system. You can't get digital surround sound from these connections.)

The one exception to this rule is devices (mainly DVD players) that have a built-in Dolby Digital or DTS surround sound decoder. You *can* connect these to your receiver using analog audio connections, but this may not be the optimal solution for the following reasons:

- ✔ You need to use six cables instead of one.
- ✔ You may lose some signal quality due to interference in the analog signal.
- ✔ You need a receiver that has the necessary six analog inputs on the back.

There are two types of digital audio connections (which we discuss in more detail in Chapter 15): coaxial and optical. Some high-end audio folks believe that the coaxial sounds better; it may have a slight sonic benefit, but not so much that regular people can tell. Just make sure that you don't buy a receiver with three optical connections and one coaxial connection, and then find you have three source devices with coaxial connections only. Oops. (If you don't know what these look like, again look in Chapter 15.)

The key measurement here is the total number of connections (as long as the types of connections match up with your other equipment, which is usually not a problem because most source devices have both kinds of connectors on back). Look again at the devices with digital connections mentioned at the beginning of this section. Count how many of those devices with digital outputs you have. Do the math. Many inexpensive receivers have only three digital inputs (some even less). If all you have is a DVD player, you'll be fine. After a few years of home theatering, however, we bet you'll have multiple devices with digital outputs, so plan ahead.

Analyzing analog audio inputs

Now that we spent all that time telling you how much better digital inputs are than analog inputs, why are we emphasizing analog inputs' importance now? Well, first of all, they're not really that awful. We think digital connections are the way to go when they're available, but analog is just fine when it's all you can get. Devices that use analog audio connections include the following:

- Older CD players (without a digital output)
- External radio tuners
- Analog VCRs
- Cable set-top and DSS receivers without digital outputs
- Cassette recorders
- Older game consoles (such as Nintendo 64s and the original PlayStation)
- The newest digital audio sources, SACD and DVD-Audio, which we discuss in Chapter 5

A move is afoot in the consumer electronics industry to allow digital connections for these last two devices. The connection would use FireWire, a computer technology often used for connecting portable hard drives, camcorders, and other devices, such as iPods, to PCs. As we write, a few receiver manufacturers have begun putting these FireWire ports on their receivers, but it is far from clear when and if this will ever take off.

All the devices we mention in this list — except for SACD and DVD-Audio — use a simple pair of analog audio connections, one for the left channel and one for the right. It's not hard to figure these out. Just count up your inputs on the receiver and count up your devices. The inputs on the receiver are labeled, and these labels correspond to the buttons on the front and on your remote control. It's always nice if the names on the receiver's inputs match input names on the device that you're connecting the receiver to, but it's not essential. It may not ever be possible if you have some funky device that no one ever thought of in Japan or wherever your receiver was designed.

The one exception to this flexibility in making connections are the inputs on your receiver marked *phono*. These are for your record player (phonograph) and are not standard inputs. If you have a record player, use these inputs for it. If you don't have a record player, don't use these inputs for anything else. If you do use them, it won't blow anything up, but it will sound amazingly awful and your dog will go hide under the bed until you turn it off.

For DVD-Audio and SACD players, you need a special set of analog inputs with six connectors. These formats can support multichannel audio (five channels plus a subwoofer for bass), and therefore need the extra inputs. Many newer receivers have a six input section (called a 5.1 analog input), so you can use a SACD or a DVD-A player.

Some receivers also have a section on the back with six (or more!) inputs for an *external decoder*. These allow you to hook up a newer decoder in the future. The idea is that the future decoder will handle surround sound formats that weren't even thought of when the receiver was designed. A nice bit of futureproofing.

Some receivers also have a set of six similar looking *outputs*. These allow you to bypass the internal amplifiers in the receiver and use a set of separate, more powerful amplifiers to drive your speakers. Again, this is a nice feature to look for if you think you might need more power some time in the future.

Verifying video inputs

When hooking up a home theater, some folks try to connect all their video devices directly to the TV or display, but they usually don't succeed because most displays have a rather limited set of inputs on the back (though some have a ton). We prefer to connect all our video devices directly to the receiver and let the receiver *switch* (that is, select) which video source goes to the display. It's just easier, neater, and simpler that way.

We're talking about the video signal coming out of these devices here. They all have an audio signal as well (for the soundtrack), and that should also be connected to the receiver using one of the two methods described in the previous sections. You won't get any surround sound if you don't perform that basic step.

As we discuss in Chapter 15, there are three primary types of video connections (in order of worst to best): composite, S-Video, and component. (There are also digital connections for *some* HDTV tuners and sources, but these connections are designed to connect directly into the TV.) Virtually every A/V receiver has yellow color-coded, composite video inputs on the back. (They're usually directly next to the audio inputs for a source device, so they'll be labeled DVD or VCR, and so on.) Composite video basically stinks (relative to the two other kinds), so use it only for low-resolution video sources, such as low-end VCRs; otherwise, just leave those composite plugs unused.

What you want to look for in a receiver are S-Video connections (at a minimum) or component video connections (on fancier, more expensive receivers). The picture quality you get when using these connections is almost always better than what you get with a com-posite video connection. S-Video connections can be found on better VCRs (the S-VHS models), DVD players, DSS receivers, digi-tal cable set-top boxes, PVRs, and on modern gaming consoles (for example, Xbox, PlayStation 2, or GameCube). Component video connections can be found on better DVD players (it's re-quired for progressive scan DVD), HDTV tuners, the gaming con-soles we just mentioned, and even on the latest PVRs (such as the ReplayTV 5000).

 HDTV signals need a special kind of component video connection called a *wideband component video* connection. Some receivers have component video connections but can't handle the higher fre-quencies of HDTV. If a specification is given, look for something higher than 25 MHz.

Until quite recently, component video inputs were a rarity on inex-pensive and even moderately priced receivers. Since the popularity of DVD and other sources that can use component video (particu-larly HDTV) has risen, however, component video has moved into the mainstream. You'll still have a hard time finding a $500 receiver with more than two sets of component inputs, but for many people, that's enough. You can use S-Video for nonprogressive or non-HDTV sources (such as a PlayStation 2), and reserve the component inputs for your progressive scan DVD and your HDTV tuner.

Many otherwise excellent displays have only a single component video input, and few displays have enough S-Video inputs for everything you might want to connect to them. This is a strong argument for finding a receiver that's got a sufficient number of inputs. Like the audio inputs discussed earlier, this is a pretty simple thing to factor in while you are shopping. Count up what you've got that uses S-Video or component video and start eliminating A/V receivers that don't have what you need from your shopping list.

Switching sources

With all these inputs, the receiver can do all the source switching for your home theater system. Plug all your source devices into the receiver, connect your speakers and display to the receiver's outputs, and let the receiver do the work of sending audio and video to these devices. As we said earlier, particularly on the video side, most displays simply don't have enough inputs to allow you to connect all the myriad video sources you have (or will soon have) directly into them. Allowing the A/V receiver to concentrate and switch between all these sources just plain makes sense.

As you audition receivers, check out the quality of their video switching. We can't give you a quantitative piece of advice here, but we can tell you to do some research. Read the reviews. Most good reviewers comment on the video switching capabilities. If you can, do your own quick test. Watch a bit of video on a DVD player hooked up through the receiver, and then try watching the same video using the same type of connection plugged directly into the display. Hopefully, you won't see a difference, but if the picture is softer or less detailed when running through the receiver, then maybe it's not the receiver you want.

Another factor to keep in mind regarding video switching is how the A/V receiver itself connects to the display. You may have a mixture of composite, S-Video, and component video connections running into the receiver from your source devices. It's very likely that you will, in fact. Some more capable receivers convert signals from lower-quality to higher-quality connections. For example, a receiver may convert all composite and S-Video incoming connections to component video. This doesn't make the picture any better, but it does enable you to use a single output connection from the receiver to the display. It also enables you to set the display on its component input and then just leave it there and forget it, which is pretty handy.

Many receivers use the home theater display to provide system controls, using an on-screen display. If your system converts composite or S-Video to a higher-quality connection, make sure it also sends the on-screen display over that connection. Switching the display back to the composite video input just to tweak a control is a real pain in the tonsils (as Pat's mom says — though he's not sure what that means).

Assessing your amplifier

Another of the essential jobs of an A/V receiver is to provide the amplification of audio signals so that your speakers can do their thing. We discuss how speakers work in the following chapter, but at a high level, let's just say that they are based on electromagnetic systems that need a lot of electricity. The electric signals coming out of audio source devices are relatively low powered. The amplifier does what its name says; it increases this power level.

Unscrambling power ratings

The first thing most folks look at when they see a shiny new receiver sitting on display is the power rating. The rating is measured in watts per channel (usually measured as RMS, or root mean square, instead of peak, which means that it is a measure of sustained power, not the highest possible instantaneous peak). The problem is that you can't take these ratings at face value, because manufacturers play a lot of interesting tricks when they give these watt ratings. The result is that a receiver can be more or less powerful than another receiver with the same rating. To really get a feel for a receiver's power, examine the following four things closely:

✔ **Distortion:** Power is measured at a certain number of watts at a certain level of *distortion* (noise created by the amplifier). You want low distortion (of course). The tricky part comes in when you examine how the amplifier's power output is measured — specifically at what distortion level it's measured. An amp that is measured, for example, at 100 watts per channel at 0.02 percent THD (total harmonic distortion, the standard measurement) is quieter and is probably more powerful than one that is measured at 100 watts per channel at 0.2 percent THD. You can really only do a direct comparison if both are measured at the same THD percentage. Another way of looking at this issue is this fact: If manufacturers measure power at a higher distortion rating, they can squeeze more "on paper" power out of the receiver.

Uh oh, too few inputs on your receiver?

Sometimes, you do your homework and buy a receiver with enough inputs, and then some new video source plops into your life unannounced, leaving you an input or two short. (Or maybe you just plain fell in love with a receiver that didn't have enough inputs. We forgive you.) What to do?

Well, first check your display for extra inputs on the back (or front). Using these isn't quite as neat and integrated as using the receiver, but doing so won't hurt your quality at all.

If you're still running short, look into an external video switcher. You can get your hands on a cheap one at any electronics or home theater store. You usually switch this device manually (meaning you walk up to it and push a button). Switchers accept composite or S-Video connections, and have a single output on the back to run to your display. If you want to go for quality (and can afford to spend a bit more), check out the Monster Cable's Entech line of products (www.monstercable.com/entech). For about $350, you can get a system that accepts composite or S-Video connections from up to four devices and converts them into a single S-Video output for connecting to your A/V receiver (or directly to the display). This system also connects the corresponding analog audio signals and features an automatic switching system. Whichever source is actively playing is switched to the output connections (you can manually override this, too).

 ✔ **Resistance:** Almost all amplifiers are rated at 8 ohms resistance (so you can compare ratings this way), but a few are measured at 6 or even 4 ohms. These lower resistances can give an artificially high power rating — be dubious.

Not all amplifiers built in to receivers (or even in separate power amplifiers) can power 4 ohm speakers without overheating, popping a circuit breaker, or just plain breaking down. Check to see if a receiver can support these lower resistances (called *impedance*) if you choose speakers that require it. This is rare unless you are buying some really high-end gear.

 ✔ **Frequency range:** Lower frequencies (the bass frequencies) require more amplifier power than higher frequencies. Because of this, some receiver manufacturers test their systems not at the full 20 to 20,000 Hz range (which is what we call *full range*), but with a limited range (such as 40 to 20,000 Hz). This can also create an artificially high power rating. Receivers that are measured at full range are often called *full bandwidth rated.*

 ✔ **Number of channels driven:** Home theater receivers should be capable of driving at least five speakers (some have amplifiers for six or even seven speakers for extra surround channels). Power ratings should state how many speakers are actually being driven when the system is tested. Preferably, all channels are driven simultaneously at the stated power. Some systems give power ratings in *stereo* mode (with only the front left and right speakers driven), which means that the power with all speakers being driven is less than the stated amount.

Determining how much receiver power you need

How much power do you need in your receiver? Well, we're going to weasel out by saying, "It depends." Which speakers you choose plays a key role here. Different speakers have different *sensitivities,* a measure of how loud they are given a certain amount of power. (The standard measure for this is how many decibels they produce with 1 watt of power at 1 meter's distance from the speaker.) A more sensitive speaker requires less amplification to reach the same volume level.

You also need to consider the size of your home theater and how loudly you plan on playing your movies and music. If you want to create permanent hearing loss, or if you have a room the size of the Taj Mahal, you might need a receiver that can pump out 150 watts per channel. If you have relatively sensitive speakers, a moderate sized home theater, and don't plan on testing the thickness of your window glass with really loud music, then a receiver with 70 watts per channel (or less) might do the trick. We think that receivers with about 100 watts per channel (honestly measured) will do the trick in just about any home theater.

Amplifiers (whether separate or in a receiver) make their power using transistors. (In the old days, amplifiers used vacuum tubes, and some really expensive high end amps still use tubes because some audio enthusiasts prefer their sound.) Inexpensive receivers use an IC (integrated circuit), which provides the power-generating transistors for several audio channels on a single chip. Better receivers have *discrete* amplifier output transistors — separate transistors for each channel. Typically, you get more power and better sound from a discrete design.

Zoning out to the rest of the house

Many home theater receivers — particularly when you start hitting about $1,000 or higher in price — include a *multizone* functionality. This lets your receiver not only control your home theater, but also provide music to other rooms in your house. A multizone receiver is a good way to get started down the whole home theater path.

The simplest multizone receivers have a pair of stereo audio outputs (not speaker connectors or amplifier channels, just outputs). These outputs enable you to run an audio cable to another room and connect to a separate amplifier and speakers in that room (or to a pair of *active* speakers that have a built-in amplifier). The key feature to look for here is that this second zone is truly a second zone. That is to say, the receiver lets you send a *different* audio source to the second room, not just the one you are playing in the home theater. So the kids can listen to Barney the dinosaur sing, "I love you," in the den, while you watch *Memento* in the home theater.

As you get into more sophisticated systems, you can find receivers with extra built-in amplifiers (so you don't need an amp in the extra room), and with extra zones (so you can send different audio sources to a third or fourth room). You may even find multizone A/V receivers that send out a composite video signal. With this signal, you can watch the video from a home theater video source elsewhere in the home.

In Chapter 17, we get into more detail about sharing home theater sources throughout the home. If you want to get really sophisticated with a true "every room in the house" system, you might need some more gear (which we discuss in that chapter).

Having fun with DSPs and decoders

Another key responsibility of the A/V receiver is to decode surround sound formats in your audio and video programming, so that sound can be sent to those six or more speakers in your theater. Two kinds of chips in the receiver handle all this digital magic: the DSP and the DAC.

Digital Signal Processors

The DSP (or Digital Signal Processor) is the brains of the decoding process. It's a chip that handles all the *steering* of surround sound, sending the right musical signals to the right channels. The DSP also can provide its own soundfield enhancements (though some people hate them and wouldn't use the term *enhancement* to describe them!). These enhancements are called *DSP Modes,* which are modifications to the signal to create delays in the sound. The delays can make your home theater sound like something else — for example, a cathedral or a smoky jazzy club (you have to provide your own smoke).

One feature that DSPs enable (and that we love!) is the ability to *dynamically compress* music and, more importantly, movie soundtracks. Dynamic compression makes the louds less loud and also makes the quiet parts not quite so quiet. When someone is sleeping two rooms over while you watch a movie at night, you don't necessarily want that *Top Gun* F-14 flying overhead at full roar. (Pat was in the Navy, and spent too much time in the Persian Gulf with jets taking off about 15 feet over his head, and doesn't ever want to hear that again, but that's a different story.) This feature, often called *nighttime mode,* is really great for family harmony.

Many receiver manufacturers make a big deal about which DSP they use. It does make a difference, and some aficionados have their own preferences. The key is that the DSP can support the decoding of the surround sound formats you want and need in your home theater. At a minimum, you should pick a receiver that can decode Dolby Digital and DTS (the plain Jane 5.1 versions of these standards), and Dolby Pro Logic (for VHS and other nondigital sources). We like receivers that can also decode Dolby Pro Logic II, which does a much better job on VHS and regular TV.

If you're getting into a 6- or 7-channel system, then you want a receiver that can support DTS-ES or Dolby Digital EX (or THX Surround EX). We don't think that's necessary for an entry-level home theater, but if you're getting fancy, heck, why not?

If you need to review these surround sound formats, you can find the details about all these formats back in Chapter 3.

Digital Analog Converters

DACs (or Digital Analog Converters) take the digitally encoded musical signals (from a Dolby Digital or DTS DVD soundtrack or the PCM from a compact disc connected digitally), and convert these digital signals into analog signals that the receiver's amplifier and the speakers can understand. Receiver vendors seem to be going through some kind of an arms race with DACs these days. Each vendor is coming out with models that have new DACs with even higher capacities.

DACs are rated by the frequency of digital signal and number of bits they can decode (for example 96 kHz and 24 bits). We've seen receivers with *multiple* DACs (up to 16 in a single receiver) rated at 192 kHz and 24 bits. You should choose a receiver with at least 96 kHz/24-bit DACs. If digital connections for systems such as SACD or DVD-Audio ever become common, those higher capacity DACs will become a minimum recommendation (today, they are not, in our minds).

Sometimes, you don't want to mess with all that digital stuff. Analog signals coming into the receiver are typically converted to digital signals (using ADCs — the opposite of DACs). The digital signals run through the DSP and are then converted back to analog signals with the DACs. Many audio purists feel that all this conversion can create minor (but to them, not insignificant) distortions in the audio. If your receiver has *analog bypass,* you can stay in straight, good old fashioned, pure analog all the way to the amplifier section. We recommend analog bypass for the analog inputs from an SACD or DVD-Audio player, as well as for turntable inputs. Some receivers automatically bypass the digital stuff for these inputs, whereas others have a switch on the remote. Some don't bypass it at all; so if you want this feature, check to see if your receiver will give it to you.

Dealing with bass

Connecting a subwoofer (or more than one if you love the bass) to your home theater is an essential part of providing the sound for your movies and TV. The majority of subwoofers are *active* (they have their own built-in amplifiers). So you need an output on your A/V receiver to connect a standard analog audio cable to the subwoofer. On most receivers, this output is labeled the *LFE* (Low Frequency Effects) channel — the ".1" part of 5.1/6.1/7.1 channel surround sound formats. We highly recommend you get a receiver with this output, and most will have one.

The other subwoofer-related thing to look for is an *adjustable crossover* that lets you select which audio frequencies go to the subwoofer and which go to the main front speakers. Different speaker systems sound better with the crossover set at different frequencies. If you have small bookshelf speakers in the front, you might set the crossover to a higher frequency. If you have a set of huge tower speakers with giant woofers (bass speakers) of their own, you might set the crossover to a lower frequency and let the subwoofer concentrate on only the really deep sounds.

We discuss speakers in more detail in Chapter 11.

Interfacing with your receiver

A/V receivers control a lot of things in your system, such as selection of audio and video sources, volume, surround sound formats, relative volume levels for surround speakers, and more. You interface with the receiver through the buttons and knobs on the front and, more importantly, through the remote control.

The receiver gives you feedback on your control actions through one or both of two means: lights and displays on the face of the receiver and an on-screen display on your television set. We like on-screen displays (they're easier to read), and we'd be willing to bet you will, too. However, you're not going to find this feature on most inexpensive receivers.

Whether or not you have an on-screen display, we think that checking out how the receiver's interface works is important. For example, most receivers use menu-driven controls (like the menus in a computer program). In some cases, you need to push a lot of buttons and navigate through several menus to get to important controls. That's okay for things you set once and forget about (such as your initial setup), but such controls are a real pain for procedures you do over and over again (such as selecting a video or audio source). We like systems that have easy-to-understand menus, and *direct access* to key functions (meaning you have to press only one button to get to them).

When evaluating a receiver's interface, you also want to check out the remote control. These days, most A/V receivers can control other devices (such as DVD players). Many remotes are *learning* or *programmable* ones that can control devices from other manufacturers. Cheaper programmable remotes work only with equipment from the same manufacturer. When you start getting fancy, you find remotes that are backlit (so you can see them in the dark) or even *touch screen* remotes (with a touch-sensitive LCD panel instead of a million tiny little buttons). We talk about remotes in much more detail in Chapter 14.

Making the Separates Decision

As you start moving up the price scale, you begin to reach a decision point: Do you want to stick with a (very very good) all-in-one high-end A/V receiver, or do you want to move into separates? *Separates* break down the functions of the receiver into three (you guessed it) "separate" components: a radio tuner, a power amplifier (or power amplifiers), and an A/V controller. You can probably guess what the tuner and amplifiers do; the controller performs the switching and *preamplification* tasks (basically, adjusting the levels of audio signals to control your volume), and includes the DSPs and DACs that do surround sound decoding and conversion of digital audio into analog audio.

You might go with separates for a couple of reasons:

✔ **More flexible:** A separates system lets you choose exactly which components you want. Like the amplifiers from Brand X, but the controller functions from Brand Y? Mix and match! Separates give you a more flexible upgrade path, too.

If you buy a Dolby Digital and DTS 5.1 decoder, but someday want to move up to Dolby Digital EX (or some future surround sound format), you only need to upgrade the decoder, not the whole system. Keep in mind that you might have to buy extra amplifiers for extra surround sound channels, but that's easy to do.

✔ **Better performance:** A/V receivers can offer really excellent sound quality, but for that last little bit of sonic realism, separates can offer the ultimate in sound. Putting all the electronics for your A/V components in separate chassis can reduce the possibility of these electronic gizmos interfering with each other and causing distortions in your sound. For example, many folks going the separates route buy fancy *mono* power amplifiers — a separate amplifier (with its own power supply and other internal components) for each channel. Most people don't have the space, budget, or (to be realistic) the need for such a setup. But it's a nice possibility to consider.

We talk about separate components in more detail in Chapter 20, where we talk about moving up to the high-end of home theater. If you can afford the additional expense, you might want to consider using separates. If you don't want to spend any more than you have to and prefer the simplicity (and space savings) of an all-in-one solution, stick with an A/V receiver.

Chapter 11

Strictly Speakering

● ●

In This Chapter

▶ Understanding speaker bits and pieces

▶ Flanking your system to the left and right

▶ Surrounding yourself with a diffuse soundfield

▶ Managing bass expectations

● ●

*A*lthough your TV display often hogs all the attention in your home theater, the speaker system is what really makes your theater sing, literally.

Speaker systems don't get the attention they deserve. Many people actually see the speaker system as almost an afterthought — something that is bundled with the receiver or other equipment. Speakers have a double curse: They lack oodles of fancy features or display screens, and the features they do have are tied up with very technical descriptions that most people can't decipher.

Not paying enough attention to your speaker system is a huge mistake. People notice bad audio a lot faster than they notice bad video. In this chapter, we explain how to evaluate your speakers, and we discuss issues to think about when buying speakers for your home theater. In Chapters 16 and 17, we talk about how to install your speakers and tweak them to perfection.

Understanding How Speakers Work

Unlike other components in your system, speakers are differentiated by somewhat obscure technical characteristics more than anything else. An understanding of how speakers work will help you understand us when we talk about making sure your speakers are in phase and things like that.

Drivers

In actuality, speakers are relatively simple devices. Basically, you have an enclosure (typically a box) into which speaker drivers are attached. The *drivers* are the round elements that many people call the actual speakers (they're not). The drivers look like cones or horns (or even ribbons or domes), and in fact, the large surface area of the drivers is called the *cone* or *diaphragm*. These surfaces move back and forth to make the sound. If you have ever pulled the front screen off your speakers or have seen speakers without their front grille on, you've seen speaker drivers *au naturelle*.

Driver sizes

Drivers come in different sizes and modes, but generically, you'll find three types, based on the frequencies they handle:

- ✔ **Tweeter driver:** These handle the high-frequency treble range (above 2,000 Hz).

- ✔ **Midrange driver:** These, not surprisingly, handle the midrange frequencies (200 Hz to 2,000 Hz).

- ✔ **Woofer driver:** These handle the low-frequency bass range (below 200 Hz).

No single driver is well suited to handle all sounds from 20 Hz to 20,000 Hz; multiple drivers are commonly used to be able to span the full spectrum. A speaker that handles the full frequency is called, not surprisingly, a *full-range* speaker.

How drivers work

Speaker driver cones are typically made from paper, plastic, or metal. This material moves back and forth and creates changes in the air pressure (sound waves) that ultimately arrive at your eardrum and cause it to move back and forth in a corresponding fashion. This causes you to hear the sound. The cone is moved by an electromagnetic process that's caused by a coil of wire at the base of the cone, called the *voice coil*. The electrical impulses coming from the amplifier (or the amplifiers built in to your receiver) drive the voice coil and the voice coil interacts with a permanent magnet attached to the speaker's cone (or dome or whatever shape it may take). (If you want a great explanation of how speakers work in more detail, check out www.howstuffworks.com/speaker.htm.)

Drivers come in all sorts of different sizes, but in general, the larger the driver is, the lower the frequencies it was designed for. Because higher frequencies require sound waves that have high and low pressure points close together, the cone must be smaller to be able to move back and forth fast enough to keep up. Lower frequencies have to move back and forth more slowly, and smaller drivers have a hard time with these. So you find that drivers are designed for specific audio frequency ranges.

Most speakers that have multiple drivers in their speaker enclosure have *crossovers,* which divide up inbound speaker signals and distribute them to the appropriate driver.

Drivers in speaker-market lingo

You'll most often run into two types of speakers on the market:

- **Two-way:** These have a woofer and a tweeter in one speaker enclosure.

- **Three-way:** These have a woofer, tweeter, and a midrange driver in the same enclosure.

The use of the cone-shaped diaphragm and electromagnetic-powered movement is specific to the class of speakers we've been discussing, *dynamic speakers.* Generally, these are the speakers we recommend for home theater.

You may run across other speakers that are more expensive and are used for specific purposes. In most cases, we don't recommend the following speakers for home theater use:

- **Electrostatic speakers:** These are used primarily for stereo audio listening and are rare in home theater systems. They can't handle bass and are rather limited in where and how you position them.

- **Planar-magnetic speakers:** For similar reasons, these are not likely to be useful for your home theater application because they are best used for the higher frequencies only.

We mention electrostatic and planar-magnetic speakers in case someone tries to sell you some; unless you really know what you're doing with these types of speakers, you're better off spending your money on quality dynamic speakers.

The pole position

You'll also run into speakers with more than one set of speaker drivers, facing in different directions:

- ✔ **Monopole:** These speakers have all the drivers on one face of the enclosure. These can be used anywhere in your home theater. These are also called *direct radiating* speakers.

- ✔ **Bipole:** These speakers have drivers on two faces, opposite each other. These are designed for the side/rear surround speaker applications.

- ✔ **Dipole:** These speakers have drivers on two faces, opposite each other. These are designed for the side/rear surround speaker applications.

- ✔ **Omnipole:** These speakers radiate their sound in all directions, in a 360-degree fashion, and are popular for outdoor applications. We won't talk much about these here, but know they exist.

To understand the difference between bipole and dipole speakers, we have to get technical for a minute, but it's an important tangent discussion.

Harken back to your science class days when you studied topics of *phase,* specifically being *in phase* and *out of phase.* If you recall, in a general sense, something is in phase when it acts in the same pattern and time session as something else, and out of phase when it doesn't. Because controlling the way sound waves interact with each other is a key component of home theater, you have to deal with the concept of phase.

Bipole and dipole speakers are designed specifically to help contribute to your surround sound field. All you need to know for now, however, are some basics about how they work. Bipole speakers fire their cones to the front and rear (remember, they have drivers on two planes) at the same time and in phase. In other words, the cones go out or in together, in the same direction (both out or both in) and at the same time. Dipole speakers are out of phase with each other. When one side's drivers are pushing out, the other side's drivers are pulling in. See the section, "Surround speakers," later in this chapter, for an explanation of how these speakers help create surround sound.

Although the electrical phase in bipoles and dipoles is different, the basic construction of bipoles and dipoles is very similar. You can find speakers on the market that can be both bipoles and dipoles. Most of these speakers have a switch that lets you switch the mode they operate in. Some people prefer music played back through dipoles and movies through bipoles, and these speakers let you make that choice on the fly.

Enclosed for your convenience

Your speaker enclosure, it turns out, is pretty critical. You see, with all the shaking your drivers do, if you have a rather flimsy speaker encasement, then it's either going to make a lot of noise, fall apart, or both. Your enclosure should be able to handle the vibrations with ease and should add little sound interference to the sound emanating from the drivers.

You'll run into two major types of enclosures: sealed (also known as *acoustic suspension*) enclosures and ported (also known as *bass reflex*) enclosures. A *sealed enclosure* is what it sounds like; it's an airtight case. As your driver moves back and forth, the air pressure in the speaker is constantly changing. This puts extra pressure from behind on the diaphragm as it moves in and out, and that takes extra power to overcome. On the positive side, however, that extra pressure makes the cone snap back and forth faster and with more precision, giving you a more crisp and accurate sound.

A more efficient speaker design is the *ported* or *bass reflex enclosure*. In the front of these enclosures is a hole (port) that equalizes pressure between the inside and outside of the speaker. When the diaphragm moves back into the speaker, it increases the internal pressure, which is funneled out through the front port of the speaker. This augments the sound waves traveling from the speaker, and increases the efficiency tremendously. The downside is that, from a reproductive sound perspective, you may get less accurate results from bass reflex enclosure. That's because they don't have the benefit of the extra pressure influencing the reverberating diaphragm. So the speaker sound might reproduce bass notes less precisely — substituting a louder boominess for a more realistic reproduction of the low notes that doesn't have as much house-shaking "oomph."

Bass reflex enclosures can dramatically decrease your power requirements because they increase the bass output of a speaker by around 3 dB compared to a sealed enclosure. To match a 3 dB output boost through amplification, the power applied to the speaker needs to be doubled. So if a bass reflex enclosure speaker were powered with a 150 watt amplifier, a sealed enclosure speaker would require a 300 watt amplifier to produce the same output. That's pretty awesome improvements.

In the end, you can be happy with either sealed or bass reflex designs. Just keep in mind that these units handle bass differently and that good design and construction can minimize these effects.

Inside, outside, upside down?

As if this is not enough thus far, you'll probably run into four generic shape and size categories of speakers, for your home-entertainment system. These four are:

- **Floorstanding:** These speakers can be as tall as you are, can handle the full range of frequencies, and may or may not own the low-bass frequencies often taken over by the subwoofer.

- **Bookshelf:** These aptly named speakers are designed for smaller footprints (the amount of space they take up). You often find them on a bookshelf or discreetly mounted on the wall. Sometimes, you see them on speaker stands to bring them up to ear-level (which is the best way to install these types of speakers, in our opinion). They are usually designed to handle the midrange and high-end frequencies and are typically mated to a subwoofer in your installation. You may hear bookshelf speakers described by the term *satellite speakers*.

- **Subwoofer:** These are larger and heavier speakers than the bookshelf models and are usually kept on the floor due to their size and weight. These contain the large drivers for low-frequency use.

- **In-wall:** In-wall speakers share most of their characteristics with the bookshelf models; these are smaller speakers designed more for the midrange and high-end frequencies. Although some have enclosures that are mounted into the wall, the majority of these systems use the wall's own enclosed nature as its enclosure. The drivers and other pieces and parts (like the crossovers) are mounted in a frame mounted flush with the wall or ceiling.

In general, in-wall speakers are more for whole-home background music and to contribute to the surround sound of a home theater. For the most part, the benefit of these speakers is their ability to be located in places that have more aesthetic than acoustic appeal. They stay tucked away in corners or low on walls, but their acoustical contribution is mainly for background and surround types of sound.

Also, depending on the construction of the walls themselves, in-wall speakers that lack their own enclosure may spread sound along the wall rather than direct sound forward. If you find yourself planning in-wall speakers, take some extra time to study up on the best ways to optimize their location and performance.

Stereostone Age

We talk in Chapter 22 about outdoor applications of your home theater, but in advance, we want to introduce you to outdoor speakers, because they are pertinent for your gardens, pool areas, and soon-to-be-outdoor theater greens.

All the discussion in this speaker section is pertinent to shopping for outdoor speakers. One of the leading vendors is Stereostone (www.stereostone.com), which makes speakers in all sorts of simulated rock forms and colors, like brown sandstone and black lava. There are omni-directional speakers, subwoofers, and even stereo fountains. You can get them with or without visible grills in the layers of the rock, and with volume controls for individual speaker control. All this in weatherproof enclosures that start as low as $150 and go up to $1,000 for the most sophisticated models.

Active and passive speakers

Finally, all speakers, regardless of the number of drivers, pole type, enclosure type, or whatever, fall into one of two categories: active or passive. How they're classified depends on their relationship to the amplifier driving them.

The vast majority of speakers are passive. A *passive* speaker doesn't have a built-in amplifier; it needs to be connected to your amplifier through normal speaker wire. This speaker level signal has been amplified enough to drive the speakers sufficiently.

Active speakers, on the other hand, have a built-in amplifier and are fed by a low-level (line-level) signal passed along an interconnect cable originating at your preamplifier or controller. Because the amplifier is an active electronic device, it needs power, and so you have to put any active speakers near a power outlet.

For most home theaters, the subwoofer is probably going to be your only active speaker (though you can also find passive subwoofers, and some high-end home theater systems use these). There's no practical reason for any of your other speakers to be active. Active speakers limit your ability to pick amplifiers tailored to your home theater and are generally more expensive options than what we've been talking about. They are also much harder to find. Most active speakers either fall into the low price/low-end category (designed for hooking into PCs or portable CD/MP3 players), or the really high end (where the speakers cost $5,000 to $10,000 *each*).

Connections are everything

When connecting your receiver or amplifier to your speakers, you're pretty much going to find two types of connectors: spring clips and five-way binding posts. Spring clips are considered the lower end of the two, and most audiophiles tend to put them down. You see, spring clips have more exposed wiring, less surface contact, and greater likelihood of signal degradation over time, due to this exposed wiring. Five-way binding posts, on the other hand, have a much more flexible connection structure. Not surprisingly, you can connect at least five ways. There is a large washer-like area at the base that allows for more extensive contact with bare wire, pin-form connectors, spade lugs, and banana plugs. There's too much to try to put into words here, we recommend that you get someone at a stereo store to show you a five-way binding post. Just know that the five-way binding posts are the way to go if you have a choice.

Setting Up Surround Sound

Whew. You still with us? Well if you are, the worst is behind you. Now, you can apply all this newfound knowledge to a discussion of your surround sound system. In this section, we talk about the different speakers found in any home theater system — the center channel speaker, the left and right front speakers, the surround channel speakers, and the subwoofer. To see what a surround sound setup looks like, see Figure 2-1 in Chapter 2.

Center speakers

We start with the center speaker. On the one hand, the center speaker is probably the most important speaker in your system; on the other hand, it's optional. How can that be, you ask?

Well, many people say the center speaker is optional because the left and right speakers can handle the sound that comes from the center speaker. However, we think that you miss out on a lot, and we don't recommend this setup at all. The front center speaker, we feel, is critical and not at all optional. But some budget crunchers will try to convince you that it is.

Now, why is it critical? Ah, our favorite subject. The center speaker anchors your on-screen dialogue and serves as a seamless connection between your left and right speakers. As that boat zooms by left to right, you don't want to have a gap in the middle of your soundfield (a concern as screens get larger and larger). Center speakers are usually located behind the screen or above or below displays, so that you can localize the on-screen sound as much as possible.

To achieve this seamless harmony with the left and right front speakers, your choice of center speaker is important. Don't skimp on the center speaker in favor of your other front speakers. Each speaker (left, center, and right) is equally important and should be of similar size, similar capability, and preferably come from the same manufacturer. In fact, if you can use an identical model speaker for the center, left, and right speakers (we talk about them in just a second), do it. Many folks can't do this because they've chosen tower speakers for their left and right speakers, and can't possibly install a tower speaker on top of their display as a center channel speaker. (And if you're not using dipole or bipole speakers for your surround channels, you should consider using another identical pair of speakers for your surrounds as well.)

 Make sure any speakers that will be close to a cathode ray tube (direct-view) video display are *video shielded* — especially the center speaker. If not, the speakers will cause picture distortions on your screen. This is most important for your center speaker (which may rest directly on top of your display), but can also be an issue for your left and right speakers if they too are close to the display.

Left and right speakers

We've cheated somewhat by talking a lot about the front left and right speakers already in this chapter. If possible, these speakers should be

- ✔ Full-range speakers (even if you plan on using a subwoofer).

- ✔ Ear-level (even if using bookshelf-style speakers). If the speakers are large, keep the tweeters at ear level.

- ✔ Of similar performance capability as the center speaker — preferably from the same manufacturer.

We talk in Chapter 2 about whether you can use your existing speakers with your home theater, and the bottom line is that if you do, try to buy a center speaker from the same manufacturer and class for the best results.

In an ideal world, you use exactly the same model of speaker for your center, left, and right speakers — all your front speakers. This isn't always practical, but we highly recommend you buy all three of these speakers from the same manufacturer and make sure that the manufacturer has designed them to be *timbre matched* — in other words, that they sound alike. This ensures that you get a more seamless listening experience.

Surround speakers

No matter what the setup of your speakers for surround sound — whether you have two, three, four, or more side and back speakers — your surround speakers play a fundamentally different role than your front speakers. You want things highly localized in the front part of your soundfield, but the surround field is more diffuse.

Now we can get back to the bipole/dipole speakers we discuss earlier in the chapter. Recall that the purpose of the center speaker is to provide highly localized speaker information; it's coming from the center of the screen. There's a high correlation between what you see on the screen and where the sound comes from.

And likewise, the left and right speakers are to provide more lateral, but still highly localized and directed, sound. Together, the three represent the frontal face of your home theater sound experience. When there is a specific sound — the clash of swords, the shout of the main character, the click of a trigger being pulled back — the sound comes predominantly from these speakers.

The surround speakers have almost the opposite duty. Although you will hear discrete sounds from your surround speakers, their main duty is to create the sense of environment, the background, the unobvious. So if there is a howling wind, the pitter-patter of a rainstorm, or the background of a busy city, it comes from these speakers.

Reviewers tend to talk about the *diffuse sound* of the surround sound speakers because they often are not really making any specific sound per se, but a cacophony of sounds that together create an atmosphere. And where the front speakers (the center, left, and right) are arrayed at or around your ear level, the surround sounds tend to work higher, to the sides, and behind you, enveloping you in the surround soundfield.

Surround sounds tend to rely less on direct radiated sound and more on reflected and indirect sound. Just like in a city where sounds bounce off buildings, or in a stadium where it's sometimes hard to localize a specific noise.

Bipole and dipole speakers, mounted on the sides of your room with front and rear facing drivers, contribute to this diffuse and reflected sound. Dipole speakers tend to be preferred for home theater applications because, relative to bipole speakers, they bleed out less sound to the sides and therefore are better at nonlocalized sounds. In comparison, bipole speakers tend to have more sound seep out from the sides, which makes them less diffuse.

Recall from Chapter 3 that there are several different modes of surround sound, often dependent on the encoding of your source input. There is a fair amount of debate about the appropriate speaker to use to create surround sound. For instance, Dolby Pro Logic encoders have a monophonic surround channel with a limited range of frequencies supported; by comparison, Dolby Digital encoders plan for full-range speakers. So do you use full-range speakers that are more directional, in order to take advantage of the newly enabled signals of Dolby Digital? Or, do you use more diffuse speakers to add to the shared atmosphere of the "surround"?

The choice isn't clear-cut. In general, we advise you to focus on creating a broad, diffuse soundfield to the sides, back, and top of the room. A good installation uses dipole speakers to help provide localization where needed. For the higher-end encoding, such as THX Surround or DTS-ES, where there are at least four surround sound speakers, we suggest four dipole speakers — two on the sides and two in the back. You set up your two back surround speakers so that their drivers are in phase with one another. This maximizes the ability to create a specific sound image right behind you and serves as a good solution for home theater surround sound issues.

 Some folks (typically on the high end of the home theater spectrum) recommend using direct radiating speakers for your surrounds. (In fact, DTS recommends this for DVDs encoded with their surround sound system.) We think that for most people, dipoles are a better bet, mainly because, for most films, audio engineers mix the sound specifically for the diffuse speaker arrays used in theaters. So the majority of DVDs have been designed specifically for dipole-style speakers for your surrounds.

Subwoofers in the mix

Most subwoofers have floor-based enclosures with active speaker systems (that is, with built-in amplifiers) for driving the low bass frequency ranges. Your biggest decision comes in *bass management*. That is, how do you want the bass signals in your system to be handled? You have a couple of options:

Getting heady(phones) at home

You will see advertisements for Dolby Digital 5.1 headphones. Hopefully, you've understood enough in this chapter to say, "How can you cram five speakers and a subwoofer into a set of two-speaker headphones?" Hey, good question!

It's simple. No matter how many speakers you use in your system, you supposedly are still listening with two ears. These headphones basically try to reproduce what is arriving at your ears by using digital signal processors (DSPs). Dolby has gone one step further, with a Dolby Headphone encoder (www.dolby.com/dolby-headphone/) that simulates Dolby Digital 5.1 over the two headphone channels. Pretty cool if you ask us.

If you plan on using headphones a lot (perhaps because your spouse does not like the movies you watch, eh Pat?), check if your receiver supports Dolby Headphone.

 ✔ The subwoofer can complement your full-range front speakers, providing for an even fuller bass signal.

 ✔ The subwoofer can handle all the bass, giving your front speakers the ability to focus on the mid- and high-range frequencies.

Most home theater experts will advise you to move all bass to the subwoofer. This results in more power and attention to the mid- and high-frequency drivers and less strain on the amplifier and speaker systems. This setup also gives you a more dynamic range, because the bass can go lower than most full-range speaker woofers can themselves (hence the term, *subwoofer*).

If you have a modern A/V receiver, you use a standard line level audio interconnect cable to connect your subwoofer to the receiver (we talk about these cables in Chapter 15). If you're using an older receiver as a stopgap until you purchase that nice new Dolby Digital A/V receiver, look for a subwoofer that also accepts *speaker level* connections. These connections enable you to run the speaker wires from your receiver to the subwoofer, and then on to your front right and left speakers. The wires aren't nearly as good as the cable, but they work.

Many subwoofers come with an Auto On/Off function that turns the active subwoofer's amplifier on and off with the presence of a signal. So the amplifier turns itself on when you're playing music or a movie soundtrack and then off again a few minutes after you're done. Pretty handy.

Recall, the subwoofer is usually powered by its own amplifier. As such, there is a volume control and a phase adjustment switch. You adjust the volume when fine-tuning your system and pretty much leave it at that setting. Your phase adjustment switch is sometimes a +/–180 degree switch and sometimes a continuously variable switch from 0 to +/–180 degrees (preferable). This comes into play when trying to fine-tune your system vis-à-vis your front left and right speakers. You adjust this so that the sound coming from each is relatively in alignment, despite the fact that the sub-woofer and front speakers may be located at different distances from the listeners. By adjusting the phase, you can move the timing of the sound coming from the subwoofer.

In Chapter 21, we explain how to link your bass with *transducers,* to provide a truly ground-shaking home theater experience.

Chapter 12

Picking a Display

· ·

· ·

*W*e spend a lot of time in this part of the book talking about the audio systems that envelop you in surround sound and aurally immerse you in a movie. But let's face facts, we call it *watching* a movie because that's what we do. The audio creates the ambience, but the display is what you focus on. So choosing a high-quality video system that can properly display the content you want to watch — whether it is on a regular TV, DVD, or even HDTV — is essential.

In this chapter, we talk about two of the most popular kinds of displays:

 ▻ **Direct-view TVs:** These units use a picture tube, just as TVs have for decades.

 ▻ **Flat-panel TVs:** You can hang these newer models on your wall or stick them just about anywhere.

In Chapter 13, we continue our discussion of displays and talk about displays that use projector systems.

 You may already have an idea about what kind of display you want to buy for your home theater, but we urge you to at least take a quick spin through Chapters 12 and 13. You might find out something surprising and change your mind!

Learning the Lingo

If you're shopping for a TV for your home theater, you're probably going to run into sales people, Web sites, and brochures full of acronyms and unfamiliar terms. Unfortunately, the technology industry tends to market its products with a list of features that are designed to bludgeon you upside the head and leave you with glassy eyes and a credit card in your hand.

We're here to help. The following sections cover some of the most significant features and performance stats that you'll hear as you shop and, more importantly, explain what they mean!

Screen size

We won't insult your intelligence by telling you what screen size means, but we will tell you how it's measured. With a single exception (screens for front-projector systems), displays are measured diagonally. This is important to keep in mind because 16:9 and 4:3 screen sizes can't be directly compared diagonally — it's an apples and oranges thing. For example, a 16:9 32-inch screen is about 28 inches wide and a bit less than 16 inches high, while a 4:3 32-inch screen is 25.6 inches wide and a hair over 19 inches high.

Before you buy any television, you need to consider the size of your room and your expected seating distance from the display. As a gut reaction, most people think, "Bigger is better," when it comes to TV, but in fact, that's not really the case. Just as a TV can be obviously too small for a room (try sitting 15 feet back from a 27-inch TV), so too can a TV be too big. And we're not just talking about being physically too big to fit in the room (or to look acceptable to your spouse, décor-wise), but also being visually too big.

Every video display has some sort of line (or in the case of flat-panel displays, pixel) structure. The picture you see on your screen is made up of a series of individual points of light. Generally speaking, the bigger the screen, the bigger these individual points are. When you sit back a reasonable distance, your eyes can't discern these individual items, but if you get too close, they can. (Don't believe us? Go turn on any TV in your house and walk right up to it. Take a look. See?)

Because line or pixel size depends on the size of the screen, the distance at which you can make out this structure varies by screen size. (The number of lines or pixels being displayed plays a part, too, which makes this effect slightly less noticeable on HDTVs that fit 720 or more vertically measured lines on the screen, instead of 480.) Table 12-1 is a rough guideline for screen size versus distance from the screen.

Table 12-1   Screen Size and Viewing Distance

Traditional Analog TV		HDTV	
Size	Viewing Distance	Size	Viewing Distance
27 inch	6 feet, 9 inches	30 inch	6 feet, 3 inches
32 inch	8 feet	35 inch	7 feet, 4 inches
36 inch	9 feet	40 inch	8 feet, 4 inches
40 inch	10 feet	45 inch	9 feet, 5 inches
50 inch	12 feet, 6 inches	55 inch	11 feet, 6 inches
55 inch	13 feet, 9 inches	60 inch	12 feet, 6 inches
60 inch	15 feet	65 inch	13 feet, 6 inches

Source: Crutchfield Corp. (www.crutchfield.com)

Aspect ratio

We already let the cat out of the bag on this subject (several times throughout the book), but let's repeat it because it's important — displays can be shaped for widescreen material (16:9) or for traditional TV viewing (4:3).

You can view either kind of material on either direct-view or flat-screen TVs, but you might want to pick one over the other based on what you view more. As we discuss each type of display, we talk about what aspect ratio we recommend for that type of display. Generally speaking, we recommend 16:9 aspect ratio displays, but we do think that 4:3 aspect ratios are the best choice for most people using direct-view TVs, mainly because it's a lot easier to find direct-view TVs in this aspect ratio. If you really want widescreen and a direct-view, some models are on the market. You just have fewer choices.

Picture adjustability

Any display allows you to adjust the specific settings for your picture (and this is something we highly recommend you do). To do so, you typically use an on-screen display and your remote control.

Most people think of these settings as something to do once and never change. In fact, different environments might call for different settings. You might have one setting for the darkened room home theater environment and another setting (that deals with ambient light better) for the brightly lit Super Bowl party.

Some systems let you save these settings as presets so that you can quickly access a certain group of settings without having to manually readjust every setting each time you want to recreate your settings. It's nice to be able to press a few quick buttons and get things back to the optimal movie-watching settings without readjusting your picture manually.

Connections on the back

Although many display manufacturers offer an almost bewildering array of connectors on the back of the TV, we don't think these connectors are really much of an advantage. We recommend that you connect all your source devices directly to your A/V receiver, not your display, to simplify both hook-up and operation.

We do recommend, however, that you choose a display that has connectors for your antenna and/or cable system and at least one connector each for composite, S-Video, and component video connections (as well as their associated audio connections). Displays that have more than one set of component video connections can be very useful (in order to connect, for example, both a DVD player and an HDTV tuner). Because many A/V receivers can't accept this high-quality connection, you may need to connect DVD players and HDTV tuners that use component video connections directly to the TV.

Connections on the front

If you own a camcorder or some other portable video source device (such as a laptop computer that you may wish to occasionally connect to your home theater display), you may want to choose a display with a set of A/V connectors on the front of the unit. It's a lot easier to make quick, temporary connections this way than it is to try to climb behind your display and hook up things.

Monitor versus television

When a display comes with a built-in TV tuner (so you can plug in an antenna or a cable connection and immediately watch TV), we call it a *television*. Some displays, such as projectors and plasma displays, often come without any built-in TV tuning capabilities; we call these displays *monitors*. In fact, some monitors don't have a built-in audio speaker, so they don't offer even a minimal audio capacity. (We don't think this is a huge deal, because any home theater worth its salt already has a good audio system, but for casual viewing, like watching the news, you may not want to fire up your audio system.)

Contrast ratio

If you look at TVs on a showroom floor, you might not ever realize this (because the displays have their brightness cranked up), but displays should be capable of showing both dark and light scenes. For example, you want to be able to see the flash of the artillery in *Saving Private Ryan,* as well as the soldiers seeking cover in the shadows.

There's a measurement for how well a display can show both bright brights and nuanced darks: contrast ratio. You'll see this as a numeric ratio, something like 500:1, representing the whitest white compared to the blackest black. Typically, direct-view (tube) displays and projector systems that use CRTs have the highest contrast rations, whereas systems using plasma or LCD technologies have the lowest. When it comes to contrast ratio, a higher ratio is better.

There isn't a standardized, approved way of measuring contrast ratios, so one manufacturer's 100:1 may not be the same as another's. You need to rely on magazine and online reviews and use your own eyes in a thorough test drive at a dealer's showroom. We like reviews that include a professional calibration of the display, because that shows the display's true "ultimate" capabilities. When you do a test drive, use some of your own DVDs that you know well.

Comb filter

Many video sources (such as broadcast NTSC television or com-posite video connections from source devices such as VCRs) send both the color (chrominance) and brightness (luminance) parts of the video signal as a single, combined (or composite) signal. Inside the TV, a device called a *notch filter* or a *comb filter* is used to sepa-rate these signals.

If signals aren't properly separated, you see moving dots of color around the edges of images, a phenomenon called *dot crawl.* Notch filters are the least effective at this process, whereas the various kinds of comb filters do a better job. You'll find three kinds of comb filters in direct-view displays:

- ✔ **2-D comb filter:** This is the least effective (and least expen-sive) kind of comb filter, though it is better than a notch filter.

- ✔ **3-D comb filter:** We're talking middle ground here — better than 2-D, but not as good as the digital comb filter.

- ✔ **Digital comb filter (sometimes called 3-D Y/C):** Found in more expensive direct-view sets, the digital comb filter uses more sophisticated (and digital!) signal processing to separate chrominance and luminance. This is the king of the hill, when it comes to comb filters.

When you connect sources to your display using S-Video or com-ponent video cables (discussed in Chapter 15), chrominance and luminance are separated in the source device, not in your TV. In this case, your display's built-in comb filter is bypassed.

Resolution

As we discuss in Chapter 4, the resolution of a display is a measure of how precise and sharp a picture your display can create. For standard definition programming — such as NTSC television and, to a degree, DVD — this isn't a really huge deal. (Any display can handle the 480 vertical lines of resolution of these formats — which is not to say they'll all look the same!) As you start getting into HDTV sources (and even widescreen "anamorphic" DVDs), however, resolution becomes a really big deal.

Generally, display vendors spend most of their time talking about the *vertical* resolution of their sets, which corresponds to the most commonly discussed resolutions of HDTV, like 720 or 1080. Some displays (particularly those that have a fixed pixel system, such as

LCD or plasma) give resolution in terms of both horizontal and vertical number (similar to the way resolutions are discussed in the computer display world). So you might see, for example, a plasma display with a resolution of 800 x 600. In this case, the 800 refers to horizontal resolution (the number of pixels, or individual points) across the screen, and 600 refers to the vertical number (like the scan lines on a conventional TV).

Scan type

In Chapter 4 (again — it's a chapter you shouldn't skip!), we talk about the two *scanning* methods that video displays use — interlaced and progressive. Traditional TV systems (such as NTSC, the standard TV system in the United States) use an *interlaced* scan, where half the picture appears on the screen at a time. The other half follows an instant later ($\frac{1}{60}$th of a second, to be precise). The interlaced system relies on the fact that your eyes can't really detect this procedure in action — at least not explicitly. In a progressive scan system, the entire picture is painted at once, which greatly reduces the flickering that people notice when watching TV. Progressive scan is available throughout the range of TV types we're about to discuss. We highly recommend progressive scan if it fits into your budget, because the picture appears much smoother and more like a film. (You can get direct-view progressive scan TVs for under $1,000 these days.)

Scan frequency

Scan frequency is something you might not hear much about unless you're buying an HDTV or a high-end projector system, but if you're shopping in the higher end of the market, you should know what scan frequency is. At a high level, scan frequency (which is measured in kHz — thousands of cycles per second) is directly related to the interlaced and progressive scan types that we discuss in the preceding section. Standard NTSC video, which is interlaced, puts out 15,734 scan lines per second. 15.75 kHz is the commonly rounded version of this number. When you start getting into progressive scan video (using, for example a progressive scan DVD player), you effectively double this scan frequency to 31.5 kHz. HDTV systems can go even higher. If you're looking into projector systems (which we discuss in the following chapter), you'll hear a lot about scan frequencies.

Getting Ready for HDTV

Before we start talking about the physical differences between the various categories of displays (differences such as picture tube or no picture tube), we want to cover one even higher-level distinction. That distinction is the following: Is the display capable of playing back HDTV at full resolutions?

We talk a lot about what HDTV is in Chapter 4, including the fact that next-generation digital TV (also called ATSC) has a bunch of different formats. Two of those formats, 1080i and 720p, qualify as high-definition television, or HDTV.

Deciding on HDTV or a traditional NTSC TV is probably the most important decision you can make if you're buying a new display unit for your home theater, but we think home theater shoppers won't need to agonize over this decision for much longer. That's because we think almost all displays that are appropriate for home theaters will soon be capable of displaying HDTV. At the very least, we feel that moving up to HDTV capabilities won't be much of a price jump. If you can afford it today (and you can get HDTV-ready sets for under $1,000), we highly recommend that you get an HDTV or HDTV-ready display now.

We talk about HDTV back in Chapter 4. Now, we want to talk about the characteristics of TVs and displays that can play back HDTV programming. The first layer of the HDTV onion that we should peel back is the concept of an *HDTV* versus an *HDTV-ready* system. An HDTV has the following key characteristics:

- ✔ **Resolution:** Can display true high-definition signals with at least 720 lines of horizontal resolution (in other words, 720 lines of picture data stacked up on top of each other vertically on the screen).

- ✔ **Aspect ratio:** Has a widescreen aspect ratio of 16:9.

- ✔ **Tuner:** Has a built-in TV tuner, which is capable of decoding any over-the-air broadcast format within the ATSC digital television standard. (HDTVs that get their HDTV programming from an internal DSS receiver are also called HDTVs, even though they don't fit this definition strictly.)

An HDTV-ready set, which is much more common on the market today, must meet only the first two requirements. Many direct-view (tube) HDTV-ready sets meet the second requirement only because of an "anamorphic squeeze" mode (discussed in "Sticking with the tried-and-true," later in this chapter), not because the sets are physically shaped in the 16:9 aspect ratio.

Will my HDTV work next year?

Seems impossible to even consider doesn't it? HDTV is the newest thing around, just barely on the market, and already we're asking a question like this? Well, although it would take a degree of contempt for (or ignorance of) the customer, which we don't think the HDTV industry will let happen, it *is* possible that some buyers of HDTV technology may find their sets unable to connect in the not-so-distant future.

The issue is copy protection. Many movie and TV studios want to have some control over your ability to make copies of digital content sent to your HDTV (not all, to be fair — a few actually support technologies such as the D-VHS we discuss in Chapter 6). So a new type of connection technology called *DVI* (Digital Visual Interface), which supports a copy-protection system called *HDCP* (High Definition Content Protection), has been developed for HDTV-ready TVs, set-top boxes, and HDTV tuners. Only some of today's HDTV ready systems have this connection built in. If you buy one, and a few years down the road want to hook up a new HDTV tuner, you might find that DVI is the only interface available on new HDTV tuners, which will leave you no way to connect your expensive, HDTV-ready display to HDTV content.

Could happen. Probably won't. But we wanted to mention it as something to think about before you make an investment in HDTV. Keep in mind that this issue (not having an HDCP-enabled DVI port on your HDTV-ready display) won't keep you from using any HDTV tuner you buy along with the display (or the built-in tuner if you buy a true HDTV). It'll just keep you from having all the flexibility you might want. We recommend getting a unit with DVI (even though we're not all that keen on the concept of HDCP), as long as it fits in your budget and satisfies your theater needs. (We prefer the FireWire system for digitally connecting HDTV devices, but unfortunately, the market seems to have chosen DVI.)

All four types of displays we discuss in this book — direct-view, flat-panel, front-projection, and rear-projection systems — can be built as an HDTV or HDTV-ready system. And just like non-HDTV versions of these displays, a huge range of sizes and shapes is on the market. You can buy a 14-inch LCD (Liquid Crystal Display — which we talk about later in this chapter) HDTV for a bedroom or kitchen, or you can buy a $60,000 HDTV-ready projector that requires professional mounting and calibration and gives you an HDTV picture the size of some movie theater screens. You can find a vast range of options in the HDTV world.

As we discuss the different types of displays in this chapter (and in the following chapter when we discuss projectors), we talk about the strengths and weaknesses of each type of display in overall terms (HDTV, NTSC, DVD playback, you name it — when we say overall, we mean overall). Remember that *any* of these systems can be used for HDTV (of course, not *every* or even most models within these groups can display HDTV signals). We mention any special HDTV considerations as we discuss each type of display.

Choosing a TV

As you shop for a display, you'll find that, beyond all the brand and size choices, you need to make some high-level decisions about what kind of display you want. For many people, a display (or TV) means the traditional tube television that's been around for decades, but new technologies have made flat-panel screens (which have no tube and are only a few inches deep) into a viable choice as well. In this section, we talk about some of the pros and cons of these types of displays. (Don't forget that we also talk about projection TVs in the next chapter.)

Sticking with the tried-and-true

Admit it. You say it, too. "What's on the tube?" C'mon, we all say it. And for good reason — the vast majority of TVs are *direct-view CRT* (or cathode ray tube) models. You know what they look like — kind of big and bulky, with a big (and relatively heavy) glass tube inside.

The CRT itself is a vacuum tube (so don't drop it — well, don't drop any television, if you can help it, especially not on your foot) with an electron gun at the back, and a *phosphor* coating on the inside of the screen (the part you look at). When a CRT operates, the electron gun shoots a beam of electrons on that phosphor coating. In reaction to being bombarded by these electrons, the phosphor coating lights up. A color CRT actually has three electron guns — one each for red, green, and blue. This combination of colors (often called *RGB*) can be combined on the screen to produce any color on the screen.

Because CRT TVs are an old technology, many people skip right past them as they shop for a home theater display. We're not convinced that's a good idea. Direct-view TVs have a few significant things going for them:

- **Cheap:** Because the factories and machines and technologies behind CRT are old (though constantly refined), CRTs are rather inexpensive to build (HDTV models are not nearly as cheap). This gets passed on to the consumer in the form of lower prices (capitalism at work!), making direct-view televisions the cheapest you can buy.

✔ **Work well in a bright room:** The contrast ratios and overall ability to crank out the light are typically highest on direct-view displays. If you can't create a dark environment for your home theater (something we think is really important, but which we realize isn't always possible), a direct-view TV may be your best choice. Another reason to choose direct-view is because you like to have your buddies over for the big game in the middle of a bright day.

✔ **Better at black:** Not only are CRTs brighter than other display types, they're also better at creating dark images than most other kinds of displays. So if you like to watch a lot of *film noir* or anything that has dark scenes (with people lurking in the shadows), you'll appreciate the fact that direct-view displays let you see details that can be lost on other sets.

Like anything else, getting a direct-view TV has some drawbacks. Whether these drawbacks are enough to drive you to a different display type really depends on how important the strengths we just listed are to you. Here's what to keep in mind as you make this decision:

✔ **Limited size:** Although CRTs are relatively easy and cheap to make, the manufacturing process does become difficult when CRTs reach a certain size. Huge vacuum tubes aren't easy to create, and as the screen gets bigger, keeping the electron guns properly aimed is also a big issue for display designers. When you start looking at displays bigger than about 40 inches, you won't find CRTs in your size range.

✔ **Heavy and bulky:** You certainly can't hang a CRT on the wall (like you can with the plasma displays we discuss in a moment). In fact, if you go for a bigger screen size, you can't even lift your direct-view TV (direct-views bigger than 36 inches often weigh over 200 pounds). And weight isn't the only issue — direct-view sets usually have 2 or 3 feet of electronics and tube behind the screen. So if you're tight on space but desire a big screen, don't be surprised if a direct-view doesn't work for you.

✔ **Lower resolution:** For NTSC and DVD viewing, CRT direct-view displays (at least high-quality models) can meet the resolution demands of the source material. But when you start getting into HDTV sources, you'll find that direct-views can't keep up. They *can* provide excellent pictures, but if you were to compare them side by side with a plasma or projection TV, you'd find that most direct-view HDTVs don't match up, at least in terms of resolution.

If you have the money to spend (and it won't be cheap), you can get many of the benefits of a direct-view TV, without the drawbacks, by investing in a CRT-based projection TV. We discuss these TVs in Chapter 13.

If a direct-view TV fits into your budget, room, and lifestyle, there are a few things you look for. (As an aside, one of Pat's college professors automatically gave an F to anyone who used the word *lifestyle* in a paper, so he loves to sprinkle it in his writing now.) Consider this a checklist of sorts, but keep in mind that some TVs can have all these things and still not be all that great. Others can be great even though they're missing a feature or two. So the following items are recommended but not essential:

- ✔ **Flat-screen:** Older TVs had a curved screen surface (the actual front of the screen that you watch), but many newer models have a truly flat-screen surface. (This is different than a flat-panel, where the whole display is flat and thin.) The biggest advantage of a flat-screen direct-view TV is the fact that this screen is much less susceptible to reflections and glare from light sources in your home theater.

- ✔ **Aspect ratio:** For most display types, we recommend a 16:9 aspect ratio that is optimized for widescreen movie viewing. When it comes to direct-view sets, however, we usually recommend the more traditional 4:3 aspect ratio.

  We have two reasons for this recommendation. First, the vast majority of direct-view sets on the market come in the 4:3 shape, so it's much easier to find a good 4:3 set. Second, the phosphors on direct-view sets tend to become dimmer with use, and because most broadcast material today is still 4:3, a 16:9 direct-view display could end up with an unevenly lit picture on the edges. If you watch *lots* of 16:9 material, consider a widescreen CRT, but if you don't, look at 4:3 displays with *anamorphic squeeze* (which we discuss in the following section).

- ✔ **Anamorphic squeeze:** Often called *raster squeeze,* this is a neat trick that lets you watch anamorphic DVDs at full resolution on 4:3 aspect ratio, direct-view TVs. (This isn't a feature you find or need on fixed-pixel displays, such as LCD or plasma.) The squeeze basically re-aims the electron guns' beams (the raster) to create a 16:9 window within the 4:3 screen. At first glance, this looks a lot like a letterboxed video picture on your screen, but instead of wasting lines of resolution to draw black bars, this refocused beam uses the entire 480 lines to create the video you're watching. The result is a sharper, brighter, and better-looking picture. Some displays have an automatic system for detecting 16:9 sources and turning on this mode, and others have a button on the remote to activate it.

If you use this mode, make sure you've set your DVD player to "think" it's connected to a 16:9 TV. Otherwise, you don't get anything out of your display's anamorphic squeeze function.

Thin is in — flat-panel TVs

The coolest development in the TV world in years and years has been the advent of the flat-panel (notice we didn't say flat screen) display. These are TVs that you can literally hang on the wall. Flat-panel TVs make use of technologies such as LCD and plasma to create a TV that is barely bigger than the screen itself. These displays have a small frame around the edges of the screen and are about 3 or 4 inches deep. There are some tradeoffs to flat-panel displays, but if you can live with them, you can definitely find a place in your home theater for a flat-panel — literally!

Many flat-panel displays ship as monitors only. They don't have the built-in TV tuner, so you may need to buy a separate tuner. This isn't an issue if you have a DSS receiver or digital cable set-top box. If you're using basic analog cable or a broadcast antenna, however, you need something to tune in your TV. One easy way to do this is to simply use the TV tuner built in to your VCR. To get HDTV, you need an HDTV tuner.

Demystifying LCD

If you have a laptop computer, a digital watch, a handheld computer, or just about anything electronic, you've probably seen, touched, felt, and used a liquid crystal display, or LCD. We first saw LCDs on digital watches back when we were kids (we thought they were cool) and never imagined the size they'd grow to. We certainly never thought LCDs would one day display high-resolution images with millions of gradations of color. But that's exactly what they can do, and are doing, in an increasing number of homes and home theaters.

Despite these amazing changes, LCDs tend to be the smallest displays (and therefore the least suitable for many home theaters). The process of "growing" LCD crystals is quite complicated, and the bigger the crystal, the harder (and more expensive) it is to make. Most of the LCD displays top out at about 24 inches — smaller than all but the tiniest of the other kinds of displays. So LCDs are typically used as computer displays or as small (but high quality) televisions in dens, bedrooms, and kitchens.

We're talking about direct-view LCD displays here (where you look directly at the LCD, just as you look directly at the picture tube with direct-view tube TV). LCDs can also be used in projector TVs (both front and rear), and we talk about them in the next chapter.

A few companies make mega-big LCD displays. As we write (early 2003), we've seen prototypes for LCD displays as big as 52 inches diagonally. And new technologies, such as O-LED (Organic LED), promise LCD-like displays in ever bigger sizes in the future. We've even seen prototype systems that seamlessly combine three smaller (and easier to build LCD panels) into a larger single panel — making a cheaper big LCD.

Most LCD television monitors are built in the widescreen 16:9 aspect ratio, although some vendors sell 4:3 versions (which are more typical for PC screens). We prefer the widescreen versions of LCDs, as 16:9 LCDs don't tend to "wear out" unevenly (like direct-view CRTs do) when used to display 4:3 video programming.

LCD displays have a couple of particular strong points when it comes to playing video:

- ✔ **Extremely high resolutions:** LCD displays can easily reach HDTV resolutions (in fact, most LCD displays do).

- ✔ **Excellent color:** LCDs offer exceptional reproduction of colors, with the potential for beautifully recreated colors across the spectrum. This differs from other flat-panel displays (such as plasma systems), which often tend to inaccurately display certain colors.

- ✔ **PC monitor capable:** This probably won't surprise you, because you're probably familiar with LCD screen monitors. Most LCD television displays can also do double-duty as a PC monitor, plugging directly into any PC with a standard PC video cable.

- ✔ **No *burn-in*:** If you play a lot of video games, watch the stock ticker on MSNBC, or do other things with your display that involve a lot of *static* content (images that don't change or move around), you can end up with those images permanently burned into the phosphors on your screen. When these images become permanently etched into the phosphor, you see them even when you're watching something else. Because

LCDs use a separate backlight, instead of creating their own light with phosphors, they are immune to this problem (plasmas are not, by the way).

✔ **Inherently progressive:** Unlike direct-view systems, LCDs don't display their picture using electron guns scanning lines across a screen. Instead, LCDs use millions of tiny transistors that can be individually controlled by the "brains" inside the display. This means that LCDs can easily handle progressive scan sources, such as progressive scan DVD and HDTV — unlike some direct-view systems that simply can't scan fast enough to display progressive video.

Besides the size limitation we discuss earlier in this section, consider a few other problem areas before you buy an LCD system as your primary display in a home theater:

✔ **Expensive for their size:** Although LCD displays tend to be less expensive than the plasma flat-panels we discuss next, they're much smaller than the plasmas and much more expensive than direct-view displays. The huge price drops that have hit the LCD computer monitor world have yet to hit the LCD television market. At the beginning of 2003, you could expect to pay about $1,000 for an HDTV-ready, 17-inch LCD display. For the same price, you could buy an HDTV-ready, 32-inch direct-view set.

✔ **Poor reproduction of blacks:** Compared to direct-view tube displays, LCDs do a poor job of reproducing black images. Darker screen images never show up as true-black, but rather as various shades of gray, and actions happening in these darker areas are difficult to discern.

✔ **Limited viewing angle:** Although they are getting better (due to some intensive efforts by manufacturers), LCDs typically have a poor viewing angle. If you are not sitting nearly perpendicular to the screen, you don't get a good picture.

✔ **Limited brightness:** Because LCDs use a backlight shining through the liquid crystal, most of the light is absorbed. As a result, the LCD displays have lower contrast and are harder to view in a brightly lit room (the picture appears washed out), compared to direct-view TVs.

Staying on the cutting edge with plasma

Perhaps the coolest thing to come down the home theater pike in quite some time (maybe ever!) is the larger, flat-screen monitor that uses plasma technology. A plasma screen contains literally millions of gas filled cells (or pixels) wedged between two pieces of glass. An electrical grid zaps these pixels and causes the gases to ionize (the ionized gas is plasma — hence the name). The ionized gases, in turn, cause a layer of phosphor on the outside layer of glass to light up (just like the electron gun in a CRT causes the phosphor to light up on the front of the tube). Figure 12-1 shows a plasma display unit.

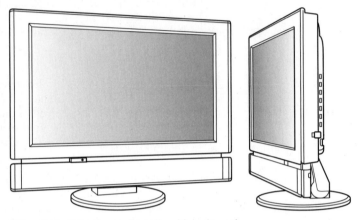

Figure 12-1: Hang it on your wall — it's a plasma!

Plasma displays have really captured the attention of the home theater industry (and of home theater consumers) because of the sheer size and quality of the picture they can produce. They're also known for their compact size. Plasma displays are available in 42-, 50-, and even 60-inch sizes. Even at the larger sizes, the display itself is usually no more than 5 or 6 inches deep — and suitable for wall hanging! All the plasma displays in these sizes (which are by far the most common, at least in the U.S. market) have a 16:9 aspect ratio.

Other benefits of plasma displays include:

✓ **Excellent brightness:** Because plasma displays use the direct lighting of phosphors (instead of a backlighting system like LCDs), they can have an extremely bright and crisp picture, just like a direct-view CRT TV. In fact, because each pixel is controlled directly by the electrical grid behind the plasma cells, the brightness tends to be extremely even across the screen. In a CRT, the electron guns shoot at the phosphors from differing angles depending upon which part of the screen the gun is creating, which can cause uneven brightness, unless the CRT is well designed.

✓ **High resolution:** Although not all plasma displays can reach HDTV levels of resolution (many "inexpensive" $3,000 plasma models can't show true HDTV), they do typically provide greater resolution than CRT displays. This is especially true of the more expensive HDTV plasmas, which can often reach higher horizontal resolutions that direct-view sets can't match. Just about all plasma displays on the market are 16:9 aspect ratio sets, which is also essential for HDTV viewing.

✔ **PC monitor capable:** Like LCD screens, most plasma displays can be plugged directly into any PC (not just home theater PCs with special TV video cards) to act as a gigantic PC monitor.

✔ **No geometric distortion:** In a direct-view display, the electron guns that shoot their beams on the phosphor screen are in a fixed location (the center/back of the tube). The angle at which these beams hit the phosphor varies; in the middle of the screen, the angle is perpendicular, but the angle is quite different at the corners of the screen. This can cause distortions in the picture — *geometric distortions* caused by this changing angle. In a plasma display, each gas pocket is at an identical angle (and distance) to the phosphor it is lighting up, so you don't get distortions around the edge of the picture.

✔ **Progressive by nature:** Like LCD displays, plasma systems don't use a scanning electron beam to create a picture. Instead, all the pixels on the screen are lit up simultaneously. So progressive video sources display progressively on any plasma system; you don't need to buy a special progressive set like you do with direct-view displays.

✔ **A wide viewing angle:** Unlike LCDs (which often have problems in this regard), plasma displays have a good picture even when you are sitting "off axis" (not perpendicular to the screen surface). In a smaller room, where some of the seating might be at a rather acute angle from the screen, the wide viewing angle can be a big plus.

Of course, the plasma equation has a few downsides (besides the fact that a lot of us can't afford the $8,000 it costs for an HDTV plasma):

✔ **Susceptible to burn-in:** Any system that uses a phosphor screen to display video can fall victim to the phosphor burn-in mentioned earlier in this chapter. If you do a lot of video gaming or stock/news ticker viewing, you need to be aware of this fact. Although burn-in can also be an issue with a direct-view set, it's an even bigger issue with a plasma considering the price. You can't remove burn-in after it's happened; you need to either live with it or replace the display.

You can minimize burn-in on any display by calibrating the set properly and reducing the brightness from its (usually too high) factory setting.

✔ **Shorter lifespan:** Another phenomenon of any phosphor-based display system is that eventually the phosphors "wear out" or lose their brightness. Like burn-in, this degradation also happens to CRT-based direct-view displays, but it often happens faster with plasma displays. Given the considerably higher cost of a plasma, your dollars per hour of viewing is much higher. Before you buy, check the manufacturer's specifications on *hours to half brightness* (the point at which the display is only half as bright as it was when new). For example, if this specification is 20,000 hours, and you watch the set for 6 hours a day, it will be effectively worn out in about 9 years. If you have kids, keep in mind that 6 hours a day is *not* an excessive estimate for how long the television may be turned on every day.

✔ **Less than perfect color reproduction:** Although plasma displays are capable of producing a breathtaking array of colors, all the sets built to date have had an unfortunate tendency to make red colors look more orange than true red. This has held true on just about every plasma set out there. Only a few factories in the whole world make some key components for plasma screens; so all these sets share certain characteristics, and this is unfortunately one of them. We're sure that this problem will be solved over time, but it is something to keep in mind (particularly if you're a Cincinnati Reds fan!).

✔ **Poor reproduction of black:** Although plasma displays are an equal to direct-view sets in terms of absolute brightness, they fall short in the contrast ratio comparison. Like LCDs, plasma displays have a really hard time reproducing black, so black scenes end up being reproduced as shades of gray.

We think that these shortcomings are far from fatal. We love plasma displays, but we realize that they aren't for everyone. In many home theaters, perhaps the biggest factor supporting the plasma display (besides the undeniable Wow factor that comes out every time you look at one in action) is their amazing compactness relative to screen size.

There's an acronym in the industry, SAF (or spousal acceptance factor), that absolutely applies to the plasma display (actually, the term is WAF, but we're being politically correct here). If your spouse isn't really into the concept of a home theater and hates the idea of a huge TV cluttering up the family or living room, a plasma may be your home theater salvation. You don't even have to tell him or her you wanted one anyway (because of the awesome picture). Grumble a little bit and get some brownie points out of your purchase!

Chapter 13

Projecting a Good Image

. . . .

. . . .

*W*hen you go to the movies, the images you see on the screen are projected onto that big screen in front of you. If size matters to you (and if you have the room in your home theater — and seats far enough away from the screen), then you too should consider a projector for your home theater's display system. Even if size isn't a huge deal to you, you may decide to go with a front-projection system because they can offer the ultimate in home theater image quality.

In this chapter, we talk about the two types of projectors available for home theater: all-in-one rear-projection systems and movie projector-like front-projection systems. We also talk about the different kinds of projector systems found in both front and rear projectors. And, finally, we get into the choices you'll find for separate screens (needed if you buy a front-projection system).

For many home theater enthusiasts, a theater isn't really a theater unless you have a projector. Until the advent of the plasma flat panel (discussed in the previous chapter), projectors were really the only choice for big screens (bigger than the approximately 40-inch limit of CRT direct-view TVs, at least). And while 60-inch plasmas are now on the market, you still need a projector system to get a really big picture (front-projection screens can be as big as 10 feet or more *across*!).

In fact, if money is no object in your home theater, you'll find that just about every home theater installer, reviewer, and expert out there will direct your attention to a top-of-the-line, 9-inch, CRT (cathode ray tube) front-projection system (we explain what this means shortly). This is really the ultimate in home theater video reproduction — providing the most awesome, film-like images you can get at home.

But projection systems don't need to break the bank either. Rear-projection systems (RPTVs) are perhaps the best value in home theater, at least in terms of bang for the buck. For a few thousand bucks (or even less, as new technologies like DLP (Digital Light Processor) begin to saturate the market), you can get a picture as big as a plasma, in full HDTV glory. You can't hang one of these units on the wall, but visually the picture is at least as good as (and often better than) plasma, for thousands less. In particular, RPTVs are much better than most plasma displays at reproducing blacks onscreen, which means you get superior reproduction of darker scenes when you're watching movies or television.

Choosing between Front and Rear Projection

The first big decision to make when evaluating projection systems is, for most people, the easiest: front or rear projection. We say this is the easiest decision to make, because we find that most people choose a rear-projection system. They are cheaper (generally speaking, though high-end rear projectors can definitely cost more than low-end front-projection systems), and they are easier to set up and integrate into your home theater.

Having said that, let's define what the difference between these systems is. It's quite simple, really:

✔ **Front-projection:** A front projector is very similar to a movie projector (except it doesn't use film). It includes a projector unit (which is usually mounted on your ceiling but can also be on a lift, on a floor mount, or in the rear wall) and a separate screen. Video sources (such as DVDs, cable, and satellite TV) are routed into the projector, which then turns these signals into light. Then, the light is (ding ding ding, you guessed it) *projected* onto a separate screen that's mounted on a wall in the front of your home theater. Figure 13-1 shows a front-projection system.

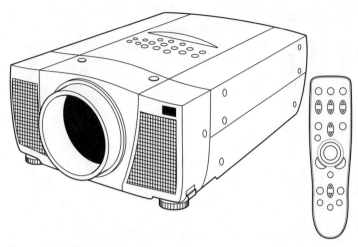

Figure 13-1: A front-projection system.

✔ **Rear-projection:** These are the traditional big-screen TVs that have been sold for years and years. If your Uncle Vinnie got a big screen back in 1987 for Superbowl XXI, this is what he has. Now some people, having seen the lousy, washed out picture on Uncle Vinnie's TV, think that rear projectors trade picture quality for size. Nothing can be further from the truth. A good quality, well set-up rear projector can offer an awesome picture. A rear projector TV (or RPTV) has both parts of the front projector (the projector and the screen) in a single, all-in-one box, and the projector illuminates the *back* of the screen instead of the front. Figure 13-2 shows a rear-projection system.

RPTVs are great. In fact, we think they may be the best value in home theater big screen displays. But they do have two limitations: a limited viewing angle and size. Because of the way video is internally reflected toward the screen in these sets, you need to be perpendicular to the display (or near-perpendicular) to see a good picture. Keep that limitation in mind as you consider an RPTV. If your home theater room is set up with widely dispersed seating, an RPTV may not be your best choice. Also, rear-projection TVs can be very deep and overwhelm a room with their size. For some, this is a limitation.

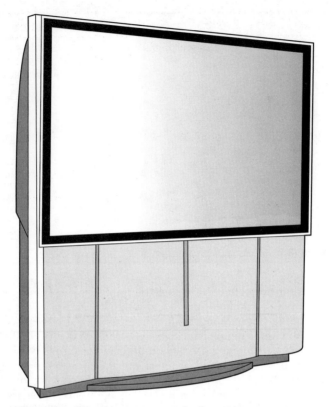

Figure 13-2: The all-in-one, rear-projection system.

Now, we've already come right out and said that for most people —
most people, not *all* people — rear-projection systems are probably the best choice. As we mention earlier, the lower cost and
easier setup make rear projectors more consumer-friendly. (You
don't have to spend nearly as much time getting the projector
properly aligned and aimed at the screen with a rear projector —
though you do have to spend *some* time doing this.) But with the
advent of new, computer-based technologies such as DLP (Digital
Light Processor) chips, front projectors have begun to drop in
price from the stratospheric ($20,000 to $60,000) to the reasonable
(under $3,000), and the setup of these new systems is easier, too
(which we explain in a minute). Rather than take up your valuable
reading time with a long-winded description of the relative benefits
and shortcomings of these two types of projectors, we've created
the handy-dandy Table 13-1 to enlighten, educate, and energize the
home theater portion of your brain.

Table 13-1	Comparing Front and Rear Projectors	
Characteristic	*Front Projector*	*Rear Projector*
Screen size	Gigantic	Merely huge
Price	Moderate to astronomical	Moderate to high
Aspect ratio (4:3 or 16:9)	Fixed or flexible (depends on technology)	Fixed
Picture quality	Great to astonishing	Great to astonishing
Setup	Moderate to complicated	Easy to moderate
Installation	Moderate to complicated	Easy

Selecting a Projection Method

As you move past the rear- versus front-projection decision, you'll find that you really haven't decided anything at all. Four main technologies that are currently on the market do the actual work of converting electrical video source signals into light that can be projected onto the screen. Each of these can be found in either front-or rear-projection units. Keep in mind, however, that new variants of these technologies, as well as entirely new ways of projecting video, are being invented all the time.

Catching on to the cathode ray

We cover the CRT, or cathode-ray tube, in Chapter 12, so we're not going to get into a long discussion about what they are or how they work here. However, that good, old-fashioned tube is not only the heart of most conventional TVs, but also the centerpiece of the most sophisticated, highest-quality projector systems (which is to say, the most sophisticated, highest-quality displays, period).

CRT projectors, particularly front-projection systems, can provide the highest resolution (including full HDTV support), the most excellent color, and a bright picture with a superb contrast ratio. (If any of these terms seems unfamiliar to you, refer to Chapter 12.) CRT projectors also provide the best reproduction of black tints — significantly better than any of the other projector types available.

Not all CRT projector systems can display HDTV. Plenty of inexpensive systems that provide only a big-screen NTSC (National Television Standards Committee) picture are still on the market. These mainly consist of RPTVs — most CRT front-projection systems *are* HDTV-capable. These systems can't display progressive scan DVDs or HDTV broadcasts either. Most of the newer systems that manufacturers are releasing these days, however, qualify as HDTV-ready. This means they don't have a built-in HDTV tuner, but they can be connected to an external tuner and display HDTV at either the 720p or 1080i resolution. As you move up to larger sizes of CRT projectors, you'll definitely want a system capable of displaying progressive, higher resolution images, to reduce the appearance of visible scan lines (as we discuss in the previous chapter).

Unlike direct-view CRT displays, which use a single picture tube, CRT projectors use three separate tubes — one each for red, green, and blue. The extra tubes make the setup and calibration more complex, because the light projection from these three CRTs must be *converged* (aligned so that they each hit the screen at the same place). If you've seen bad projection TV before, with inaccurate color reproduction and colored "halos" around objects, you've probably seen a system that has not been properly converged. It's not pretty. Convergence on projection systems tends to drift over time, so you need to think about resetting the convergence a couple of times a year. Luckily, many RPTVs now include an automatic convergence system that simplifies this process. In Chapter 18, we discuss how you can do your own calibration or hire a professional to calibrate your projection system.

Perhaps the biggest factor to consider when comparing CRT projectors is tube size. In the RPTV realm, this isn't a huge deal. Almost all RPTVs have the same size (7-inch) tubes, but front projectors have tubes in the 7-, 8-, and 9-inch size ranges. Bigger tubes bring with them sharper, more detailed pictures, but at a considerably higher price. In fact, the price differential between a 7- or 8-inch projector and a 9-inch model can be striking. You can get a decent 7-inch front projector for under $10,000 (still a lot), but 9-inch CRT projectors usually start off in the $30,000 (and up!) range.

Keep in mind three things about any CRT projector system (front or RPTV):

> ✔ **Brightness can be an issue:** This isn't a major problem for RPTVs, where the tube is relatively close to the screen, but in a front projector environment, the CRT is the least bright of all the alternatives. Imagine trying to light up a screen across the room with your old direct-view TV (not really a fair comparison, but the technology is very similar), and you'll understand

that a CRT doesn't throw off a ton of light. The other systems we discuss use a separate (high-powered) light source, which gives them greater brightness. So a CRT front projector works best in a room with very little ambient light; in fact, near total darkness works best. (In fact, total darkness gives you the best picture with any front projection system.)

✔ **Tubes wear out:** Just as direct-view CRTs lose brightness over time, so do CRT projectors. In fact, because CRT projectors need to be set up to project more light than a direct-view TV (especially front projectors), CRT tubes in a projector tend to wear out even faster. Check the manufacturer's specifications for how quickly its tubes lose brightness and plan on budgeting some home theater money for new tubes based on those specifications. This isn't a cheap fix. You can spend thousands of dollars on new tubes every time you need to replace them, so read the fine print.

✔ **Tubes can get burn-in:** *Burn-in* occurs when static content, such as video games, permanently alters the phosphors on your CRT, so that you always see, for example, a ghost image of Halo's weapons status on your screen. If you (or your kids) play a ton of video games, we suggest you look at one of the other projector technologies we're about to discuss. Burn-in can also be a problem when the CRTs have a fixed aspect ratio. For example, if you have 16:9 (widescreen) tubes, and watch a ton of 4:3 (traditional square screen) content, you can end up with uneven brightness on the tubes. This occurs because the center of the tube is constantly in use, but the edges are used only occasionally. See Chapter 12 for more about burn-in.

We've given you a quick overview of CRT projectors. CRT RPTVs are the kind of product you can buy, install, and set up on your own, if you want to. We think that a CRT front projector is something you *need* professional help with. That includes help choosing the right model and an associated screen and help installing, configuring, and maintaining the projector. It's a huge investment, and you should find a dealer you're comfortable with who can help you down this path.

Projecting with LCDs

LCD technologies have been used for years and years for relatively low-quality projectors — the kind you might have in the conference room at work, for projecting those ubiquitous PowerPoint slides on the white board during mind-numbingly boring meetings at work.

Well, the LCD has come of age in the era of home theater, and now you can buy front and RPTV systems that are based on the LCD and that provide a high-quality (many times HDTV) picture at a price that is typically lower than that of CRT front-projection systems. (LCD RPTVs aren't much cheaper than CRT RPTVs and may even cost more.)

LCD projectors typically use three small LCD panels (a couple of inches across at most) — one each for red, green, and blue picture information. Behind these panels is a strong lamp that provides the light. LCDs (and the DLP and LCoS projectors we discuss next) are *fixed pixel* displays, meaning that they display video at a certain resolution. For example, Sony's most recent LCD RPTV displays at 1366 pixels horizontally and 768 pixels vertically (this exceeds the 720 vertical pixels required for 720i, so the set is HDTV-ready). An internal device called an *image scaler* converts the incoming signal (such as 480p from progressive scan DVDs or 1080i from an HDTV broadcast) to the 1366 x 768 resolution for display. LCD projectors are inherently progressive, so even standard NTSC broadcasts are converted to a progressive scan mode for display. We discuss inherently progressive systems in more detail in Chapter 12.

The quality of the image scaler — how well it converts other signals to the fixed pixel resolution *native* to the LCD — is a key factor in a projector's picture quality. In Chapter 20, we talk about external image scalers (and related devices such as line doublers and quadruplers) that can improve the picture quality of a projection system — not just fixed pixel displays, but also CRTs.

Because you never know who'll come up with a better system the month after this book is printed, we generally avoid dropping brand name recommendations. However, we find that scalers from one company, Faroudja (www.faroudja.com), are always excellent. You can find many different brands of projectors (and HDTVs in general) that use Faroudja chips to scale, or *upconvert,* images.

LCD projector systems have a couple of big advantages, when compared to CRT projectors:

   ✔ **Lower cost front projectors:** Although CRT front projectors can cost an arm and three legs, you can buy a quality LCD projector for less than $10,000.

   ✔ **More compact RPTVs:** Because the LCD panels and the lamp are small, LCD RPTVs can be much thinner than CRT RPTVs. Although many CRT systems can be 3 or more feet deep, LCD systems can be less than 1.5 feet deep. That helps a lot in small rooms, and with that SAF (spousal acceptance factor) we discuss in Chapter 12.

✔ **Brighter than CRT:** The separate lamp used in CRT projectors puts out a ton of light (you wouldn't want to have someone shine one in your eyes close up!). The result is a brighter picture that can tolerate more ambient light in your home theater.

✔ **Don't need to be converged:** Despite the fact that an LCD projector contains three LCD panels, it has only one light source. So you don't need to converge the picture like you do with a CRT projector. This makes the setup much easier for mere mortals.

✔ **Burn-in isn't a big issue:** Plug in that Xbox or PlayStation 2 and play all the games you want. Because LCD systems don't use phosphors, they can't get permanent burn-in like CRTs (or flat-panel plasma systems) can.

Of course, there's got to be a downside, right? LCDs don't do a couple of things well:

✔ **Relatively poor black performance:** LCD projectors, like LCD direct-view sets, can't display true black tints well. Dark scenes end up being gray instead. So when the Orcs are sneaking up on Frodo from the mouth of that dark cave, you can't see them all that well.

✔ **Limited resolution:** Today's LCD panels can reach HDTV resolutions (at least 720p resolutions), but most can't display the full resolution of 1080i content. To do so, the LCD panels need a resolution of 1920 x 1080, and none we know of are there yet.

✔ **The lamp will wear out:** Nothing lasts forever, and the high-output lamps on LCD projectors tend to wear out after a few thousand hours of use, which is faster than the tubes on a CRT. But the LCD lamps cost a lot less to replace (hundreds instead of thousands of dollars).

✔ **The "dead pixel" problem:** If you own a laptop computer (or a desktop computer with an LCD display), you may be familiar with the issue of *dead pixels.* These are usually minor manufacturing defects that cause individual pixels to not light up when the display tells them too. Because the relative size of pixels in a projection system is large, you may notice a dead pixel on your screen (and be very annoyed by it). Many manufacturers think that having a few dead pixels is just part of doing business, and they will not replace your LCD panels except in extreme cases. As a result, it is a good idea to find out the manufacturer's "dead pixel policy" before you buy.

✔ **The "screen door":** When LCD images are projected onto big screens (like the ones you find in a front-projector system), you can begin to see the pixel structure of the LCD itself. By this we mean the physical structure of the LCD that separates the individual pixels. Because of the way LCDs are constructed, you can look closely at a large projected image and see dots of lighter and darker areas — like you're looking at the world through a metal screen door. We should emphasize that this isn't a huge issue. This "screen door" effect is sort of like the scan lines on a CRT system, in that you really only notice it if you're too close to a big image.

Deciding on a Digital Light Processor

Texas Instruments has developed (over the course of many years) a completely new way of projecting video called the DLP (Digital Light Processor). DLP has created a whole new category of inexpensive projector systems and has also lead to a digital revolution in those old-fashioned movie theaters you used to go to before you got a home theater. If you were lucky enough to see *Star Wars: Episode II — Attack of the Clones* in a digital theater, you have already seen (a super high-end, expensive version of) DLP in action.

The DLP is an entirely digital process that utilizes a semiconductor generically called the *DMD* (or digital micromirror device). The DMD contains over a million incredibly tiny, hinged mirrors. Each of these mirrors represents a single pixel on your video image. The DLP chip's electronic logic controls the hinges on the mirrors, turning them so that they either reflect light (onto your screen) or block it (creating a dark spot on the screen). When the DLP's "brains" turn these mirrors on and off, the mirrors create different levels of light between black and white that result in a *grayscale* version of your image. A device called a *color wheel* filters light from a lamp (like the lamps found in LCD projectors), reflects this off the mirrors on the DLP chip, and provides the color in your image. This is really a Mach III fly-by of the details of DLP; if you want to know the nitty gritty, check out Texas Instruments' site on the technology, at www.dlp.com.

The DLP system we just described, with the color wheel, is called a *single chip* DLP solution, and is by far the most common in consumer DLP projectors. Movie theater projectors (and a few ultra-expensive home theater models) dispense with the color wheel, and use three DLP chips (one for red, one for green, and one for blue). These three-chip projectors can produce more gradations of color than a single-chip system but cost a heck of a lot more.

When looking at DLP projectors, the most important factor to consider is the capabilities of the DLP chip, which is the heart of the system. Like LCDs, DLPs are fixed-pixel displays, and Texas Instruments has a couple of chips on the market with different aspect ratios and different resolutions. Early DLP chips were designed for 4:3 video reproduction (with a lower-resolution, 16:9 mode), but current models are designed for 16:9 aspect ratios.

Some DLP chips can reproduce HDTV resolutions. Other, less expensive versions cannot. All DLP chips that we know of can reproduce 16:9 widescreen progressive scan video (which is 848 x 480 pixels), but the fancier versions can reproduce 720p HDTV signals. The latest and greatest DLP chip (and given the nature of the computer industry, this will change relatively soon) is called the HD2, which offers a 16:9 aspect ratio and a 1280 x 720 pixel resolution.

Even if a DLP projector can't reach HDTV resolutions (and none that we know of can yet display 1080i HDTV content at its full resolution), their internal image scalers can downconvert higher resolution HDTV signals and display them at their native resolution. The result can look pretty darned good, especially on a reasonably sized screen (meaning, something smaller than 10 feet across).

DLP projectors share many of the advantages of LCD models: low price, compact size (with particularly thin RPTVs possible), and immunity from image burn-in. They also share some (but not all) of the same drawbacks: less resolution than the best CRT systems (at least with today's chips) and less than perfect reproduction of blacks (but better than most LCD projectors). DLPs don't have the screen door issue we mention earlier and, additionally, have one big advantage over the other types of projectors we've discussed so far: They are brighter (and therefore better in rooms that aren't too dark). In a DLP chip, light from the lamp is reflected off the mirrors, but in an LCD, light is transmitted through the liquid crystals, which causes a decrease in brightness.

We love the future of DLP projectors (both front and rear). They have great pictures, are relatively inexpensive, and are a snap to set up. As the technology matures, we think this may end up being the predominant projection system of the future. Given the nature of the microprocessor business, we think that DLP chips will get much cheaper and much more capable faster than you can bat an eye. You can already buy a good-quality (but non-HDTV resolution) front-projection DLP system for under $3,000 (check out www.plushometheater.com for their Piano models).

Looking at Liquid Crystal on Silicon

Another "projector-on-a-chip" system that has hit the market in recent years is the LCoS (Liquid Crystal on Silicon) system. A couple of different manufacturers are making LCoS systems, but the most prominent to date has been JVC, with a system that they call D-ILA (Digital Direct Drive Image Light Amplifier). We're puzzled by the acronym, but we guess DDDILA is too hard to remember.

LCoS systems are basically a new variant of LCDs. LCoS systems still use liquid crystals, but instead of transmitting light through the liquid crystal (like an LCD does), LCoS reflects the light like a DLP, resulting in a significantly brighter image.

LCoS systems are very new on the market, but like DLP, they show a lot of promise. As we write, LCoS projectors (both front and RPTVs) that can reproduce the full 1920 x 1080 resolution of 1080i HDTV have been announced (and shown at trade shows). These sets aren't cheap, but they're the only sets (besides a mega-expensive, 9-inch CRT projector) that can do that!

Keeping Other Features in Mind

Regardless of technology, keep in mind a few other things when evaluating projection systems:

- ✔ **Fixed versus variable focal length (front projectors only):** Some front-projection systems (including many fancy CRT models) have what's known as a *fixed focal length*. This means for a given screen size, the projector must be placed a fixed and predetermined distance away. This can limit your placement in the room. If a heating duct on the ceiling is right where the projector needs to be, that's too bad. Projectors with variable focal length can be placed in different spots to fit your room's layout, and then adjusted to focus on the screen properly.

- ✔ **Light output (front-projection only):** We've already discussed the various projector types with regards to their relative brightness. But within these categories, projectors vary from model to model in their overall brightness. This is measured in *ANSI Lumens* and is a good measure of how well a system will work in a bright room. Brighter, high-end projectors are often rated at 1,000 or more Lumens, whereas cheaper ones are often below 500. We don't recommend that you use any projector in a brightly lit room, but if you simply can't make the room dark, go for a brighter unit.

Just because you can crank your amp up to 11, doesn't mean you should (excuse the shameless, pop culture, *Spinal Tap* reference). As we explain in Chapter 12, you shouldn't leave the brightness on your direct-view system cranked up all the way, and the same rule applies to a projection system. In Chapter 19, we talk about how to set up your brightness (and a bunch of other) settings on your display.

✔ **Aspect ratio:** In the RPTV world, systems have a fixed aspect ratio. They're either 4:3 (standard squarish TV) or 16:9 (widescreen). We recommend you get the widescreen version, unless *all* you watch is *Leave It to Beaver* reruns. Some front projectors also have a fixed native aspect ratio, but many systems can be adjusted to work at either aspect ratio. If you don't have a choice, go with the widescreen, and if you pick a system with an adjustable aspect ratio, enjoy it!

✔ **Projector noise:** Many front projection TVs employ a cooling fan — particularly LCD and DLP systems, which need bright (and hot!) lamps to create the picture. DLP systems may also make an audible noise when the color wheel spins. Keep in mind the fact that in a small room, you may hear these noises, which can be annoying. Try to audition your projector in your dealer's showroom, and pay attention to the noise it makes. You've got to live with it once you buy it!

✔ **Everything we discuss in Chapter 12:** This is our convenient catch-all category. In Chapter 12, we list a ton of things to consider when evaluating a display system, such as the number of inputs, the adjustability of the system, and so on. We really don't feel like repeating ourselves, and we don't like typing that much (or even cutting and pasting!) either. So go read the beginning of Chapter 12, because it all applies here, too.

Selecting Your Silver Screen

As they say in the Ginsu Knife ads, "But wait, there's more!" We've talked about the projectors themselves, but in the case of front projection systems, we've only talked about half the equation. You gotta shine that nice, high-def image onto something, and we definitely don't recommend an old bed sheet or the wall. You need a real screen — just like a movie theater.

Screens come in a couple different forms:

✔ **Portable screens that sit on a tripod:** You can fold these up and put them away when you're done (but who's ever done with a home theater?). These are a bit less than optimal (if you take them down, you need to get them back in *exactly* the same spot or refocus the projector — if it can even be focused!). We don't recommend these at all.

✔ **Retractable screens:** These can be manually or electrically powered. Although nothing is cooler than pressing a button on the remote and having the screen come down, this setup will cost you, compared to the manual version. You also need to make sure these systems are properly installed so that they are flat (otherwise the image can be distorted) and periodically check to make sure they haven't become misaligned with use.

✔ **Fixed wall and ceiling mounted screens:** If you've got a dedicated home theater where you'll never want to hide the screen, these are probably the best way to go.

Even more important than the form are the technical characteristics of the screen. The big three are the following:

✔ **Gain:** Gain is a measure of how reflective the screen is — how much of the projector's light gets bounced back to your eyeballs. There's a standard industry reference for gain, and systems that have exactly as much gain as that reference are rated at a gain of 1. More reflective (high gain) screens are rated greater than 1 (say 1.2), while less reflective (low gain) screens are rated below 1 (many are rated at 0.8). Generally speaking, match CRT projectors with high gain screens (between 1 and 1.3, though you can go higher if needed). Brighter, fixed-pixel systems like LCD or DLP can use a low gain screen (0.8 or higher).

✔ **Viewing angle:** Most display systems have a limited angle (from perpendicular) in which they look best. Sit outside that angle, and the picture becomes very dim. For front-projector screens, this viewing angle is inversely proportional to gain. In other words, the higher the gain, the smaller the angle in which viewers will get a good picture. For this reason, you are best off choosing the lowest gain screen that works with your projector in your room. This is why low gain screens are recommended for fixed-pixel projectors; LCD, DLP, and LCoS projectors have got light to spare, so why not trade some of it off for a wider viewing angle. Viewing angles are usually listed in a number of degrees (like 90). Your viewing angle is half this amount (45, in this case) on either side of perpendicular.

✔ **Hotspotting:** One reason why you shouldn't use a screen with too high a gain for your projector is the *hotspotting* phenomenon. When this occurs, one part of the screen is brighter than the other parts. Typically, the center of the screen gets too bright, relative to the edges, which makes the picture on the edges appear washed out.

✔ **Aspect ratio:** Screens are available in either the 16:9 widescreen or 4:3 aspect ratios. You should, of course, choose the same aspect ratio as that of your projector. You can buy (or make your own, if you're crafty) *masks* to cover the unlit portions of the screen when you're watching material of a different aspect ratio. So you can cover the sides of the screen with a mask when you're watching a 4:3 TV show (more *Leave it to Beaver?*) on your 16:9 screen.

Choosing a screen is not something for the faint of heart. Find out what screens your projector manufacturer recommends, ask your dealer what he or she recommends, and if at all possible, look at your projector (or the identical model) on the screen before you buy.

Chapter 14

Remote Controlling Your Home Theater

・・・

In This Chapter

▶ Controlling your home theater from your couch

▶ Checking out types of remote controls

▶ Understanding remote control features you might want

▶ Using your PDA as a remote

・・・

*R*emote controls have come a long way since the first universal remote controls hit the market, allowing you to control multiple devices from one remote control. In this chapter, we introduce you to your world of options. Today, you've got all sorts of options: tiny, large, color, touch-sensitive, voice-controlled, time-controlled, and on and on. You can spend $19 on a great remote, or $5,000. You can keep it confined to your home theater or go whole home.

Sifting through Remote Control Options

The remote control is nothing more than a means to communicate with your system, in order to tell it what to do. The term *remote* just means you don't control the device manually. Let's treat the remote control as an *interface,* and say that you can interface with your system in multiple ways.

Types of remotes

Hundreds upon hundreds of remotes are out there. Generically, they fall into the following categories, which are presented in increasing order of functionality and desirability:

- ✔ **Standard/dedicated remotes:** These are the device-specific remotes that come with your system. If you stopped here, you'd have ten or so remotes on your coffee table!

- ✔ **Brand-based remotes that come with a component:** Brand-based remotes are those that work with all sorts of devices from the same manufacturer. For instance, the RCA remote you get with an RCA DSS receiver usually has buttons for your RCA TV and your RCA VCR. There are buttons for each of the devices supported.

- ✔ **Third-party universal remote controls:** Many leading electronics brands sell so-called *universal remote controls*. These remotes supposedly work with any electronics device by way of on-board code databases. These remotes generally come with manuals that walk you through setting up your remote for your specific components. This environment is ever-changing, however, and we've found that you get what you pay for. We've never been happy with cheap universal remotes (like the $20 "do everything universal" remotes you see at the mega sized electronics stores). Some capability is always missing. We prefer the slightly more expensive *learning remotes.*

Most A/V receivers and TVs and many DVD players come with a universal remote, but most don't have a lot of functionality on other brands of equipment, just the basics.

- ✔ **Learning remotes:** Learning remotes can learn codes from your existing remote controls. You simply point your remotes at each other, go through a listing of commands, and the remote codes are transferred from one to the other. These remotes have a higher success rate than universal remotes, because you are essentially using the same codes as your present remote — not codes that a database says *should* work. Some learning remotes have an on-board, preprogrammed database against which they try to match the codes being learned; others are completely learning-based. The downside of a completely learning-based remote is that, if you lost your original remote, it's almost impossible to train the remote.

- ✔ **Programmable remotes:** Programmable remotes allow you to create *macros,* which are sequential code combinations that do a lot of things at once. So say you wanted to watch a movie on a DVD. You could program a macro to turn on your TV, receiver, and DVD player; set the receiver to the appropriate source and output modes; and start the DVD in the tray — all from one button. Now, if it could only cook the popcorn, too. . . .

- ✔ **Computer-based remotes:** Computer-based remotes take advantage of the growing number of computing devices around the home to provide remote control capabilities. This category includes PDAs, Web tablets, portable touch screens, and PCs. Home control software that can drive your lighting, heating, and other environmental controls in addition to your home theater needs, is also in this group.

- ✔ **Proprietary systems:** There are a number of closed-system control devices that enable you to integrate control of all your home theater devices on a single control system. Companies such as Niles Audio (www.nilesaudio.com) and Crestron (www.crestron.com) are renown for their control systems.

Remote control features

For as seemingly simple as a remote control is, the world of remotes is insanely complex. This section discusses some ways in which remotes have gotten more complex lately.

Radio frequency (RF) versus infrared (IR)

It used to be that all remotes were infrared-based. Now, many are touting RF connections, which is in many ways better than IR. First, RF signals tend to go farther than IR. Second, you don't need to point the remote at the TV set; RF can go in all directions, even through walls and cabinet doors. The biggest downside of RF remotes is that you can't easily integrate them into one remote (such as a learning remote) — at least not yet. Still, we prefer RF to IR if we can get it.

Most home theater equipment uses an IR remote control system, so if you use an RF system, you'll need to have some equipment to convert the RF to IR to control these IR-only devices. We talk about how to do this in Chapter 17.

Touch screen displays

Color and grayscale displays are replacing hard buttons on remotes, enabling them to be far more programmable and customizable for your system. It's not unusual that your remote would connect to your PC today in order to establish its screen look. We are finding that standalone touch screens are even replacing remotes.

New control options

We think two-way operation and voice control are innovations that will grow in popularity. With two-way operation, higher-end remotes can interact with the controlled unit to determine its *state*. If a unit is already on, your programmed macro won't turn it off at the start of its session. And with two-way operation, you can check your actions to make sure they were carried out, too.

And with voice control, you even talk to your remote control (and even to other microphones in your home theater). Want the volume turned up? No problem: "Higher volume please." (Have we reached a new threshold when a couch potato does not even have to lift a thumb?) Voice control functionality is making its way into a lot of devices, including PDAs and standalone Web tablets, making voice control a key future item in your home theater.

Another interesting innovation is the docking cradle. A cradle might enable your remote to get charged up, to access the Internet for revised programming schedules, or to update its internal code databases. (We think docking cradles are really a covert plot to make sure you always know where your remote is located.)

IR (infrared) emitters/blasters

When one IR device wants to control another device, it often sends signals to the other device's IR port through an *IR blaster* — a small device that sits some distance from (or in the instance of very small versions called *emitters*, is taped to) the IR port. Many PC applications interface with your home theater system through an IR blaster (to do things such as change the channel on your satellite receiver to start recording a program). You might find you have several IR blasters for different devices in your system. No one feels this is the best long-term approach, as newer devices allow for direct data interface via Ethernet, low-speed data connections, or even RF. But for now, IR blasters are the only options for many older systems.

Within specific brands of A/V gear, you will find that they have IR ports for interconnecting and sharing IR data directly into the motherboard — bypassing the IR port. This is one of the benefits of using a single manufacturer for your gear. Examples of this include systems like Sony's S-Link, which uses a special cable to connect Sony equipment with each other.

For the rest of this chapter, we focus on some of the highlights of this section — the things that we think you'll likely run into or want to have.

Going Universal

Universal remotes are constantly changing and vary in price from about $25 on up. They can have backlit buttons, touch screens, color screens, voice commands, and so on. A lot of it depends on what you really want out of a remote control. The more you spend on your entertainment system, the more you'll probably spend on your remote controls.

Here are some examples of some of the neater remotes you can get:

✔ **X10 5-in-1 Remote** ($49, www.x10.com): This IR-based remote not only controls your home theater system devices, but any X10-driven devices as well (using RF). Want to turn down all the lights prior to your 'show'? No problem, connect them to X10 outlets and control them remotely with one button.

✔ **ATI Remote Wonder** ($49, www.ati.com): The ATI Remote Wonder was originally packaged only with ATI's great All-In-Wonder PC cards (see Chapter 8). Now, you can use this remote for any PC application. It is RF-based and comes with a small RF receiver that plugs into any Windows-compatible PC's USB 1.1 port. A great low-cost way to control your PC.

✔ **InVoca Model 24984 Voice Activated Universal Remote with LCD Display** ($99, www.invoca.com): This remote converts spoken words into infrared remote control signals. It recognizes 50 voice commands and performs multiple-step macro functions. It can even support personal voice commands for up to four family members.

✔ **Philips Pronto line of remotes** ($199 to $999, pronto.philips.com): Philips has a solid line of remote controls that have defined the leading edge of home theater remotes in a lot of ways. The $999 fully programmable and learning Pronto Pro TSU6000 features a 256-color, high-resolution touch screen and 8MB of memory. The user can fully customize button colors, channel icons, and even background color. Plus, with IR/radio frequency capability, the unit allows the user to control infrared devices in cabinets or in other rooms with the simple addition of a Philips RF receiver, available as an option for $149.

Of course, many more remotes are on the market. A great site to check out remote control options is Remote Central (www.remotecentral.com). They have great reviews and track the newest remotes on the market.

Remotes for the rest of the family

Got kids? Try the weemote, from Fobis ($24.95 from www.weemote.com). This is a remote designed just for kids ages 3 to 8, so you can limit the channels they watch and make them responsible for their own remotes (in other words, keep their paws off yours). A typical setup with a cable-ready TV takes about five minutes.

You can go universal with your remote in another sense: You can control your home theater from anywhere in the home! We talk more about these capabilities in Chapter 17.

Programming on Your Remote

We mention earlier that remotes are becoming learning-friendly and programmable. Nothing exemplifies this more than the $299 Harmony SST-768 Remote Control (www.harmonyremote.com). The 768 helps you do more than control different devices. It helps you control different actions. Harmony's remote has an LCD screen and links to your PC via a USB connection to program the remote to tie together multiple actions at once, in order.

Let's say you want to listen to a CD on your AudioReQuest CD server. You have to turn on the TV, set it to video mode, turn on receiver one, set it to CD, turn on receiver two, set it to CD, scroll down to your desired playlist, and hit Play. Harmony reduces this to a simple one-click task. It makes schedules and listings available on your remote's screen, and when you click it, all the requisite actions on your CD player, receivers, TV set, and so on are done in one quick series of signals from the remote to the devices. So Harmony is designed to help you perform activities such as watch TV, play a CD, play a DVD, and so on. That's what we call click and play!

Harmony is also a learning remote, and the latest version has added number buttons, a docking and recharging station, and bidirectional RF to a PC home server or set-top box for automatic updates. Très cool. For the price and simplicity, every home theater owner should check out these Harmony remotes.

Watch this!

We're not sure this is what your momma meant when she said to watch TV, but check out Midas from UEI (www.uei.com). Midas is a contemporary looking watch with coverage of most remote control functions for TVs and cable boxes. Well, it solves the problem of losing your remote in the couch!

Using Your PDA as a Remote

Want to use your PDA as a remote control? A couple of solutions are out there. Philips has ProntoLITE ($19.95) for turning Palm-based PDAs into a universal remote control. Universal Electronic's Nevo (www.mynevo.com) has a more "on-board" remote control operating system solution, initially built into Compaq's iPAQ Pocket PCs. The aforementioned Harmony Smart State technology is being ported to PDAs, too.

For people who want the flexibility of a big color screen, these programs allow you to take advantage of the dropping costs of PDAs to get a world-class universal remote. Neat idea if more PDAs ship with it on-board. Check out your PDA's home page on the manufacturer's site for any information on remote control software.

Other devices are sporting IR interfaces and can become remotes too, namely Web tablets and standalone touch screens. Philips and Intel have codeveloped a platform (iPronto) that combines home theater system control and 802.11b wireless broadband Internet access. With iPronto, you can control your A/V system components, check out program guides, and surf the Web from a tablet-like platform. Users can easily control devices through the high-resolution touch screen LCD, combined with a customizable user interface and exterior hard buttons. The system features a built-in microphone and stereo speakers, allowing users to listen to MP3s from the Internet and to be future-proof for applications such as voice recognition and telephony. Way cool. Initial pricing is $1,699.

Crestron rules the upper end of touch screen options, as discussed in detail in Chapter 20. Crestron's color touchpad systems are to die for, or at least second mortgage for.

Part IV
Putting It All Together

"Well, there goes the simple charm of sitting around the stove surfing the Web on our laptops."

In this part . . .

So you know what stuff you need to buy to get into home theater, and you may have even bought it. Well, if you're like us, buying stuff is a reflexive act. We could do it in our sleep. The hard part is figuring out how to hook it all up. Fear not — Part IV to the rescue.

First, we talk about the cables and connectors you can use to connect the components of your home theater together. This is really an important section to read, because in many cases, there's more than one kind of cable you can use, and there's definitely a hierarchy. Some of these cables are simply much better than others in terms of creating a home theater that looks and sounds like it should.

Next, we talk you through the "insert tab A into slot A" aspect of connecting a home theater. Now, remember that this advice is generic. Home theater equipment vendors are always coming up with their own little "modifications," making it hard to give concrete advice that applies in every single situation. But we get you 99 percent of the way there.

We also talk about how to do some nontraditional things with your home theater. First, we discuss how to connect your home theater components into a whole-home network that lets you view, listen to, and control expensive home theater gear anywhere in your home. We also give you some details about how to hook up the home theater PCs we talk about in Part II, so that you can bring the power of the PC (and the Internet) to your home theater!

Chapter 15

Home Theater Cable Basics

*O*ne of the most puzzling, infuriating, blood-pressure-raising tasks in the putting together of a home theater is finding the right kind, size, shape, and length of cables. Someday in the not-so-distant future, if the copyright lawyers don't get in the way, there may be a single type of digital cable that can be used to connect everything together. We may soon see an even better solution to the cabling problem: inexpensive yet high performance wireless systems that connect between components.

We can dream of the day when complex cabling is no longer necessary, but it has not yet arrived. In this chapter, we discuss the different kinds of cables required to hook up the common components in a home theater and those needed to share your theater with the rest of the house. In many cases, there's more than one way to hook one component to another, in which case we tell you which cable is best.

Working with Short Run Cables

Most of the connections you make in a home theater are *short runs* — that is, connections between components that are sitting just a few feet from each other (or at least within the same room). The cables you use for these connections are typically called *interconnects*. Later in this chapter, we talk about the long run cables that make up the infrastructure of a whole-home audio and video network.

Choosing quality cables

We should take a moment here to talk about cable quality —
right up front, in the beginning of the chapter. You can get audio
(or most any kind of cable) for free in the box when you buy new
equipment. Or you can go out and pay literally $1,000 a foot for
the double secret mojo cold fusion reactor-type cables. In case
you think we're kidding, we're not (well we are about the cold
fusion part). Some people pay thousands of dollars for each cable
in their system. Our take on the matter is this: Don't use the free el
cheapo cables that came in the box, because you get what you pay
for; don't pay $1,000+ per cable unless you are both rich and
absolutely convinced that you can hear an improvement in your
sound or see an improvement in your video. There's a happy
medium. Bottom line: Yes, there is a difference in cables, but no,
you don't have to pay a ton for good cables.

Look for cables that use oxygen-free copper (OFC) conductors
and have gold-plated surfaces on the jacks. Oxygen-free copper is a
purer form of copper, and the gold-plated surfaces resist corrosion.
Use the shortest run of cable possible, because the longer that
audio signal is traveling over the cable, the more likely the signal
will be audibly degraded by interference or *attenuation* (the weak-
ening of the signal as it travels over any cable).

Literally dozens of companies make high-quality cables
(most at a wide range of prices), such as Monster Cable (www.
monstercable.com), Kimber (kimber.com), audioquest (www.
audioquest.com), and more. (By the way, there are so many good
cables out on the market, please don't feel like our short list is anywhere near exhaustive. We could have filled a page with company
names.)

Joining the RCA mania

The most common type of connector in any home theater is the
standard analog *audio interconnect*. Traditionally, these cables
came in pairs, for 2-channel (stereo) audio connections, but in the
realm of the home theater, with its multiple surround sound channels, cables don't always work in neat pairs. You may find yourself
using these cables individually (like the cable that connects a subwoofer to the receiver or controller) or in big bunches (like the six
cables that connect an SACD (Super Audio CD) or DVD-Audio
player to the receiver).

Audio interconnects use a standardized jack known as an *RCA jack,* which is nice, because any audio interconnect with RCA jacks will plug into any corresponding RCA plug on a piece of A/V equipment. Figure 15-1 shows an RCA plug on a stereo (dual) pair of audio interconnects.

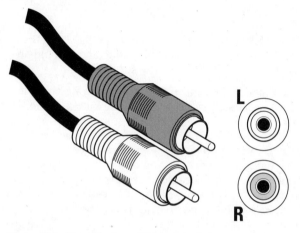

Figure 15-1: The ubiquitous RCA jack and plug.

If you go shopping for audio interconnects, you'll find a huge array of different cable constructions. The typical audio interconnect is a *coaxial* cable, which means that there are two electrical conductors surrounded by a shielded jacket within the cable. This jacket is called *shielded* because it is designed to keep stray electromagnetic energy from getting into the conductors and causing interference with the audio signal. But you'll find a lot of variation out there, and some cables are unshielded but twisted. (Twisting has a similar effect to shielding — due to the black art of physics, twisted cables can *cancel out* interferences.)

Connecting your speakers

Another cable that you'll find in every home theater (except for those that use active loudspeaker systems, which we discuss in Chapter 11) is the speaker cable. Speaker cables are used to connect the outputs of the power amplifier or the amplifier section of the receiver to the speaker. These cables carry the high-powered electrical currents required to move the internal components of the speaker (the magnets which move the drivers, as described in

Chapter 11). You need one pair of speaker cables for each speaker in your system (except for the subwoofer if it's an active system — which most are — and which will use an analog audio interconnect cable instead).

Some expensive speaker systems can use two pairs of speaker wires per speaker. These systems are either biwired or biamped:

- ✔ **Biwired:** Two sets of speaker wire connect to the same output on the receiver or power amplifier, and you plug them into two sets of terminals on the speaker itself.

- ✔ **Biamped:** The speaker uses two separate amplifiers — one for the low-frequency drivers and one for the higher-frequency drivers.

Because they typically go for longer distances (especially in the case of surround speakers), and carry more electrical current than interconnects, speaker cables are considerably more beefy and thicker than interconnects. The thickness of speaker cables (or the conductors within, to be precise) is referred to as *gauge* (using a standard system, AWG or American Wire Gauge). The lower the gauge, the thicker the conductors.

Thicker conductors have less electrical *resistance* to the current flowing through them. Too much resistance is a bad thing (it can alter the audio signal), and the longer the cable, the greater the resistance the signal faces while traveling over the cable. We recommend cables of no more than 16 gauge thickness, and prefer 14 gauge cables. For longer runs of 40 feet or more, such as runs to surround sound speakers in a large room, we recommend moving down to 12 gauge cables, if they fit your budget.

If you want to hide your speaker cables in the wall (or if you're running speaker cables through the wall for a multizone audio system), you need to get cables that are specially designed for this purpose and that meet electrical code requirements. You should choose cables that have been certified for this purpose by Underwriters Laboratories (UL-certified), and that meet the *CL3* specification.

Unlike audio interconnects, which share the common RCA connector, you have a ton of connector choices when it comes to speaker cables (these connectors are sometimes called *terminations*). The most bare bones approach is to just use the bare wire itself (stripped of any insulation), but we highly recommend you don't do this. You typically don't get as good a connection, and the bare wire ends can corrode over time, making the connection even worse (and impacting your sound quality).

You'll see three main types of connectors (besides the bare wire) on the market:

- ✔ **Pin connectors:** These look like they sound — a straight or angled pin at the end of the wire (though it's not sharp, so you won't put your eye out). These work best with the spring-loaded clip type of speaker connectors, which you find on less expensive receivers and speakers. Pin connectors also work with the preferred five-way binding posts found on better models. (We talk about five-way binding posts in Chapter 11.)

- ✔ **Spade lugs:** These U-shaped connectors fit behind the screws on a five-way binding post (you slide the open part of the U over the post and then screw down the plastic nut). Spade lugs can provide the tightest, most reliable connection you can get (because of that screwing down).

- ✔ **Banana plugs:** If you squint really hard, these plugs may actually look like bananas, but they look more like pin connectors that are fat in the middle. By bowing out in the middle, they provide a tight fit into the binding post. Banana plugs come in single and dual configurations. The dual variety is just two banana plugs (one for each wire in the pair of speaker wires) stuck together in the same housing.

Figure 15-2 shows the pin, spade lug, and banana plug, and Figure 15-3 shows a five-way binding post.

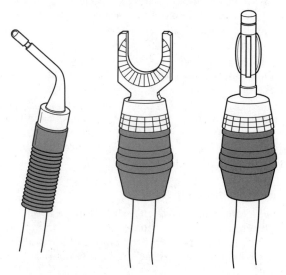

Figure 15-2: From left to right, a pin connector, a spade lug, and a banana plug.

Although the spade lug provides the ultimate in speaker wire connections, we think the banana plug provides a connection that's very close in quality. The banana plug is also much easier to use because the banana just slides into the binding post (nothing to tighten or adjust).

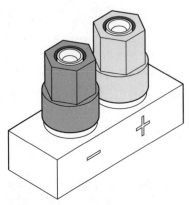

Figure 15-3: The five-way binding post is your friend (it's most versatile).

Using digital interconnects

With the advent of computer-chip-laden receivers and DVD players, home theater has moved home A/V gear into the digital age. True, CD players have been digital for years, but for the majority of people, all the digital stuff happened inside the CD. The connections between the CD player and the receiver were all analog. Surround sound (specifically, digital surround sound systems, such as Dolby Digital and DTS) has made the digital interconnect commonplace.

As we mention throughout the book, digital audio interconnects (used to connect DVD players, HDTV tuners, video game consoles, and more to the A/V receiver or controller) are divided into two main types: coaxial and optical (or Toslink).

Coaxial digital interconnects

The *coaxial interconnect* looks an awful lot like a single (mono) audio interconnect. It's got standard RCA jacks on both ends and a coaxial cable between them. Put the analog audio and coaxial interconnects side by side on a table (unlabeled of course), and you really can't tell them apart. But the conductors inside coaxial cables are of a different construction that's designed to handle the higher frequencies of digital signals. You shouldn't use standard audio interconnects in place of a coaxial digital cable. It's tough to explain the difference in sound you may experience if you use the wrong kind of cable here, but if your digital audio just doesn't sound *right,* check to see if you've got the correct digital interconnect hooked up.

Coaxial digital interconnects are not the only example of other cables in a home theater that use RCA plugs and look like audio interconnects, but are not. Both the composite and the component video cables we discuss shortly also appear to be identical to audio interconnects, but in fact use different internal conductors and designs.

Optical digital interconnects

The Toslink optical connector uses fiber optics instead of copper cabling and carries the digital signal as pulses of light, instead of as an electrical signal. The connector on a Toslink interconnect, viewed head-on, looks like a nice little house in suburbia — except most houses don't have a laser flashing out of the side of them (well at least ours don't — we won't presume to speak for you). Figure 15-4 shows the Toslink cable connector.

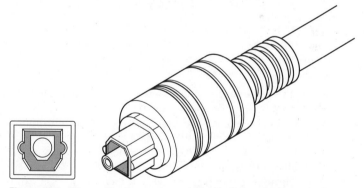

Figure 15-4: Fiber optics in your house! The Toslink optical interconnect.

The *female* Toslink connector (on your receiver or DVD player or wherever you're plugging a Toslink into) is usually covered by a little removable dust cap. If you don't take off this cap, you're going to curse like a sailor trying to plug in that cable.

Using analog video connections

The majority of video connections in a home theater are made using analog connections (though we talk later in the chapter about some new digital systems used for making video connections between HDTV tuners and HDTV monitors). You'll find three types of *short run* analog video connections in a home theater.

Before we talk about the connection methods themselves, let's discuss what kind of signal they carry. There are two components to a video signal — the *luminance* and the *chrominance*. The luminance provides the video display with the brightness information that determines which parts of the screen are darker or lighter. The chrominance adds information about what color each segment of the screen should be.

There is a definite hierarchy among video connections. One is visibly worse (in terms of picture quality) than the other two, and of the two superior methods, one is better (though not as significantly) than the other. In ascending order (worst to best), these connection types are as follows:

- ✔ **Composite video:** Both luminance and chrominance are combined into a single signal. The *comb filter* inside the display (discussed in Chapter 12) separates these two components and sends them to the appropriate internal circuitry.

- ✔ **S-Video:** In S-Video, luminance and chrominance are separated onto two separate signal paths, so the signal can bypass the comb filter in the TV. This usually results in a much clearer picture, with more defined colors and images.

- ✔ **Component video:** Component video separates the signal even further, providing one path for luminance information, and then providing two separate paths for chrominance information. Component video connections can be further enhanced in a *wideband* component video connection, which allows the higher frequencies needed for HDTV to travel from the source (such as an HDTV tuner) to the HDTV monitor.

So the big difference between composite (the lower-quality video signal) and S-Video and component video connections is the fact that the better connections carry luminance and chrominance information separately. Why is this a big deal? After all, the display has a comb filter to take care of that problem. Well, comb filters do an imperfect job at separating these two signals and can leave visible *artifacts* in your picture. You want the sharpest, most colorful picture you can get, don't you?

In some cases, you might not choose the highest-quality connection available to you. We talk about these in Chapter 16, when we discuss hooking up your home theater.

Both component and composite cables use standard RCA connectors and bear a striking resemblance to the analog audio interconnect (and the digital coaxial interconnect, for that matter). Composite video cables are loners (you need just one), and component video cables travel in small packs of three (often labeled Y, Pr, and Pb).

Composite video cables are usually color-coded yellow (that is to say, the connector usually has a yellow ring around it, or the rubber boot around the connector is yellow in color).

S-Video is an unmistakable beast, with its own special connector (the S-Video connector of course). This connector has four small pins that correspond with four small holes on the S-Video plug on your gear. Figure 15-5 shows an S-Video connector.

S VIDEO OUT

Figure 15-5: Separate out that chrominance and luminance with S-Video.

S-Video connectors can be a real pain in the butt to line up and connect. One set of pins is slightly more widely spaced than the other (the bottom ones are farther apart). If you're really killing yourself, check to see that you aren't pushing this cable in upside down. A little plastic doohickey keeps you from really messing things up, but bent pins are far from unknown to first-time S-Video users.

Employing digital video connections

The consumer electronics industry (in association with the content providers) has been working overtime to develop some digital video interconnection systems that satisfy the following requirements:

- ✓ **Preserve the digital signal:** The video connection systems we discuss earlier in "Using digital interconnects" are all analog systems. They carry analog video signals, not digital ones. Nothing is inherently wrong with analog connections, but they are more susceptible to interferences and other losses of signal quality when compared to digital connections. And in the case of digital signals (such as HDTV and other ATSC digital television broadcasts), there's really no reason to convert to analog until the very last minute (inside of the display itself). As Dick Vitale would say, "Keep it digital, baby!"

- ✓ **Minimize cables:** Some of these analog connections (particularly component video) also require multiple cables per connection. So if you want to connect the component video output of your HDTV tuner to your receiver, and then on to your display, you need six cables (three for each link). Add a DVD player using component video into the mix, and you've got six more cables. Pretty soon you have spaghetti.

- ✓ **Provide copy protection:** These analog connections don't have any inherent copy protection systems. If there's one thing that content providers (movie and television studios) want to prevent, it's people copying their content. They don't even really want to let you make copies for personal use, such as copying *CSI* when you're out of town on business so that you can watch it after you come home.

We discuss the available, digital video connection options in the following sections.

FireWire

One of the first systems for digital video crossed over from the computer industry: FireWire, which is also called IEEE 1394 or i.LINK, depending on who's talking. Apple Computer originally developed FireWire for connecting peripheral devices to Macintosh computers. Companies such as Sony picked up on the technology and began incorporating FireWire into its camcorders and PCs, and FireWire grew from there. (The FireWire in camcorders is often called *DV.*)

Some HDTV tuners and HDTV-ready displays include FireWire connections, as do a few other devices (such as JVC's D-VHS), but as we write, FireWire appears to be becoming less common as a means of connecting HDTV devices together.

So why do we mention it? Well, for starters, you can still buy HDTV systems that use FireWire. Additionally, FireWire is beginning to become more common in the audio side of the home theater. The DVD Forum (a coalition of companies that helps develop the DVD standard) has recently approved FireWire as a connection method for the audio output of DVD-Audio players. When these players (and compatible receivers or controllers) hit the market, you'll be able to replace those six analog audio interconnects with a single cable. That will be nice!

 Although DVI, FireWire's biggest competitor in the digital video connection world, appears to be winning the war over digital video interconnects, battles are still being fought, and the tide may turn. So don't count FireWire out completely yet.

Digital Visual Interface

One reason that FireWire is becoming less common in the digital video world is the success of its competitor, *DVI* (Digital Visual Interface). DVI is another technology adopted from the computer world, where it was originally developed as a means of connecting computers to digital LCD screens. Along the way, DVI picked up a strong copy protection system called HDCP (discussed in Chapter 12) and became a favorite of the HDTV industry.

HDCP makes DVI a relatively *dumb* connection — all it does is send video in one direction (for example, from the tuner to the display), and HDCP won't ever let you make a digital copy of what you're watching (so forget taping that *CSI* episode on your D-VHS). Figure 15-6 shows a DVI connector.

Not all devices with a DVI connector incorporate HDCP. For example, LCD computer monitors may use DVI without HDCP. If you connect an HDCP-enabled HDTV tuner to a non-HDCP display using a DVI cable, you can't get a full HDTV signal. Instead, the signal is converted to a lower resolution.

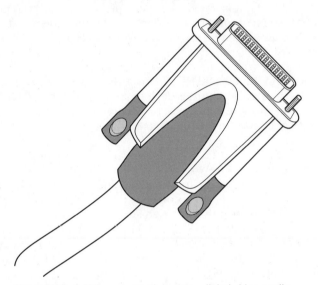

Figure 15-6: A DVI connector for yummy digital video quality.

Serial Digital Interface

You can find a lower-speed digital video interconnect called *SDI* (Serial Digital Interface) on a limited number of home theater devices. Because SDI is a relatively low-speed connection, it can't handle HDTV. SDI is used only for standard definition content (NTSC). The vast majority of people will never even run into an SDI connector in their home theaters, because it's just not that common.

Working with Long Run Cables

When you start thinking about connecting your home theater to the rest of your home (perhaps to share a video source device with TVs in other rooms), you will run into a new set of cables. These *long run* cables are designed to minimize signal loss and get your audio and video to any spot in the house. Although you can distribute audio and video around the home in many ways, the three most common ways are the following:

✔ **RG6 coaxial cabling for video:** This cable (which we describe later in this chapter) is used for carrying video signals (and the associated audio tracks) from antennas, satellite dishes, and cable TV feeds from the street. With devices called *modulators,* you can actually create in-house TV channels and use this cable to share your own video sources with other TVs in the house.

✔ **Speaker cabling for whole-home audio:** We discuss speaker wires (appropriately rated for in-wall use) in the section, "Connecting your speakers," earlier in this chapter. You can use this same speaker wire to connect a multizone receiver (or a separate whole-home audio system) to speakers throughout the house.

✔ **Category 5e (CAT-5e) network cabling:** This is the cable used for computer networks — the stuff you put in your walls if you are creating a whole-home network. With the appropriate gear on the ends of these cables (we discuss this in Chapter 21), you can use this cable to carry audio and video signals.

Going with RG6

Coaxial cable (usually just called *coax*) is a metallic cable most often used for transmitting radio frequency (RF) signals, such as broadband television video and radio signals. Coaxial cable contains two conductors, or axes, to carry data. A layer of dielectric insulating material surrounds a single, center conductor. The other conductor is a metal shield, usually made of a braided metallic wiring, that goes around the dielectric (insulating) layer. The outermost layer of coax cable is an insulating jacket. The connectors on an RG6 cable are known as *F connectors.*

You may encounter coaxial cables labeled RG6QS or RG6 Quad Shield, which means that the cable has additional shielding beneath the cable jacket — four layers, as the name implies. These layers provide additional protection against interference from external sources. Because of this extra shielding, we recommend you use Quad Shield coax. It doesn't cost a lot more, and it's worth the investment.

CAT-5e cabling systems

If you've ever spent any time building, designing, or just using a computer network, you've encountered CAT-5e cabling. CAT-5e is a type of UTP (unshielded twisted pair) copper cabling and can be used for phones, computer networks, home automation networks, and audio/video distribution systems. CAT-5e cables typically consist of four pairs of wire (eight total conductors) wrapped in a single jacket. The ends of CAT-5e cables are terminated in connectors known as *RJ-45 jacks*, which look exactly like the common RJ-11 phone jack, only wider.

CAT-5e cabling can be used to connect your home theater to your computer LAN and through this LAN to the Internet. For example, CAT-5e connectors are commonly found on MP3 servers, PVRs, and increasingly on audio source devices that are designed to play back Internet radio stations or MP3 files located on a computer in your house. CAT-5e cabling may also be used to connect the A/V source components in your home theater to other rooms in the house. (We discuss systems that do this in Chapter 17.)

There is actually a range of Category-rated UTP cables (for example CAT-3 cabling is often used for telephone wiring). CAT-5e is the current "top-of-the-line" UTP cabling, suitable for very fast computer networks, but a newer standard (CAT-6) is under development as well and should become common over the next few years.

Each piece of a CAT-5e system (the cables themselves, the RJ-45 jacks, and so on) is subject to the CAT-5e rating system. If you use CAT-5e, make sure *all* the pieces and parts are rated CAT-5e. The "weakest link in the chain" rule applies here. Any piece that's rated below CAT-5e brings the whole system down to that lower rating. Many A/V-over-UTP systems require CAT-5e and don't work well on identical-looking, but lower-rated cables. All CAT-5e cables and connectors will be clearly marked with a label of some sort, so just read the fine print (on the cable itself) to be sure.

Identifying Other Cable Odds and Ends

We'd like to end this chapter with a hodgepodge listing of other cables and connectors that may show up in your home theater. These connection systems are less common than the ones discussed in preceding sections, but none of them is a complete stranger to the world of home theater. This is particularly true if you are hooking your home theater into a whole-home network or when you are connecting PCs and other computer-like devices (such as PVRs or MP3 servers) into your home theater.

Wireless connections

Wireless networking technologies have made a huge splash in the computer networking world — everyone, it seems, has gone crazy for a system called *Wi-Fi* (a type of wireless computer *LAN* or local area network). (Read our books *Smart Homes For Dummies* or *Wireless Home Networking For Dummies,* both published by Wiley Publishing, Inc., for a ton of information about this technology.)

As more people begin to use PCs and the Internet in their home theaters, this technology is increasingly moving from the computer world to the consumer electronics world. Many manufacturers, such as NETGEAR (www.netgear.com) and D-Link (www.dlink.com), are creating devices called *Wi-Fi Ethernet Bridges* specifically for home entertainment/home theater gear. These bridges make it easy to connect Internet-capable, home theater gear with an Ethernet port into your home's Wi-Fi network. (Ethernet is the common computer network that uses CAT-5e cabling and RJ-45 jacks.) For about $100, you can buy one of these bridges and use a short length of CAT-5e cabling to connect it to your PVR (personal video recorder), MP3 server, home theater PC, or even your gaming console (such as Xbox or PlayStation 2). The bridge then connects wirelessly (using radio waves) to your DSL or cable modem, through a device called an *access point.*

If you don't have a wireless network but want to connect some distant source devices (such as a PC in your home office) to the home theater, you can also use a purpose-built wireless system. An example is X10's Entertainment Anywhere system (under $100 at www.x10.com). These systems also use radio waves to communicate but can't connect to PC LANs like Wi-Fi systems can. Instead, they connect directly to the source device and receiver, using composite video cables and stereo audio interconnects. Purpose-built wireless systems have two units — a transmitter that connects to the source device and a receiver that connects to your A/V receiver or directly to your display. They aren't the ultimate in high-end signal quality (they don't take S-Video or component video connections), but they make connecting remote devices quick and easy.

RS-232

If you've ever connected a modem to an older PC, you've probably used an RS-232 connector and not even known it. RS-232 is a standard computer communications system that's more commonly known as a *serial* connection. Until the advent of the USB system (discussed in the following section), RS-232 was the standard connection for modems, handheld computer cradles, and many other PC peripheral devices.

In the home theater world, RS-232 is *not* used for carrying audio and video. It is, however, often used for connecting A/V components to automation and control systems (such as the Crestron systems we discuss in Chapter 14). You can also find RS-232 ports on the back of many advanced A/V receivers, where they can be used to connect the receiver to a PC for upgrading the software system within the receiver.

USB

USB (or Universal Serial Bus) has pretty much replaced RS-232 in the PC world. These days, most printers, external modems, handheld computers, portable MP3 players, and other PC peripheral devices connect to PCs via USB. In the home theater world, USB can be found on the back of many computer-like source devices (such as MP3 servers and PVRs). USB has not yet replaced RS-232 for connections to automation and control systems (but probably will eventually).

The most common use for USB in a home theater is in conjunction with a Wi-Fi system. You can outfit source devices that can connect to the Internet with a USB Wi-Fi network adapter. This adapter enables you to connect back to the Access Point and out to the Internet. USB is also used for remote control connections for PCs. The remote control receiver for the PC connects to the PC via a USB cable.

IR connections

In Chapter 17, we talk about ways that you can connect your home theater to speakers and displays in other parts of your home, using a whole-home entertainment network. As we discuss earlier in this chapter, you use RG6 coaxial cable, speaker wire, and/or CAT-5e cabling to carry your audio and video around the house. There's one other piece to this whole-home puzzle, however. You need some sort of system for controlling remote devices when you are watching them (or listening to them) in a different part of the house. If the phone rings, you want to be able to turn down the music or pause the movie.

Most A/V systems use IR (infrared) systems for their remote controls. IR is a great system, but because it uses a beam of light to carry control signals, it can't penetrate walls (unless you have a glass house, we suppose). So you need some sort of wired system that can carry IR signals from remote locations back to your home theater. (You can also find wireless alternatives from companies such as X10.) You can set up an infrared system in four ways:

- ✔ **IR cabling:** Many home networking vendors sell three conductor cables specially designed for carrying IR signals from remote locations back to the home theater.

- ✔ **CAT-5e cabling:** If you're using CAT-5e cabling for audio and video distribution (using some of the systems we discuss in Chapter 17), you'll find that these systems have a built-in capability to carry IR signals for remote controls. If you're not using one of these systems but have put CAT-5e cabling in your walls when building your home, you can use extra (unused) CAT-5e cables in place of the IR cabling we just mentioned.

- ✔ **RG6 coaxial cabling:** Using special devices called *IR injectors* (available from vendors such as ChannelPlus, www.channelplus.com), you can carry IR signals over the RG6 coax that you use for distributing cable or broadcast antenna TV signals.

You can't use an IR injector on the RG6 cables used to connect a DSS dish to DSS receivers.

- ✔ **Proprietary systems:** If you opt to install a high-end automation system, such as those from Crestron, you need to use special proprietary cables from the manufacturer. For example, Crestron uses its own special cable called CrestNet.

Chapter 16

Hooking Up Your A/V System

In This Chapter

▶ Planning your gear layout

▶ Hiding wires

▶ Connecting to the receiver

▶ Making the video connection

▶ Adding PCs and gaming systems

▶ Powering your system

*Y*ou've picked a room, collected all your A/V gear, opened the boxes, and *oohed* and *ahhed* at your shiny new stuff. Now it's time to get down to the work of hooking up your home theater. At first glance, this can seem like a daunting task. You have a lot of cables and connectors to deal with, and even to the experienced home theater folks, the back of an A/V receiver can be confusing at first. The key is to take a methodical approach. With a few key concepts in mind, hooking up an A/V system can be easy and even fun!

In this chapter, we talk about where the various pieces and parts of an A/V system should go in your home theater and how they should be connected to each other. However, the advice we give in this chapter is generic in nature. Although the majority of home theater components connect in a similar fashion with identical cables and connectors, there are always a few differences among different brands and models. For example, what we call CD Audio In might be labeled CD Line In or even Aux In on your receiver. For the exact terms and procedures that apply to your system, you need to read your manual.

Planning the Room Layout

After you've read those oh-so-fun manuals, you might think it's time to start plugging away. The temptation is to get things hooked up and working. You want to watch a movie *right now,* admit it . . . so would we. But by devoting a few minutes to planning out your next steps, you can make the process easier and get better results when the time comes to watch and listen to your system.

At a minimum, your home theater has six speakers (counting the subwoofer). Each of these speakers has a role in creating the illusion of being "in the action" when you watch movies or shows (or listen to multichannel audio on DVD-A or SACD). So you've got to get the speakers in the right spot, relative to your listening position. Incorrectly positioning your speakers creates gaps in the soundfield that surrounds you. These gaps can be distracting or downright annoying and can also cause room interactions that reduce the fidelity of the audio you are re-creating.

No matter what you do, your speakers interact with your room, creating echoes and reflections that have some impact on the sound. The key is to reduce the negative effects of these interactions and, instead, to use them to your advantage.

Getting the front speakers in place

The front speakers — left, right, and center — provide the bulk of the sound you listen to while watching a movie. One of the key jobs of these front speakers is to provide a realistic reproduction of dialogue — you want people in the middle of the display to sound like they're right in front of you, and those on the left and right to sound like that's where they are. Proper placement of these three front speakers is essential in creating this effect and minimizing any gaps in the speaker's coverage (so when dialogue moves from side to side, it does so seamlessly). Keep the following points in mind when setting up your front speakers:

✔ **Set up your center channel speaker first:** The placement of the left and right speakers is dependent upon this.

✔ **Make sure the front surface of the center channel speaker is flush with the display:** Most center channel speakers are designed to be placed directly on top of the display. Keep the front surfaces of both flush with each other to minimize reflections. If your equipment physically permits, you might try to get the front of the speaker (the baffle), *in front of* the surface of the screen. (This is really hard to pull off in the real world, which is why we recommend just making them flush.)

✔ **Keep the right and left channel speakers the same distance from your listening position as the front speaker:** Some place the three front speakers in a straight line across the front of the room. This actually makes the center speaker closer to you than the others, meaning sounds from the center speaker reach you sooner than sounds from the others. Instead of a line, the front speakers should form an *arc* in front of you, in which each speaker is the same distance from your primary viewing position (or the middle of the viewing position, such as the center of a couch or the middle of a group of seats.

✔ *Toe-in* **the left and right speakers:** The front panels of the left and right speakers should be placed so that they are aimed directly at (or immediately behind) your seating position.

✔ **Place the left and right speakers at a 45- to 60-degree angle from the listening position:** Start off with the speakers at the wider angle. Place each speaker 30 degrees to the right or left of the center speaker from your viewing position, as shown in Figure 16-1. If you find, while listening to movie soundtracks, that sounds seem unnatural and too widely spaced, you can move the right and left speakers closer to the screen. Conversely, if it's hard to distinguish right from left from most seating positions, spread them a bit farther apart. When you do so, maintain the arc we just mentioned.

✔ **Place the speakers in a position where the tweeters are at or near the viewers' ear level:** Keep in mind the seated height of your viewers in the seating you've selected, and adjust your speakers accordingly when selecting stands or wall mounting. Even if you have floorstanding speakers, you can buy small stands to raise the height, if necessary. If your center speaker is up above you (maybe you've put it on top of a gigantic RPTV), you can at least aim it down towards your listening position. Our technical editor (who's a genius at this stuff) likes to use rubber wedge-shaped doorstops under the backside of the center speaker to do this aiming.

Dealing with surrounds

Many people think of their surround sound speakers as their rear speakers. Indeed, many receivers label the surround outputs as Rear, so people imagine that these speakers need to be along the back wall, behind the listening position. This isn't always the case — particularly with the bipole or dipole surround speakers, which are the most common kinds (we prefer dipoles).

5.1 channel surround sound

For 5.1 channel surround sound, we recommend you place bipole or dipole surround speakers along the side walls (preferably mounted on the side wall). Position them even to or slightly behind your home theater seating, and about 2 feet above the listeners' seated ear level. If you are using direct-radiating speakers for your surrounds, the best placement is behind the listeners, aimed so that they radiate (face, in other words) toward the *back wall.* That might sound a bit counter-intuitive, but if you face them directly toward the listening position, you don't get the diffuse surround sound that you're looking for.

Other types of surround sound

If you're using Dolby Digital EX or DTS ES, you have an extra speaker (or two) to deal with. These systems have side surrounds (which are placed like 5.1 channel side surrounds) and *center surround* channel speakers (one or two, depending upon whether you're using a 6.1 or 7.1 channel setup).

These center surround speakers should be placed behind the listener. In a 6.1 channel setup, they go directly behind the listening position. In a 7.1 channel system, the two center surround speakers should be placed along the rear wall, on either side of the seating position.

Placing the subwoofer for optimal bass

You'll often hear people talk about low-frequency sounds being *nondirectional,* which is a fancy way of saying that you can't really locate where they are coming from by ear. Proponents of this concept will tell you that your subwoofer can be hidden well out of the way — under the proverbial end table, far away from the action. Subwoofers are nondirectional, to a degree, but putting your subwoofer too far away from the rest of your speakers (and from your listening position) can lead to situations where you do hear where the bass is coming from. Indeed, if you move your subwoofer too far to the left or right, the bass isn't well integrated with the sound coming from the other speakers. In most cases, it's actually better to not hide the subwoofer. Treat it like any other speaker — show it off!

Many vendors recommend that you place your subwoofer in a corner. This placement reinforces the bass significantly, and we think this is a good place to start. However, in some rooms, you can get too much reinforcement of your bass in the corner, and you end up with boomy sounding bass. What we mean by *boomy* is that the bass notes become indistinct; you just hear a low-frequency sound, and can't really distinguish between the different frequencies. So if someone's playing a Bach fugue on a pipe organ, you don't hear the distinct notes. If this happens to you, try moving the subwoofer out from the corner a bit.

One good (if slightly unscientific) way of finding a place for your subwoofer (after you've got it hooked up, of course) is to swap places with it. Put the subwoofer right up where you sit and turn on some bass-heavy music (or a bass-heavy movie soundtrack). Walk around the room until you find the place where the bass sounds best. Now, swap back by putting the subwoofer in the spot where the bass sounded best.

Figure 16-1 shows a typical 5.1 channel surround sound speaker configuration. As we discuss in the previous sections, the center and front left and right speakers are equidistant from the viewing position, with the left and right speakers 45 to 60 degrees apart. The surrounds are beside or slightly behind the comfy home theater seats, and the subwoofer is placed along the front wall of the room.

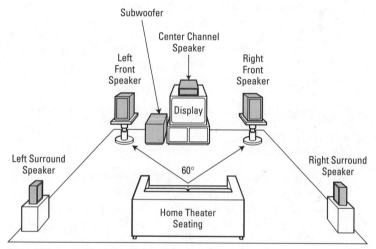

Figure 16-1: Getting those speakers in place.

Hiding Unsightly Cables

One drawback of a surround sound audio system is that having those speakers alongside or behind your seating position makes hiding the speaker cables difficult. Now, some people out there love the look of fancy speaker wires (Pat's got a set of Kimber speaker cables that he just loves to stare at). But for most people, speaker cables are an unsightly reminder of all the work they've put into building their home theaters, and hiding these wires is a good thing.

The best way to hide cables, if you can pull it off, is to put them inside the wall. If you've got a basement or attic over your home theater room, using in-wall speaker cabling is pretty easy. Just make sure you've got the proper kind of speaker cable (UL-rated CL3 or higher), and that you use a thicker cable (lower gauge), such as 14 or even 12 gauge. See Chapter 15 for details about cables.

Sometimes, you just can't get your cables in the wall. For example, Pat's house (like many in southern California) doesn't have a basement, and the ceiling over his home theater is raised to the roof (no attic access). In these cases, you can try to hide your cables under carpets or rugs. If that doesn't work, you might consider installing a *raceway* along the baseboards of your room that can contain the wires, or even consider using thin (but wide) flat cables. For example, Monster Cable (www.monstercable.com) sells flat speaker cables in its "Invisible out of wall" series. Taperwire (www.taperwire.com) also offers flattened versions of most wiring you find in the house — including speaker cables — so it's easy to hide. These flat cables are pretty hard to see when placed along your baseboards and can even be painted to match your wall colors.

Attaching Components to the A/V Receiver

Getting your speaker cables and speakers mounted in place is a good first step. Hooking up the rest of your A/V gear is the next step. (Keep in mind that you might have to go back to the speakers and tweak the placement of at least some of your speakers after everything is up and running.)

Spaghetti isn't just what's for dinner. It's also what you get when you pull out all the cables you bought for your home theater components. There sure is a lot of wire behind the scenes in today's home theater (we hope that this will decrease over time as digital connections, such as FireWire, become more popular). Luckily, any home theater worth its salt has a device — the A/V receiver or controller — that provides a central connection point for all these wires. Also, if you have a rack for your gear, the rack should have a good cable management system to help you out. We talk about racks in Chapter 23.

At the highest level, connecting components into your home theater is as simple as using the right cables to connect them to the back of your A/V receiver (or controller). With very few exceptions, you don't connect other components directly to each other. Let your A/V receiver do its job!

Hooking up your speakers

The next step is to connect your speaker wires to the appropriate speaker outlets on your A/V receiver. This is a pretty simple process, but there are a few things to keep in mind:

- ✔ **Keep your speakers in phase:** Each speaker wire consists of two conductors, a positive and a negative (usually color-coded red and black, respectively). If you connect these out of phase (that is, the positive on the receiver to the negative on the speaker, and vice versa), you hear a definite impact on your sound. Specifically, your speakers can't create the appropriate *soundstage,* so sounds that are supposed to clearly come from the right or the left won't. (By the way, *right* in this context means to the listener's right when facing the display or the front of the room.) Most speaker cables are also color-coded red and black to make this job easier (or you may have a white stripe on the jacket of one of the conductors in the speaker wire).

- ✔ **Make sure you have a tight connection:** For the best sound quality and for a connection that won't stop working over time, make sure your speaker connections are solid. We like banana plugs or spade lugs on five-way binding posts because you can get these suckers nice and tight. Make a good connection the first time, and you won't need to touch it again for years. We discuss these different connections in more detail in Chapter 15.

- ✔ **Don't forget to connect the subwoofer:** Most subwoofers are *active* speakers (they have their own built-in amplifiers), so you don't use speaker wires to connect them. You need a long analog audio interconnect cable, which runs between the Subwoofer Out or LFE output on the back of your receiver and the input on the subwoofer itself. Make sure you get a cable that's long enough to let you move the subwoofer around, because you many need to reposition your subwoofer as you discover how it interacts with your home theater's room.

Connecting to the A/V receiver

Take a look at the back of a typical A/V receiver, like the one shown in Figure 16-2. Wow that's a lot of jacks, huh? Well, they're not all back there for show or to make the designer happy. They're there to give you a flexible home theater .system that can do what you need it to do.

Each component in your A/V system has a set of audio and/or video connections to your A/V receiver. The receiver itself connects to your speakers and to your display (with another set of audio and video cables).

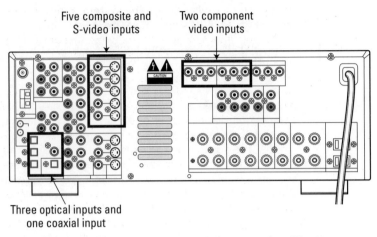

Five composite and S-video inputs

Two component video inputs

Three optical inputs and one coaxial input

Figure 16-2: Check out the connections on this A/V receiver. Wow!

First, connect audio interconnects and video cables to each of your source devices. Keep the following things in mind:

- ✔ **Keep your right and left in mind with audio cables:** Any device that connects with analog audio cables has two connections (the cables themselves usually, but not always, come in attached stereo pairs). One jack (the right) is usually colored red, and the other white. Make sure that you connect the left output on the source device to the corresponding left input on the back of your receiver.

- ✔ **Use digital audio connections whenever possible:** Use coaxial or optical digital audio cables to connect DVD players, game consoles, DSS receivers, or any source that has a digital audio output. If you want to use Dolby Digital or DTS with any of these sources, you *must* use the digital audio connection.

- ✔ **Keep track of which connections you use on your receiver:** One nice thing about the standardized connections used in home theaters is the fact that you don't have to plug sources into jacks that correspond with that device on your receiver. For example, if you have a video game console (but no Game inputs on your receiver), but no laser disc player in your system, you can plug the game console into those laser disc inputs on the receiver. This is where keeping track of your connections comes in handy. In order to send the audio and video from the game console to your speakers and display, you have to select the laser disc input on your receiver. You might even want to make a little cheat sheet to keep near your system (with all your little home theater quirks written down), so the rest of your family can run the system. Fancy A/V receivers and controllers may even have *assignable* inputs that let you select (or even type in with your remote control) the names that correspond with each set of inputs on the back of the receiver or controller.

✔ **Use an extra set of audio and video cables to connect your recording systems:** Your receiver has an extra set of A/V output connectors that correspond with its VCR inputs (usually labeled VCR1, VCR2, and so on). When you connect your VCR or PVR (personal video recorder) to these inputs, use an extra set of cables to connect the receiver back to the inputs on these sources (labeled Audio In and Video In on the back of the source). This lets you route audio and video through the receiver for recording purposes. (You may not be able to record DVDs this way because of DVD's Macrovision copy protection system, which we discuss in Chapter 6.)

✔ **Use the highest-quality video connections available to you:** Use component video if your sources have these connections. Otherwise, use S-Video for sources, such as DSS receivers, that don't have component video connections. Some sources (such as many VCRs) have only composite video connections.

After you've connected all your sources to the receiver, you can connect the receiver to your display unit using one or more video cables (we discuss this shortly), and a set of analog audio interconnects.

Using this set of audio cables between the receiver and the display may seem to be a bit of cabling overkill. After all, you've already got a surround sound audio system connected to the receiver. We find that, sometimes, we just want to use the built-in speakers in our display, like when we flip on ESPN to catch the college basketball scores, and then turn the TV back off. If you don't think you'll ever do something like this, you can skip this step.

A step you won't want to skip is connecting the receiver to your display with video cables. If you have source devices connecting to the receiver with different kinds of video cables (for example, component video for the DVD and HDTV tuner, S-Video for your PlayStation, and composite video for your VCR), you may have to use more than one cable to connect the receiver to the display. That's because most receivers don't have the ability to *transcode* (or convert) video signals to a different type of connection. A few (mainly expensive) receivers have this ability, so you can use a single connection (S-Video or component video, depending upon the receiver) between the receiver and the display.

If you connect a source to your receiver using an S-Video or component video cable, but use only a composite video cable to connect the receiver to your display, you'll find that you get sound, but no picture, when you try to play that source.

Getting television signals

TV comes into your system from a cable TV service, a DSS satellite dish, or an antenna for broadcast TV (or in some cases, from a combination of these devices). Regardless of the system, an RG6 coaxial cable connects these TV sources into your system.

If you use an antenna for non-HDTV over-the-air broadcast TV (or for nondigital cable without a converter box), this connection is usually pretty simple. Connect the coaxial cable coming out of your wall outlet to the Antenna/Cable In input on the back of your VCR, and then run another short length of RG6 coaxial cable from the Out to TV output on the back of the VCR into the Antenna/Cable In input on the back of your display. (**Note:** Your cable company may have installed a similar RG59 cable instead of an RG6 cable, if you're running your own cable, we recommend you use RG6.)

If you've got digital cable (or analog cable with a converter), a DSS dish, or if you're picking up over-the-air broadcast HDTV signals, you need to run the RG6 cable to the appropriate set-top box, DSS receiver, or HDTV tuner. These devices are connected through your A/V receiver, just like any other source device. You can use the receiver to send the video from these sources to your VCR for recording (if it's allowed).

If you're using broadcast HDTV and you've got a true HDTV (with an integrated tuner), you can connect the coaxial cable running from this antenna directly to the back of your display.

If you've got digital cable, you may want to route your cable signal through the VCR before you connect it to your set-top box. Many digital cable systems transmit a number of channels using standard analog cable channels that your VCR can tune into. Routing this cable through the VCR lets you record those analog channels while your set-top box is tuned to a different channel (analog or digital) for simultaneous viewing.

Adding your gaming console or Home Theater PC

Very few A/V receivers have made provisions for connections from game consoles or Home Theater PCs (HTPCs). Although these devices are too new to have been incorporated into most receiver designers, that is no reason to give up hope. You can still get these devices hooked into your surround sound system and display.

The key thing to keep in mind is that HTPCs and game consoles are really no different than any other source device. They have analog and digital audio connections. They have composite, S-Video, and (in many cases) component video outputs. Your receiver doesn't care whether these signals came from a DVD player or an HTPC. Neither does your display.

So connect these devices just as you connect any of the other source devices we mention earlier in this chapter. Keep the same rules in mind: Use digital audio connections, if you can, and use the highest-quality video connection system that the device supports.

As we hint at earlier in this chapter, you probably won't find any inputs on the back of your receiver marked HTPC or Xbox. So find an unused set of inputs and use them.

If you have one of those fancy touch screen remote controls that we discuss in Chapter 14, you may be able to program the remote to use the actual name of the device you are using. So even if the HTPC is connected to the VCR2 input on your receiver, you can make the remote button say HTPC. With this setup, the babysitter can easily use your home theater. (We're not sure whether or not that's a good thing.)

Powering the Network

After you've made all the connections, the temptation to plug everything into the wall and get going is strong. Hold off for one more step: making the power connections safely. We're not talking about your personal safety here, but the safety of your equipment. You probably forgot about these cables (we did), but you should have some plans for these, too. There are lots of them, and they certainly get in the way a lot.

You'll have to confront two big issues: the number of connections and the quality of the connections (or, put another way, where to plug them in and how to keep your gear from getting fried).

You will simply have way more power cables than you think. The great thing about power management is that you can add connections as you need more with few issues. So if you need more outlets, no problem — just add some more interconnection devices. The overall power usage of your home theater is relatively light, compared to, say, a dishwasher, so in general, daisychaining devices (plugging several into one outlet) is not a huge problem.

 Some home theater components — high-powered receivers or power amplifiers and large displays — do draw a lot of current. It's always best to plug these items directly into your surge protector (which we discuss next). Other items, such as DVD players or CD players, can safely be plugged into either the surge protector or into one of the auxiliary outlets on the back of another piece of equipment (many receivers have such outlets).

 Two kinds of outlets are used on the back of receivers: *switched* and *unswitched.* Switched outlets turn on and off with the receiver, while unswitched outlets are always on. Keep that distinction in mind if you have something plugged into your receiver's power outlets that you want to use even when the receiver is turned off.

 The bigger issue is surge protection. Electrical currents are like water currents; they flow up and down, and if they get too high (a surge), it's a problem. (If they get too low (a brown-out), that's a problem, too.) You need to consider professional-class surge protection (not what you buy at Wal-Mart). One good lightning strike, and you can toast your home theater (and not in a good way). Leviton (www.leviton.com), for example, has a Home Theater Surge Protector that has nine outlets plus a neat expandable modular outlet that can handle surge protection for telephones, modems, faxes, DSLs, cable modems, computer LANs, and satellite and cable TV systems.

 If you are building from scratch or have the luxury of adding some outlets, put in electrical lines that are dedicated to your home theater and that go straight to your electrical panel, so that no intermediate devices can cause in-home surges on your lines.

In general, we also advocate whole-home power protectors that can help groom the power coming from the street. That's where some of the big surges can come from, and these surges can hit not only your home theater, but also everything else in your home. We consider these $300 to $800 "first line of defense" units a must for any home. They sit between all the electrical lines coming in and your electrical panel, truly stopping any problems before they get to your house. You can find models that also protect your satellite and cable connections at the home level, too. You can get these from Leviton and other electrical suppliers.

We talk more in Chapter 20 about power conditioning, which is the next step up after surge protection. Power conditioners use various techniques to restore your A/C power to a true 60 Hz, 120 volt signal, and can offer better audio and video performance.

Chapter 17

Plugging into a Whole-Home Network

We strongly believe that you should spend time thinking about how to exploit your investment in your home theater by taking it whole home. In many instances, you've already done the hard part by deciding that a home theater is worth the big investment to begin with. Now, telling you to take it to the limit (oops, Eagles pun) by going whole home (expanding your home theater's audio and video capabilities to other parts of your house) should not be so rough.

The point of this chapter is to expose you to some of the varied ways you can accomplish whole-home networking of your audio and video gear. If you are serious about this (and you know what's coming here, shameless self-promotion time!), we absolutely insist you think about getting our *Smart Homes For Dummies* book, because it goes into all the requisite details for you to do this by yourself.

In this chapter we talk in detail about some whole-home wiring systems that we recommend you install when you are building or remodeling your house. For most folks, the installation of whole-home wiring is *not* something that they want to do as a casual project. If you don't have a whole home wiring system in place, and can't put one in, don't freak out! We'll also talk about some solutions that use wireless networks or existing wires in your wall to expand the reach of your home theater components.

Introducing Whole-Home Entertainment

Let's talk about what it means to go whole home. If you read Chapter 2, you may recall that you need to plan around two major concentrations of equipment:

- **Wiring hub:** This is generally that place in your house where everything tends to come into the house from the outside. The electrical panel is likely there, along with your incoming telephone lines, your cable or satellite service connections, and maybe your cable or DSL modem if you were smart and planned ahead. Ideally, most of your in-home communications and information services are connected together in this area, with *home run* wires running throughout the house in a hub-and-spoke fashion. (In a home run wiring system, each outlet has a dedicated wire running directly to it from the wiring hub.)

- **Media hub:** You can consider the main home theater to be your media hub. Most of the gear we discuss in this book resides in the media hub, either on shelves out in the open or split between some gear in the open and some in a nearby equipment closet or rack.

When you go whole home, equipment also resides in your media hub and in other rooms around your house. For example, Danny has a kids' computer lab where four computers are clustered together so that his two sets of twins (he's always been an over-achiever) cannot fight over the computers to do their homework online. (Actually, Pat says he knows they are secretly playing *Civilization* and *MathBlaster.*)

In most cases, you are likely to have gear spread all over the house, particularly in the master bedroom, where you might have another TV, VCR, and cable/satellite receiver (maybe even another surround sound system), and potentially something in the kids' rooms.

So the question — and opportunity — is how can you link all your gear to minimize your costs (yes, you can *save* money by not having to buy a PVR or a satellite receiver for each room) and exploit your investment in your media hub. Well, have we got some ideas for you!

Think about what whole home means for you, because although you can grow your whole-home network, you can save money in the long run if you have a better idea of what you want to do up front. After you've already built the network, adding things can be more expensive. There's a world of difference between running an extra set of speakers to the bedroom or dining room for your audio, and wanting to have background music in every room. If your whole-home plans are relatively limited, you can almost always get inexpensive (under $100) devices that can meet these needs from Radio Shack (www.radioshack.com), X10 (www.x10.com), or SmartHome (www.smarthome.com).

But if you want to have more flexibility to mix and match in any room, or to have higher-quality connections, you may want to think about looking into a whole-home *distribution panel* for your signals. These panels, also called *structured cabling systems,* can support voice, data, and video distribution in the home. And the cost is relatively inexpensive. You can get a good panel for under $1,000 and then add jacks and wiring accordingly.

Not all distribution panels are alike. Some are for one specific application (such as video), and others allow you to select whatever you want to put on any connection. For example, a CAT-5e-based system (using that standard computer-network cabling) might let you put phone, computer data, video, or audio on any line. You merely change out the outlets at the terminating end according to your needs in that room.

You can find a list of structured wiring vendors on the Web site for our book, *Smart Homes For Dummies.* Check it out at www.smarthomesbook.com.

At a bare minimum, a structured cabling system should provide:

✔ **A flexible telephone network** using high-quality, unshielded twisted-pair (UTP) phone cabling and a modular, configurable termination system in the wiring closet (the central location where all of these systems are connected together)

✔ **A computer network** of CAT-5e (the standard for Ethernet computer network cabling) UTP cabling for data networking

✔ **A centrally distributed coaxial cable (usually RG6 — the standard video cabling) network** for distributing video signals

✔ **An all-in-one modular termination panel** to neatly terminate all this network wiring in your wiring closet

✔ **Customized wall outlet plates** to provide connectors for your phone, data, audio, and video outlets that can be easily changed and reconfigured

Connecting to a Whole-Home Audio System

Whole-home audio is a pretty simple baseline that a lot of people consider when moving out of the home theater and into the other parts of the house. After all, the first step can be as easy as merely stringing another set of speaker wires from your multizone-capable A/V receiver (we talk about these in Chapter 10) in your home theater to, say, remote speakers located in the dining room. Keep in mind, however, that the limitations of a whole-home audio network are based on your A/V receiver. Most A/V receivers that have multizone capabilities can only support audio in one or two other rooms — not zones in every room in the house.

So if you want a true whole-home audio system, you probably need to consider installing additional equipment in the media hub (or nearby). With this equipment in place (and the appropriate wires in the wall), you can share the audio source devices in your home theater with any room in the house. In almost all cases, this system is used to provide *stereo* (2-channel) audio, not surround sound (multichannel) audio, in rooms outside your home theater. The sidebar, "The trouble with whole-home surround sound," talks about this issue a bit more.

You can get audio from your home theater to other rooms in the house in four primary ways:

✔ **Use your receiver:** As we mention earlier, many receivers (at least above the $500 or $600 price range), include multizone functionality that lets you run speaker wires or a long audio interconnect. You can really only run these into an adjacent room, not the entire length of the house, due to signal loss. This is the simplest way to get audio elsewhere in the home.

✔ **Buy a whole-home audio distribution system:** These systems come in both multizone and single zone versions (we explain the difference later in this chapter), and use their own amplifiers and control systems to send audio to any room in the house. You can buy whole-home audio systems that support up to eight or more rooms.

✔ **Use a CAT-5e audio distribution system:** These systems can distribute line-level stereo audio signals over standard CAT-5e computer network cabling. Many of these systems are designed to carry both audio and video. Some (such as the one from ChannelPlus, www.channelplus.com) can even carry the higher-quality S-Video signals and digital audio signals (such as Dolby Digital) over this network cabling. Most of these systems, however, can carry only composite video and stereo audio.

✔ **Use a wireless audio distribution system:** These are typically simple systems, designed to go from point to point (rather than cover the whole home). Many people use them to send audio from their PC to their home theater, but they can also be used to get audio from a source in the home theater to other parts of the house.

Most of the CAT-5e and many of the wireless audio distribution systems we are about to discuss can also carry video signals.

Some of the whole-home audio network systems that we talk about use CAT-5e cabling, and we expect (in the not so distant future) to see systems that can distribute surround sound audio around the house digitally, using this cable. Until these systems become available, however, we think its best to stick with good old-fashioned 2-channel stereo for whole-home audio networks.

Zoning out: Single-zone versus multizone systems

After you start sending audio to a whole-home audio network, you have some decisions to make. The biggest decision is what you want to listen to in different parts of your house. No, we're not talking about what CDs you're going to play, but rather what kind of flexibility your system has to play *different* audio sources in different parts of the house simultaneously.

In a *single-zone audio system,* you have only one audio source distributed to every endpoint across the network at any given time. You can turn various sets of speakers on or off, but you don't have the ability to listen to different audio sources in different parts of your house at the same time. A *multizone audio system,* such as the one shown in Figure 17-1, on the other hand, allows one family member to listen to, say, a CD in the family room, while another person listens to the audio channel of a DVD in his or her bedroom.

The trouble with whole-home surround sound

The stereo audio standard, in which sound is separated into two channels (left and right), still dominates music production. With the advent of home theater, however, music can now be produced using multiple channels to drive a multitude of speakers.

For the average home (read that as a nonmillionaire home), we recommend that you don't add multichannel capabilities to your whole-home audio network, at least not right now. Although you can build an audio network that goes beyond the 2-channel (stereo) limit today, the network quickly becomes extremely complicated and prohibitively expensive.

Single-zone systems are easier and cheaper to build, but obviously less flexible to use than multizone systems. The good news is that the basic architecture (the wires you've got to put in your walls) is usually the same for both types of systems. So you can install an inexpensive single zone system, and then upgrade your equipment to multizone later on.

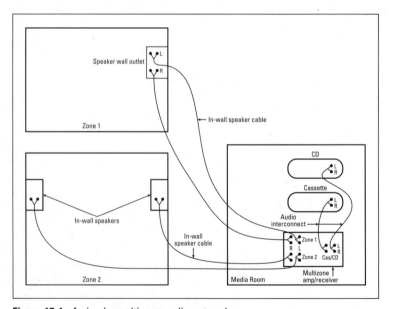

Figure 17-1: A simple, multizone audio network.

Using speaker wires to build an audio network

The traditional way to expand an audio network is to simply extend in-the-wall speaker wires from your home theater or media center to remote locations in your house (anywhere you want to have audio). Remember that you need to use UL-rated CL3 speaker wires, and given the distances traversed by these wires, we recommend 14 gauge or smaller wires. Figure 17-1 shows a simple multizone audio system. Chapter 15 explains cables and wires in more detail.

If your A/V receiver has multiroom capability, you can connect these speaker wires directly to your receiver, using a device called an *impedance matching system* (which we describe in more detail in the sidebar, "A word about impedance matching systems"). This device is necessary when you are connecting more than one pair of speakers to a single pair of speaker terminals on a receiver or amplifier.

A better way to use those speaker wire connections to remote rooms is to use a special-purpose, multiroom integrated amplifier. These devices contain individual pairs of amplifiers for each remote pair of speakers; so you don't need an impedance matching system, and you get plenty of power (and volume) in remote rooms. You can get multiroom integrated amplifiers in both single zone and multizone configurations. These integrated amplifiers are available from companies such as Niles Audio, www.nilesaudio.com.

 If you want to create a two zone audio system relatively inexpensively, look for a multizone A/V receiver that has *line level* outputs for the second zone, instead of speaker level outputs. With these systems, you can simply plug the receiver into a single-zone, multiroom, integrated amplifier using a pair of standard audio interconnect cables. Your home theater is Zone 1, and the rest of your house is Zone 2. It's not as good as a true multizone system, but a lot cheaper and easier to set up.

Besides a centralized amplifier/control system, and speaker wires in the wall, you of course need to install speakers in the remote rooms. Most folks decide to use *in-wall* speaker systems (often placing these speakers in the ceiling), but you can also install speaker terminal wall jacks, and then use standard loudspeakers. You connect the loudspeakers to these wall jacks just as you might connect them to the back of a receiver.

Controlling whole-home audio with IR

The other big challenge for a whole-home audio system is controlling your A/V components from remote rooms. Remember that most A/V components use IR (infrared) remote control systems, and that IR doesn't travel through walls and other obstacles. So you'll need a remote control system that can carry IR signals from IR sensors (that you simply aim a remote control at) or wall-mounted volume controls and keypads in your remote rooms. These whole-home IR systems typically require special 3-conductor IR cabling, but can also be carried over other cables, such as CAT-5e computer network cables or even over the RG6 coaxial cables that carry video signals around the house from an antenna or cable TV service.

You need a couple of components to connect a whole-home IR system together:

- ✔ **IR sensors or keypads in remote rooms:** These are the end of the line for your IR network. Each run of IR cable terminates in one of these devices. IR sensors and keypads send IR control signals over the IR cabling as electrical signals.

- ✔ **An IR connecting block in your media hub:** This device connects to the other end of the IR cable runs and *concentrates* the IR signals they carry into outputs that can control your A/V components. You need a connecting block because you want only one IR input connected to each component in your system, but you have IR sensors or keypads in multiple rooms. The connecting block allows, for example, the IR signals coming from five different rooms to be sent to a single CD player.

- ✔ **IR emitters (IR blasters):** These devices run from the connecting block to the components themselves. IR emitters have only one function in life: They convert the electrical control signals back into IR (light) signals that A/V components can understand.

Building a whole-home IR distribution system is a relatively complicated process. The hardest part is programming keypads and getting the right IR signals to the right A/V components. We highly recommend that you work with a professional installer if you want to implement a whole-home IR network.

CAT-5e or wireless audio distribution systems can often carry IR control signals for you, so you won't need a separate IR network.

How do I connect source devices to my multiroom system?

Most audio source devices (such as CD players) have only one set of audio outputs on the back, and you probably already have this set connected to your A/V receiver. So how can you also feed this audio into a separate multiroom amplifier system? There are two options (besides buying a second CD player).

The easiest (and cheapest) way to do this is to use a Y-splitter audio cable that splits a single pair of stereo audio signals into two pairs. One branch of the Y goes to your A/V receiver, and the other to your multiroom system. You can buy these cables at Radio Shack and similar retailers.

Some multiroom installations use separate amplifiers for each zone. In these systems, you need more than a simple two-for-one split from a Y-splitter. The solution here is to use a signal distribution amplifier. This device takes the output of a source device, splits it into multiple outputs, and then amplifies these outputs to ensure that your signal is not degraded (if you split the signal without amplifying it, it could be too weak and would cause distortion that you would hear as a background noise or hiss). This is the best approach if you are using separate amplifiers for each remote pair of speakers.

Plugging into CAT-5e

Aside from speaker cabling, you have other whole-home audio cabling options, such as CAT-5e. Systems from a variety of manufacturers can successfully carry line-level audio signals (the signals carried over audio interconnects) over CAT-5e cables in your walls. On the inexpensive end, you can get systems that convert the left and right line-level outputs of an audio device into a balanced signal. If high-end is your thing, go all the way with full-fledged, expensive audio (and video!) distribution systems that provide true multizone audio over CAT-5e.

You can distribute audio signals around the home using CAT-5e in three major ways, which we discuss in the following sections.

Point to point with baluns

Baluns are deployed in pairs for point-to-point use. A *balun* is just a little passive device (meaning it doesn't need any external power) about the size of a deck of cards, with receptacles on both sides (an RJ-45 on one side, and two or more RCA jacks on the other). One balun is associated with the source device (such as a CD player or the Audio Out ports of a receiver). This balun connects through an

A word about impedance matching systems

When we talked about A/V receivers and particularly about their amplifier sections in Chapter 10, we mentioned that many receivers have trouble dealing with speakers with an impedance (a measure of electrical resistance) of 4 ohms or less. This really comes into play in whole-home audio systems. That's because when you try to drive two sets of speakers from the same stereo amplifier, the impedance of the speakers is effectively halved. That is to say, if you plug two sets of 8 ohm speakers into a single stereo amplifier, you end up with an effective impedance of 4 ohms. Add a third set, and you're in the danger zone for most receivers.

If you've got a multizone audio distribution system, impedance isn't an issue (each pair of speakers will have its own amplifier), but in a single zone system, many folks try to cram multiple pairs of speakers onto a single amplifier. The safe way to do this is to use an impedance matching system. These systems let you hook up two, three, four, or more pairs of speakers to a single stereo amplifier, without the impedance dropping to an unsafe level. Keep in mind that the amplifier power provided to these remote speakers will be reduced as you add extra sets of speakers onto the system. So the impedance matching system will protect your amplifier, but you may not get enough power to reach the volume levels you want.

RCA audio interconnect, to the left and right Audio Out channels. Then, you plug the balun into the CAT-5e cable using a CAT-5e patch cable. At the other end of the network — down another leg of your home's CAT-5e that you've dedicated to audio — the process is reversed. The second balun plugs into the RJ-45 outlet on your wall (again using a patch cable), and then plugs into the left and right Audio In jacks of the remote amplifier or receiver that you're feeding the signal to.

Single-zone CAT-5e audio-distribution systems

In the world of audio and CAT-5e, the next step up moves beyond the point-to-point limitation of baluns and provides a single-zone, audio-distribution network to multiple locations throughout the home. These systems, from vendors such as Russound (www. russound.com) and Leviton (www.leviton.com), typically use custom faceplates that replace standard RJ-45 faceplates in each room. These faceplates have a pair of female RCA audio jacks that can connect to any standard audio source device or amplifier/ receiver. In the room containing the source device you want to share throughout the home, you simply plug a stereo audio patch cable between the device and the faceplate.

In remote rooms, you use an audio patch cable to connect the face-plate to the inputs of a local receiver or amplifier. Connecting these remote outlets is a special CAT-5e audio hub located in your wiring closet. This hub takes the source signal and distributes it to every other CAT-5e outlet connected to the hub.

Multizone CAT-5e audio-distribution systems

If you want the utmost in flexibility and capability in a CAT-5e-based audio-distribution system, you need a system that can carry different audio programs to different parts of the house simultaneously — a multizone, multisource system. Like the multizone speaker-level systems discussed earlier in the chapter, multizone CAT-5e systems are the top-of-the-line, best-you-can-buy solution. Because sending audio over CAT-5e is still new, it's not cheap. You'll probably end up paying $1,500 or more for the components alone, and that doesn't include the speakers and amplifiers or receivers in each room. And that's for the (relatively) cheap versions of these systems. Some high-end systems can cost tens of thousands of dollars. You can get systems from players such as Crestron (www.crestron.com) and Niles (www.nilesaudio.com).

Going wireless

The most popular way of getting audio around the house without a dedicated network is with an RF (radio frequency) wireless system. These come in two main flavors:

- **Wireless speaker systems** connect to the line-level outputs of a source device or preamplifier and send the signal over a 900-MHz or 2.4-GHz channel to a pair of self-amplified stereo speakers.

- **Wireless line-level distribution systems** hook up to your source components in the same fashion but send their signal to a receiver that hooks into your own amplifier and speakers on the far end.

One major potential difficulty with this sort of wireless system is that it uses a line-level input — something that most source devices have only one of. So you may run into trouble hooking up a CD player, for example, to both your A/V receiver (or controller) for local listening and to one of these devices for remote listening. Luckily, many of these units also accept the output of your receiver or amp's headphone jack, so you can avoid this problem if you have a headphone jack available. Alternatively, you can use one of the Y-splitter audio cables we mention in the sidebar, "How do I connect source devices to my multiroom system?" in this chapter. Prices for these wireless systems range from about $75 to $200. Major manufacturers include:

- ✔ Recoton (www.recoton.com)
- ✔ Paradox (www.paradoxllc.com)
- ✔ RCA (www.rca.com)
- ✔ RF Link (www.rflinktech.com)

Another cool wireless product comes from the X10 Wireless Technologies folks. (You probably know them from their infamous Internet pop-up ads on many popular Web sites.) X10's MP3 Anywhere! system works like the other systems we describe, but it's available with a feature that we think is pretty cool: X10's BOOM 2000 software. This software runs on your Windows PC and let's you remotely control and access the PC's MP3 music files, as well as CDs or DVDs played back in the PC's internal drive. RCA (www.RCA.com) has a $99 Lyra Wireless RD900W that lets you play PC-based music through the stereo, too.

Something from the "Coming Soon" department: As we write (early 2003), we are starting to see some systems come onto the market that use the 802.11 wireless computer network systems to distribute audio throughout the home. These systems are primarily being used for computer-based audio, such as Internet radio stations and MP3 files stored on a PC or *server* computer. We expect that eventually these systems will be able to carry any kind of audio signal around the home wirelessly. Prismiq (www.prismiq.com), for instance, has a $249 product that links your PC with any TV set in the house, and more products are coming.

Sharing Video Components throughout the Home

Sharing video in the home used to be a lot simpler a few years ago than it is today. This is largely due to the advent of all sorts of signal encryption and digital transmission. These have added their unique flies in the whole-home networking ointment.

At a high level, you can share home theater video signals within your home in four major ways:

✔ Use *modulators* to send your video over the coaxial cable carrying your antenna or cable TV signal.

✔ Use a CAT-5e audio/video distribution system.

✔ Use a wireless audio/video distribution system.

✔ Use a system that carries audio and video over your existing phone wires.

Using your TV cables

Most structured wiring systems include a centralized video distribution system. This system differs from the standard cable company installations in one big way. Most cable installations use a *branch and tree* architecture, with the cable coming into your house from the street and then being fed into a series of *splitters* (these are the little "one in, two out" devices that split a cable signal into two branches). A centralized video distribution system uses a special splitter, called a *video distribution panel,* that splits the incoming cable (or antenna) signal into multiple lines running to all of your TVs — each a "home run" cable in a hub and spoke architecture.

With a central video distribution panel, you can create your own inhouse television channels using modulators over your inhome coax cables. Simply put, a *modulator* takes the composite or S-Video output of a video source device (as well as the stereo analog audio outputs) and transforms it into a RF (radio frequency) signal — just like a television station does. You simply set the modulator to broadcast over an unused channel and connect it to your video distribution panel. When you want to watch that source somewhere else in the house, you just need to tune your remote TV to that station, and voilà!

Figure 17-2 shows a modulated signal (in this case, a VCR, but it can be any video source, such as a DVD player or a DSS satellite receiver).

Modulator systems don't work for everybody. New digital cable systems are designed to use all or most of the available spectrum on your home's coax network, so carving out bandwidth for your piggyback data transmission is not so easy. In many instances, it's almost impossible. You are likely better off pursuing some of the nonmodulator alternatives we're about to discuss instead.

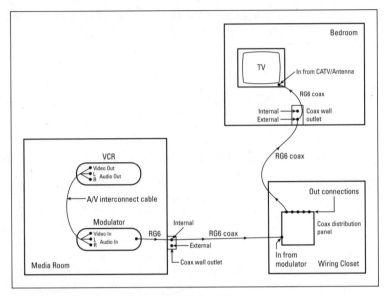

Figure 17-2: Watching a VCR in another room.

CAT-5e and wireless systems

Many of the CAT-5e and wireless systems can carry video signals. In the case of CAT-5e systems, we think that you can actually get a higher-quality video signal around the house than you can with a modulator system. That's because the process of modulating and then *demodulating* a video source (when it gets back into your remote TV) tends to diminish your picture quality. Some of these CAT-5e systems can even carry S-Video signals and digital audio for high-quality video and *surround sound* audio in remote locations (you need an A/V receiver and surround speakers in these remote locations to take advantage of this).

A simpler way of getting video around the house is to use a phone line system. The Leapfrog HomeNetwork by Terk (www.terk.com) is a device — or rather a pair of devices — that transmits video and/or audio signals from a source device (such as a satellite receiver or PVR) to a remote location over existing phone lines. The pair's transmitter half connects to the source unit's RF or line-level video and audio outputs and plugs into a standard phone jack. At the remote end, the receiver also plugs into a phone jack and connects to the RF or line-level audio and video inputs of the remote television or audio system. The Leapfrog also carries infrared control signals over your phone lines, so you can carry your remote with you to the room containing the receiver and do all the pausing, fast-forwarding, and channel-changing you like without running back and forth.

Interfacing with Your Telephone System

The days are gone when the telephone was simply something you had a conversation over. Indeed, your telephone system now is used as a data access point for dial-up Internet access, as an inbound interface to your system from afar, and even as an in-home interface to your home automation system. And you thought it was just a phone.

At the simplest level, devices need to meet baseline requirements in order to interconnect with your telephone system. Your DSS receiver, for instance, requires a phone line interface so that the receiver can access your account database in order to track online movie purchases. And some of the gaming consoles enable you to compete in multiplayer networks via dialup connections (although after you try broadband, you'll never go back to dialup).

Nothing about interconnecting your home theater to your home telephone system is overtly complex. At the basic level, you simply plug any device that requires a phone connection into the nearest outlet. If you have multiple devices, they can share a single wall outlet if you use an inexpensive 2-in-1 jack adapter ($5 from Radio Shack).

If you don't have a phone outlet nearby, you can get a wireless phone jack for around $80 that uses your electrical lines in your house to transmit your telephone communications. You plug your standard telephone line into an adapter that plugs into your electrical outlet at your home theater. Then in a room where there is an available phone outlet, you do the same, only this time you run a phone cable from the electrical outlet into the phone outlet. Shazaam! — one phone line.

Do not use a wireless phone jack with a surge protector because this may block the frequencies over which your phone line communicates. Directly plug the unit into the wall.

A nice little device is the TV Messenger (www.smarthome.com, $120), which tells you on your TV screen who is calling during your favorite TV show, so you know whether you want to get up to answer the phone. When the phone rings, the TV Messenger automatically pops up the Caller ID info on the top of the TV screen without interrupting the program. If you subscribe to phone-company voice mail, the LED blinks when messages are waiting, too. You'd only want to use this for your analog TV signals, because you don't want to limit your higher-quality DVD and other video to composite connections (all that the device offers). The TV Messenger sits in-line to your audio and video signal between the TV source and the receiver, connected via simple audio and composite video interconnect cables.

Connecting to Your Computer LAN

We talk in Chapter 2 about having a wiring closet for your Ethernet hubs and routers, in Chapter 6 about Ethernet ports on your PVRs, in Chapter 9 about gaming consoles with network interfaces, and so on. Computer networks are becoming an important part of your home theater infrastructure.

Accessing a whole-home computer network (or *LAN*) opens up your home theater to any data point on your network. A good example is Danny's AudioReQuest CD server. It has an on-board Web server that allows access to this music from wherever he wants, in the house or over the Internet. He can synchronize his boxes in Maine and Connecticut because they are connected to the Internet. As soon as he finishes this book, he's going to extend that to synching with his car stereos, too — over wireless computer network connections. The same is true with his SnapStream PVR. He can record programs while he is away and download them from anywhere on the planet. Now he can catch up on *The Sopranos* while in Kiev!

Getting your home theater devices communicating with your computer network is getting easier all the time, thanks to newer technologies, lower costs, and the equipment vendors' increased experience with the consumer market. It's getting to be almost automatic!

We talk about Ethernet networks because, frankly, you're unlikely to want to have another protocol on your computer network. There are other LAN systems (like ATM), but Ethernet really rules the computing domain.

Accordingly, it's likely — very likely — that you'll connect your home theater with your computer LAN over Ethernet connections.

So assuming this is the case, the question then becomes, "How do you interconnect with that LAN?" Well, it depends on the extent of your LAN, if it exists at all. Although we don't have space in this book to discuss all the ins and outs of computer networking, we want to offer a little guidance to help you on your way toward a whole-home computing backbone that can make use of your home theater system. Here are a few networking points to keep in mind:

✔ You can carry data signals around your house in at least four major ways: CAT-5e cabling, wireless, electrical cables, and regular phone wiring and coaxial cables. We recommend, if you can do it, that you run new CAT-5e cables through your walls to the places where you want it. If you use CAT-5e for your audio or video distribution, then you are likely building a new home or renovating your current one, and running the cable shouldn't be a problem. A wired infrastructure gives you much higher data rates, more reliability, and more flexibility for the future — and it can add to the value of your home.

✔ Wireless options are great. These are coming down fast in price, and you can build a home data network just by adding a *wireless access point* to your network. (A wireless access point is a base station of a wireless network — think of it as the equivalent of a cordless phone base station.) You then bring your devices online by adding *PC cards* (which plug into standardized PC card slots on the device) or USB-based *dongles* (or adapters) that plug into the USB ports. Most devices follow the 11 Mbps 802.11b wireless standard, but new versions for the 802.11a and g wireless standards, which provide speeds up to 54 Mbps, are now on the market.

✔ You can transmit signals over electrical cables, too, by using low-cost devices that conform to the HomePlug standard. This standard allows up to 14 Mbps transmission rates, but speeds vary substantially based on where you plug in the devices and what is turned on at any particular time. Siemens/Efficient Network's SpeedStream (www.speedstream.com) product line has gateway routers, 802.11b access points, Ethernet modules, and 802.11b PC cards that enable you to build a complete home network by doing nothing more than plugging devices into the electrical outlets. Pretty cool. In fact, a whole-home computer network for less than $500 is very cool. Want to add a room? Plug in an electrical module. Done.

✔ You can also use your coaxial cables and phone lines in your house to send signals from room to room. These use unused higher frequencies on the cable to send the data, so you can still talk on the phone or watch video at the same time. This is based on the Home Phone Networking Alliance (HPNA) standards. In general, the other options we mention are preferable to HPNA at this time, but new, faster versions of HPNA have been promised.

✔ If you have a high-speed cable, DSL, or satellite Internet connection, you have it located somewhere on your network. It does not matter where, from the home theater perspective, because there really is no specific reason the connection has to be located there. In fact, most people like it either close to their computing area or in the wiring closet, out of sight.

✔ You need a router if you want to support multiple Ethernet devices on one network and have them interface with the Internet. Often the DSL/cable/satellite modem is also a router, but not always. The router has a built-in hub that enables you to interconnect multiple data lines.

✔ If you are going to be routing video or large files over your LAN, consider getting an Ethernet *switch* instead of a hub, so that you can make sure you get all the bandwidth you need for a quality transmission. (Most routers include an Ethernet switch, but you may need an external Switch with more ports if you have lots of devices on your network.)

Although many vendors will try to push you into one solution ("You need Wi-Fi," "No, you need HomePlug"), you might find that these various networks can complement each other. You know that we think a wired CAT-5e network should be the basis of your computer-LAN infrastructure (and phone network, and maybe even your audio and video network). But we also think that all the data networking technologies can be used in concert when you build a whole-home network.

Just for fun, here are a few examples:

✔ Build a wired Ethernet LAN, but plug a Wi-Fi access point in your living room for cordless, sofa-based Web surfing.

✔ Use Wi-Fi as the basis for your home-computer LAN, but use HomePlug or HPNA to extend your network to access points in distant locations out of reach of your primary base station (such as by the pool).

✔ Use wired Ethernet for your computers, but use a HomePlug system to connect your Xbox to the broadband Internet connection for online gaming.

We could keep this list going and going, but we think you get the picture. Think creatively, and use wired and unwired technologies together to get your LAN wherever you need it to go.

Part V
Let Your Home Theater Be All It Can Be

The 5th Wave   By Rich Tennant

"Would it ruin the online concert experience if I vacuumed the mosh pit between songs?"

In this part . . .

In this part, we get a bit fancy. It's all about what to do after everything is put together. First, we discuss how to use the controls on your video systems (your television and your video source devices) to get the best picture possible.

Next, we discuss how to tweak your audio system so that you can adjust it to the dynamics of *your* home theater. Our friends in the installation business are constantly amazed at how bad good audio gear can sound, if it's not set up properly. Conversely, even modestly priced gear can sound great if it's properly tweaked.

We'll also talk about ways you can improve your home theater's environment. If you think about it, home theater is really all about creating light and sound that you can interact with. If you keep environmental lights and sounds from interfering with your theater, you can get more enjoyment out of your gear.

Finally, we talk about the high end of home theater and how to go all out in pursuit of a home theater experience. Even if you have budget limitations, you can get a preview of the future of home theater.

Chapter 18

Tweaking Your A/V System

*G*etting your A/V system hooked up can be a bit of a challenge, but it's rewarding to have all that "on your hands and knees" plug-fest work behind you. You have to take one more step, however, before you sit back and really enjoy your home theater. You need to spend some time tweaking your system — adjusting the video display and getting your surround sound set up properly.

In this chapter, we discuss ways to do these calibrations. This may seem like overkill to some folks, but it is critical. Joel Silver, the president of the Imaging Science Foundation (these are folks who know a thing or two about setting up home theaters!), tells us that over 90 percent of home theater displays are set up incorrectly. With a few tools, you can be part of the small percentage of home theater owners who are getting the most out of what they've paid for.

Calibrating Your Video

We've said it before — and we'll say it again, because it's important! — most displays come from the factory improperly calibrated. The brightness and color are set at unnatural levels in order to make the displays stand out on the showroom floor (in a brightly lit store). At these settings, if you put them in a darkened home theater, the picture looks awful.

If you have a direct-view or projection CRT (cathode ray tube) or a plasma display, you have an additional reason to calibrate your video: The overly bright settings that most of these units come with can reduce the lifespan of your display! Even if your display is not brand new or not all that fancy, a calibration can breathe new life into your picture quality.

On your average display, you (as a nontechnician) can make five adjustments. A few sets let you adjust more, and service techs with the proper manuals and codes to get into the service menus of the display can adjust just about anything. But an average person (like you or us) can adjust the following controls:

- **Contrast (white level):** Don't confuse this with *contrast ratio,* which we discuss earlier in the book (it's the ratio between the brightest and darkest images a display can create). In terms of display adjustments, your contrast control adjusts the *white level,* or degree of whiteness your screen is displaying. You see, in video displays, whites and blacks are measured on a scale called the IRE (Institute of Radio Engineers) units, which are represented as a percentage. 0 percent is black; 100 percent is white. You can actually drive your TV beyond 100 percent if your contrast is improperly set. If you do this, white portions of your picture tend to bleed over into the darker portions surrounding them.

- **Brightness (black level):** Now to throw in a counterintuitive statement, the brightness control on your display actually adjusts the *black level* that you see on the screen. Weird huh? If the black level is set incorrectly, you can't discern the difference between darker images on your screen.

- **Sharpness:** The sharpness control adjusts the *fine detail* of the picture — its ability to display minute details on the screen. If the sharpness is set too low, you have a fuzzy picture; if it's set too high, your picture appears *edgy,* often with "blobs" around the edges of objects, instead of clearly defined lines.

- **Color:** Along with Tint (which we discuss next), color is one of the two controls that let you set the balance of the colors (finally, a name that says what it means!) on your display. If your color setting is too low, images begin to appear as black and white. If it's too high, images take on a reddish tinge (for example Nicole Kidman's face will turn as red as her hair).

- **Tint (hue):** On most TVs, this control is labeled *tint,* but a few are more technically correct and call it *hue.* The tint control will adjust your display's color within a range between red and green — your job will be to find the perfect balance between them.

Almost every display we know of has an on-screen display that shows the status of these settings. Typically, you'll find a horizontal bar running across your screen, with either a moving vertical hash mark that shows your current setting, or the entire bar moves left or right as you increase or decrease these settings. Some displays also have a numeric display (usually running from 0 to 100) that shows your current setting.

We like the numeric displays, because writing down a number is much easier (if you want to recreate a setting in the future) than trying to remember exactly how far across the screen a particular bar was.

Using a calibration disc

The best way to adjust your video is to use a DVD *home theater calibration disc.* We consider these discs (which cost about $50) to be an absolutely essential investment in your home theater. Unless you've had a professional calibrate your system (or you've spent so much on everything else that you can't afford the disc), we think you simply must get one of these discs. (And no, no one is paying us to say that.)

The most common home theater calibration discs are the following:

- **AVIA: Guide to Home Theater:** Available from Ovation Software (www.ovationsw.com), this disc contains a ton of great background material about home theater. It explains a lot of the same stuff we talk about here in *Home Theater For Dummies.* It also contains a series of easy-to-follow on-screen test patterns and signals that let you correctly adjust all the settings we discuss in the preceding section. It also helps you test tones for your surround sound audio systems (which we discuss in a moment).

- **Video Essentials:** Found online at www.videoessentials. com, this is the definitive calibration disc. Two versions are available — one standard disc, and one especially for digital TVs. There's even a laser disc version available if you still have a laser disc player in your home theater. One really cool thing about Video Essentials is the inclusion of video footage that you can watch to see the results of your adjustments with actual video, instead of just on a test pattern.

- ***Sound and Vision* Home Theater Tune-up:** This one is also produced by Ovation Software (www.ovationsw.com), but in conjunction with *Sound and Vision* magazine (one of our favorites). This disc also includes tests that demonstrate aspect ratios and let you test your S-Video and component video outputs on your DVD player (to see which works better in your system).

We like all three of these discs and would be hard pressed to recommend one. The AVIA and *Sound and Vision* discs are probably the best bet for regular people (in other words, people who aren't trained video calibrators). Video Essentials is geared more for the professional. AVIA is probably a bit more detailed and comprehensive, whereas the *Sound and Vision* disc is a bit easier for first-time users. Either one (any of the three, actually) gives you a better picture.

When you buy one of these discs, you'll notice that a blue filter comes in the package. You need this filter when adjusting some of the color and tint settings on your display. You look through the filter to block out certain light frequencies.

Using one of these discs is a fairly simple process — one we don't try to re-create here step by step, because the on-screen audio and text instructions do a better job than we can in a book. Before you adjust any of these settings, get up off your comfy home theater seating and close the blinds! Ambient lighting has an immense effect on what you see on your screen (regardless of what type of display you've got in your home theater). So lower the blinds, close the door, and dim the lights. You want to adjust your picture in exactly the same lighting conditions that you'll have when you sit down to play movies or watch TV in your home theater. Then just follow through instructions on the DVD, step-by-step. It's easy, and it's even kind of fun.

When you're all done, you'll notice that your picture looks different. (We sure hope it does!) It's going to look darker. If you're not used to a calibrated video picture, this might be a bit disconcerting. Give yourself some time to get used to it, though, and you'll notice a more detailed picture, a picture that looks more like the movies. And isn't that what you're after in a home theater?

Some displays come from the factory either pretty well calibrated, or with a picture *mode* you can select on your remote that will set your picture close to the state it would be in after you manually calibrated it. Sony displays are famous for this, as are some of the high-end displays made by Loewe, www.loewe.de, and Princeton Graphics, www.princetongraphics.com. (Sony calls this their "Pro" mode.) Read the reviews before you buy. Although you still may want to tweak the display a bit with a calibration disc, it's very handy to have it be 99 percent of the way there with the push of a single button (or right out of the box).

Getting your projector in focus

If you've got a projection TV system (front or rear), and it uses cathode-ray tubes (CRTs) to create its picture, getting your set calibrated is a bit more intense. In addition to all the color/hue/sharpness/brightness/contrast stuff we discuss elsewhere in this chapter, you need to converge these displays. Converging is the process of aligning the three separate CRTs (one each for red, green, and blue) inside these projectors, so that the image projected by each CRT is exactly superimposed onto the other two. Misconvergence is obvious when you see it (the edges of images are red, green, and blue "halos" instead of a single sharp image), and is really painful to watch.

For most CRT projection systems, you need a professional to calibrate the convergence of your display. A few rear-projection models (RPTVs), from companies such as Hitachi (www.hitachi.com), are now available with automatic convergence systems. Just a few years ago (in the mid 1990s), this feature alone cost more (as an option for expensive projector systems) than the entire HDTV-ready RPTV with this automatic convergence costs today. How about that for capitalism in action? Even if you have a set with automatic convergence, you might still consider a professional calibration to get the ultimate picture from your RPTV, but the automatic convergence is much better than doing nothing.

Tuning a system without a disc

If you haven't had a chance to get your hands on one of the home theater calibration discs, but you still want to improve your picture, you can do a couple of things.

One way to get a subset of the video tests on these discs is to play a DVD that contains the *THX Optimizer*. You find this somewhere in the disc's main menu (usually in the Special Features section). Like the discs we describe earlier, the Optimizer walks you through a series of steps to adjust your display (and your audio system). You can find a list of movies (including Pat's wife's favorite, *Moulin Rouge*) that include the THX optimizer on THX's Web site (www.thx.com/consumer_products/optimizer/optimizer_dvd.html). You still need that blue filter; if you didn't get one with the DVD itself (and you probably didn't), you can get one for free from THX by filling out the order form online. (You do have to pay a couple of bucks for shipping and handling.)

We recommend that you at least rent one of the movies on the THX Web site so you can use the Optimizer. You can adjust your video just by eyeballing it. We recommend that, at a minimum, you turn down the brightness until the level is about ⅓ of the way across your screen, but using a test disc or the Optimizer is much, much easier and more accurate.

Hiring a professional

You may decide — either right up front, or after you realize that you just can't handle that remote control very well — that you want a professional to calibrate your display. Well, that's nothing to be ashamed of. In fact, if you can afford it, we highly recommend that you consider having a professional calibrate your system. They've got tools (such as light meters) that you just don't have, and their calibration is more precise and ultimately better than anything you can do with a calibration DVD and your eyeballs.

If you have a CRT front-projection system, you really *must* have a professional set it up. You'll waste tens of thousands of dollars if you don't. In fact, if you're buying any high-end display (such as that $17,000 61-inch HDTV plasma display Pat's got his eye on — don't tell his wife!), go for a professional calibration. When you start getting into this price range, you should really expect this kind of service from your home theater dealer. A professional calibration usually costs between $200 and $500, depending on what type of display you have.

If you choose to have a professional calibration done, make sure you choose someone who has been certified and trained by the Imaging Science Foundation or ISF (we mention them earlier in the chapter, you might recall). The ISF has trained (and continues to train) literally thousands of home theater dealers in the art of system calibration. You can find a trained calibration professional near you by searching on ISF's Web site at www.imagingscience.com.

Don't call ISF directly asking them to calibrate your system. Those folks know how to do it, but they're in the business of training others, not coming over to your house.

Adjusting Your Audio System

Just as your display needs a tune-up to look its best, your A/V receiver (or A/V controller, if you've gone with separates) needs a once-over to ensure you get the best possible sound from your home theater. You need to do the initial setup to make sure that your A/V receiver knows what kind of speakers you're using, and then you need to adjust the amplification levels for each speaker.

Great DVDs to put your system through its paces

After your video system is calibrated and ready to go, it's time to start watching some movies. Why not enjoy the view with some real classics, and with some newer movies that can really test the limits of your system's capabilities. For some reason, home theater enthusiasts often tend to love action movies (but hey, who doesn't?) and trot out their well-worn copies of Terminator 2 or The Matrix. These are indeed fun to watch in your home theater, and they can be demanding discs. (The Matrix, in particular, seemed to overpower many early DVD players.) But you also might want to check out some other films that show off your home theater in more subtle ways. The ISF (yep, the same guys we mention elsewhere in this chapter) has a list of films that it recommends to its affiliated dealers as great demo discs. You can find this list online at www.filmsondisc.com/ISF_Reference_DVD_Program.htm.

Get out your A/V receiver's manual before you start doing any of this. Your receiver may have different (but similar) terminology. The manual can also help you navigate your receiver's setup menu system.

Managing bass

Your A/V receiver sends low-frequency sounds to your subwoofer through its LFE (or low frequency effects) channel. Subwoofers are very good at one thing — reproducing bass notes — and not much good at anything else. Generally speaking, you want to send only the lowest possible frequencies to the subwoofer, because you want to minimize the use of the subwoofer for relatively higher frequencies.

At the same time, you must balance this requirement with the needs of your other speakers. If you've got a set of small bookshelf speakers for your center, right, left, and surround speakers, and they can't reproduce bass notes very well, you're better off letting the subwoofer handle nearly all the bass.

You need to set the speaker size for each group of speakers — center, front (or main), and surrounds. So Step 1 in setting up your audio is to go into your A/V receiver's setup or configuration menu, and navigate to the menu that lets you select your speaker size. You typically have a choice of Large or Small. The Small setting cuts off the low frequencies that are sent to your main speakers (the speakers other than your subwoofer) at a higher frequency than does the Large setting. In other words, the Small setting sends almost all low-frequency audio signals to the subwoofer, whereas the Large setting sends the low frequencies to *both* the subwoofer and your other speakers.

You'll probably find a setting in this menu for the subwoofer — an On or None setting that indicates the presence or absence of the subwoofer. Make sure you select On if you have a subwoofer.

You can use two criteria to select a setting for your speakers:

✔ **Frequency range of your speakers (best):** If you have access to the manufacturer's data about your speaker, find out the frequency range at which the manufacturer rates its speakers. (You may also find this information from a reviewer who has tested the speakers.) If the low end of the speaker's frequency response is rated below 40 Hz, set your receiver to the Large setting; otherwise, use the Small setting.

✔ **Woofer size (not as good):** If you don't know how low your speakers can go, you can use the size of your speaker's woofers as a rule of thumb. If the woofers are 6 inches or larger, try the Large setting; otherwise, go with the Small setting.

If you don't know either of these things (you can always take off the speaker's grill, and measure the woofer), start off with the Large setting. You can always switch over to the Small setting if you notice that your main speakers aren't handling the bass very well. (In other words, they're causing audible distortions with low-frequency audio tracks.)

If you don't have a subwoofer in your system, make sure you set the front speakers to the Large setting, and set the subwoofer control to Off. Even if your other speakers are small, you need to select Large here, or you'll get absolutely no bass from your system.

Setting up surrounds

After your speakers are turned on and you've selected sizes, it's time to configure your surround system. You need to configure two settings here:

✔ **Delay:** If all your speakers are the same distance from your listening position, sounds emanating from them arrive at your ears at the same time. That's a good thing, because delays in the arrival of sounds can ruin your soundfield. You want sounds to have delays only when the director of the movie

intends it (like when a footfall echoes behind you). If speakers
aren't equidistant from the listening position, your A/V
receiver can compensate with its own delay settings.

✔ **Channel Balance (or level):** Set the sound level of each
speaker so that you hear an equal volume from each speaker
during testing. If one speaker (or set of speakers) is too loud,
you experience an unbalanced soundfield while listening to
your system. (When you play back actual movies or music,
the volume coming from each speaker depends on the volumes encoded in the source material.)

Setting the delay

Depending upon your A/V receiver, you'll find two ways to set the
delay: You can enter either a distance or a delay time (in milliseconds). In either case, get a tape measure and measure the distance
to each group of speakers (center, front, and surround). You should
have to measure only one speaker from each group, because the
left and right speakers within a group should be equidistant from
your listening position. If your receiver uses distance, simply enter
the number of feet that you've just measured for each group of
speakers.

If the receiver uses delay settings in milliseconds, things get a bit
more complicated. Typically the delay settings are measured in
relation to the main (right and left) speakers. So you enter a delay
for the center channel and for the surround channel (or channels
in 6.1- or 7.1-channel systems). To do this, compare the distance of
the group you are setting to the distance of the main speakers. If
the speakers are *farther* away, you typically set the delay to 0 milliseconds. If they are closer than the main speakers, you set the
delay using the following rule: 1 millisecond's delay for each foot.
In other words, if your main speakers are 9 feet from your listening
position, and your center channel is 7 feet away, set the delay for
2 milliseconds.

Adjusting the channel balance

Your A/V receiver will have a special Test Tone mode designed for
setting your channel balance. When you enter into this mode, the
receiver generates a series of tones (at an equal amplification level)
to each individual speaker in your system. The tone comes out of
only one speaker at a time, and shifts from speaker to speaker
(either automatically, or when you press a button on the remote
control). The goal of this test is for you to set the level of each individual speaker until you hear an equal volume from each speaker.

Using test discs

The home theater calibration discs we discuss elsewhere in this chapter — such as the AVIA disc — are for more than just adjusting the video settings on your display. They also have relatively robust and elaborate audio setup sections that can supplement the test tones built in to your receiver.

For example, in addition to test tones for setting channel balance, the AVIA disc has a test that lets you verify the phase of each of your speakers. Just follow the instructions on the screen, and you can see if you've accidentally wired one of your speakers with the negative and positive terminals crossed. You can even get into more advanced tests, such as checking for room interactions with your speakers (if you're working on tweaking your speakers' positioning in the room) and voice matching, which helps you decide if certain speakers work well together.

Even though this test tone starts off with an equal amplification level for each speaker, you may (and probably will) hear a different volume level on the first round of the test. That's because different speakers have different *sensitivities*. (We discuss sensitivity in Chapter 11; it's a measure of how loud a speaker plays with a given power input.) Even if you had five identical speakers in your home theater (with the same sensitivity), their distance from your seating position and their acoustic interactions with the room can affect the volume you hear at your listening position.

As you run through your receiver's test mode, you can adjust the volume level of each individual speaker. Most people can do a good — not great, but very good — job at this by using their ears alone. To get your channel balance really nailed down, consider purchasing an inexpensive sound level meter. You can get a good one for under $50 from Radio Shack (www.radioshack.com). With a meter in hand, you can get a really accurate channel balance setting. An even better approach is to mount the meter on a tripod at your seating position — that's how the pros do it.

The test tones are also a good check to make sure your speaker wires are hooked up to the right speaker terminals on the back of your receiver (or power amplifier if you're using separates). The receiver's display (or on-screen display) tells you what speaker you should be hearing each tone from. If the display says left surround and you hear a tone from your right surround, you know that you've made a mistake!

Dealing with old-fashioned stereo sources

Although most movies are designed for surround sound listening, music is generally recorded in stereo and mixed, edited, and produced for systems with two speakers. CDs, radio, cassette tapes, and LPs are all stereo recordings. In the audio-only realm, only DVD-Audio and SACD provide multichannel surround sound-ready recordings. Indeed, not all these recordings are multichannel, as many SACDs are stereo-only.

If you take a look around your home theater, you'll see that you have at least five speakers (not counting the subwoofer). What's the deal here?

Well, most A/V receivers let you select whether you want to listen to stereo recordings in stereo or *direct* mode (through the front left and right speakers), or in a surround mode (using all your speakers). Which you use really depends upon your preference. A/V receivers can use Dolby Pro Logic II or a custom surround mode (discussed later in this chapter) to artificially create surround effects for these stereo recordings.

We prefer playing back our CDs and other stereo sources in the stereo mode. It just seems more realistic to us. If you like the surround modes, feel free to use them. It's your theater, so use it the way that makes you happiest.

Most TV shows are broadcast in stereo, and many older movies on DVD or VHS are stereo as well. For movies and TV programming in stereo (not in Dolby Digital or DTS), we like to use Dolby Pro Logic II to create surround sound.

Playing with custom surround modes

As we discuss in Chapter 10, A/V receivers and controllers use devices called *DSPs* (digital signal processors) to decode surround sound signals. These DSPs are basically powerful computer chips that can do all sorts of neat manipulations of audio signals. They're designed to tweak signals, not crunch numbers like the computer chips in your PC.

Many receiver manufacturers — the majority of them, to be honest — have harnessed this computer horsepower to create *custom surround modes* (or DSP modes), which manipulate the audio signal and create artificial surround sound modes. These custom surround modes use computer-generated models to adjust the volume and delay of signals coming from the surround and center channels in order to reproduce different "venues." For example, some receivers have a mode that tries to recreate the ambience of a cathedral, by reproducing the delays and echoes you'd hear in a real cathedral.

Most audiophiles despise these custom surround modes, feeling that they are artificial and just get in the way of the music. We tend to agree, but again, this is an area in which we leave you to your own devices. Feel free to play around with these modes and see if you like them. We won't come to your house and turn them off if you like them.

Chapter 19

Customizing Your Home Theater Environment

*I*n earlier chapters, when we talk about creating an atmosphere in your home theater, the context is adding equipment to your home theater. Building off the discussion in Chapter 2 about where to put your home theater, this chapter delves into more detail about how to craft a home theater environment that exploits your high-tech devices.

If you are building a home from scratch or renovating an area for your home theater, you have lots of things to think about. But even if you are just sprucing up your living room or that room over the garage, this chapter has a few tips for you, too.

We want to warn you in advance that some of the topics in this chapter require pretty intense construction. You need to do more research online and consult with your manufacturers and contractor, if you have one, to determine your exact course of action. We give you some manufacturer's Web addresses as we discuss different options, and we point out good resources as we go along.

Soundproofing and Improving Acoustics

No matter how good your system, if you put it in an environment that is not geared towards good sound quality, even the best audio system is going to sound horrible. The room's construction, furnishings, and window and wall treatments have a massive impact on the quality of sound from your home theater.

Many of the rooms chosen for home theaters are substantially less than optimal from a sound perspective. Your biggest enemy is vibration. Just about everything — the walls, the ductwork, suspended light fixtures, the drop ceiling — can vibrate. When a subwoofer produces its strong low-frequency acoustic energy, that sound wave travels through the room, hitting walls and ceiling surfaces. It's absorbed by the walls, which vibrate in reaction to this energy. This vibration then is conducted through solid surfaces that it's in contact with, including studs, joists, and flooring. From there, it travels up through the framing of the house, and you end up with a shaking house, making a special noise of its own. That's where you need sound planning (pun intended).

You want to try to control two major types of sound distortions:

✔ Intrusive sounds from outside your home theater coming in (and to be fair, sounds from inside the home theater from seeping out into the house and keeping mom and dad awake until the end of the midnight movie)

✔ Sound reflections and refractions from the audio system itself

If you are building a new home from scratch or doing a renovation, you have the opportunity to address this at the architectural level. You essentially want to create a room within a room, so that you can isolate and control the impact of the sound system's signals on the room itself. Seek to isolate your inside walls, ceilings, and floors as much as possible from the rest of the house.

Placing studs, doubling drywall, and insulating for sound

You want to avoid having the studs of two adjacent walls from touching each other. By doing this, you cut off a primary means for sound to travel between the room and the house (in both directions). You can also dull vibrations by adding a second layer of drywall.

To further dampen any sounds, apply insulation inside the wall cavity. (If this is a concrete basement, you need to consider a vapor barrier as well to keep moisture out of your home theater.)

Applying soundproofing between studs and drywall

Consider adding a layer of soundproofing material between the studs and drywall. This serves not only to suppress sounds going back and forth, but also as a vibration trap between the drywall and the studs themselves — further reducing unintended effects from your sound system. For instance, Acoustiblok (`www.acoustiblok.com`) sells a very effective sound barrier that comes in rolls like tarpaper.

When applying soundproofing layers, keep it somewhat limp between the studs, because you want it to absorb the acoustic energy. Also, soundproofing materials are usually pretty heavy, so be sure to buy some prime steaks and beer before you ask your neighbors to help!

Applying soundproofing to the floor

Think about a *floating* floor, which is a multilayered floor designed to isolate your home theater from the rest of the house. For example, the top floating layer might consist of tongue-and-groove chipboard, bonded to a layer of plasterboard. That in turn would be laid on a spongy layer made of some sort of mineral fiber. You could then glue the spongy layer to the existing floor or even mount the whole thing on its own joists.

Applying a soundproofing system on the finished drywall

Adding specialized sound control panels to the walls can help control refracted and reflected sounds. When placed at your speakers' first reflection points (typically the sidewall boundaries and rear wall behind the main listening position), sound treatment panels reduce your reflected sound (this reflected sound can cause a blurring of the sound image and lack of intelligibility). Sound treatments also reduce the overall sound volume in the room, enhancing low-level dialogue and environmental effects delivered over today's high-quality audio systems.

A good way to find your speakers' first reflection point is to sit in your listening position and have one of your home theater-loving buddies move a mirror along the walls. When a speaker becomes visible in the mirror (from your perspective in your comfy theater seating), you've found the first reflection point.

The following companies offer products that can be used when soundproofing your walls:

- ✔ **Kinetics Noise Control (www.kineticsnoise.com):** Kinetics Noise Control offers a Home Theater Absorption Kit that contains special decorative panels. The midwall absorptive panels take care of sound reverberation, and the triangular corner panels are specifically engineered to absorb low-frequency bass sound that tends to gather in corners. This company also makes special spring mounts for suspending your ceiling (so it doesn't rattle) and other special items for dampening other sounds in your room.

- ✔ **Acoustic Sciences (www.acousticsciences.com):** Acoustic Sciences has a neat product called the Acoustical Soffit, which is a very discreet acoustic treatment that runs around the ceiling borders of your room. This architectural acoustic component is designed to control low-end bass responses, while also serving as an internal raceway to hide wiring, HVAC, and lighting. Pretty neat idea.

- ✔ **Acoustic Innovations (www.acousticinnovations.com):** When it comes to in-room treatments, there are many different approaches, and often your taste in decorations drives your selection. For instance, Acoustic Innovations has really nice solid hardwood frames in mahogany, cherry, walnut, and oak stains for its Maestro line of panels.

- ✔ **Additional resources:** Check out other offerings from companies such as: Auralex (www.auralex.com) and Owens Corning (www.owenscorning.com).

The cost of the materials for soundproofing a home theater fluctuate, depending on what you decide to do. You can spend a few hundred dollars, or upwards of $35,000. Over time, you'll probably at least add some of these interior sound treatments to deal with the sound in the room.

Remember that your cheapest first line of sound defense is simply securing everything that is around the room, and listening for things that add noise. Subwoofers can shake things up too much;

get some inexpensive isolation pads for the subwoofer's feet. Projectors make a ton of noise, too. Consider a special mounting for the projector that contains its noise, but remember not to block the fan and airflow, because it puts off a lot of heat, too.

In Chapter 2, we discuss having a central wiring hub and a media hub for your electronics. People often have a tendency to put these all in a place where they can show them off, but with that approach comes heat and noise (from cooling fans) that you must deal with. If you can put all the power amplifiers outside the room, there is less heat and noise to dissipate, which is something to think about in your plan.

Lightproofing and Enhancing Lighting

Lighting plays a crucial role in setting the right atmosphere for your home theater. A bright light in the wrong place or the wrong glare from an open window frame can be just as annoying as someone's cell phone going off in the middle of a show.

Most home theater planners agree that the video on your display looks best when the room lights are off (or significantly dimmed), the doors closed, and the shades drawn. This is where creative use of dimmers, motorized drapes, windows, and a lighting control system can become pivotal pieces of your home theater environs.

Choosing and customizing a lighting system

Wall-mounted dimmer switches allow you to control the intensity of an individual light or series of connected lights. In most instances, this is a simple and cheap way to change the ambiance, and you can do it with $5 and a trip to Home Depot.

If you want to have real fun, then think about moving to a complete lighting control system. For as little as $300, you can get into systems designed specifically for controlling your lights within one room (your home theater). From either a wall-mounted keypad, a remote control, or both, you can turn on/off, brighten, dim, or otherwise control each light fixture in the room.

If you choose a sophisticated lighting control system (we talk about a few in this section), you can actually program the system to do some pretty elaborate lighting tricks. For example, you might set up a Preshow mode that has lights on all over the room, maybe accentuating your bar area or the couches, if you have them. You could press a Preshow button on your lighting controls to activate that mode. Then you might have a Viewing mode that would dim the sconces, cut the overhead lights, initially highlight the front of the home theater, then fade, open the curtains in front of your home theater, and start the show. (These different lighting modes are known as *scenes*.) Way cool.

With not too much more effort, you can use remote controls like the ones we talk about in Chapter 14, and integrate your electronics further. So in Preshow mode, you can control the music, and in Viewing mode, you can control the projector or display. With a good system, the macros you can set up are limitless. With the macros, you can create new modes for whatever mood.

There are new construction and retrofit solutions for lighting control, depending on whether you are building from scratch or making a system fit into your existing space with existing wiring. Systems can communicate via X10, via proprietary wireline signaling, or wirelessly. (X10 in this case is a protocol, not a company.) You can get single-room systems from players such as Leviton, Lightolier Controls (www.lolcontrols.com), LiteTouch (www.home-touch.com), Lutron (www.lutron.com), Powerline Control Systems (www.pcslighting.com), Vantage (www.vantageinc.com), and X10 (the company — www.X10.com).

Lutron's $1,800 Home Theater Package is also designed for existing rooms where rewiring isn't practical. This package includes four dimmers, a tabletop master control, and an infrared receiver so that users can control lights from their favorite universal or learning IR transmitter. Lutron also has a higher-end system that sports RadioRA, a wireless, whole-home, lighting control system that uses radio frequency technology instead of power lines for signal communication.

Introducing X10

You'll run across X10 more and more. X10 is the dominant protocol for controlling (turning on and off and dimming) electrical devices, such as lights and appliances, through your home's electrical lines. Most people type www.X10.com in their Web browsers and find X10 Wireless Technologies, a company that caters to the consumer market. X10 is now an open standard, and other companies sell devices that use this protocol as well, including Leviton (www. leviton.com) and Stanley (www.stanleyworks.com). All standards-compatible products display an X10-compatible logo on their packaging or on the product itself. When you see this logo, you know that the product works with other X10 products regardless of the manufacturer.

There are a couple of form factors for X10, the two most applicable to home theaters being wall outlet modules and dimmer switches. *X10 modules* are devices that receive and translate X10 signals to turn on and off individual lights, appliances, or other electrical devices. An X10 wall module is a small, box-shaped device that's no bigger than the AC plug-in transformers that power many home appliances, such as telephones and answering machines.

Setting up an X10 module is pretty easy. The module has a standard electrical plug on the back and a place to plug in your lamp or other device on the front or bottom. You place the device that you want to control in the On mode (for example, turn on the light switch), and then the X10 module turns the device off and on and dims as appropriate. *X10 dimmer switches* replace your normal switch and are likewise controlled via the X10 signals over your electrical lines, or manually by you at the switch.

To work in a home, X10 doesn't require specific network architecture other than your existing electrical system. X10 sends its control signals from the controller over your power lines to every outlet in the house. The controller can have remote control or PC interfaces. Figure 19-1 shows a limited X10 network.

X10 (the company) has many cheap, easy-to-install, X10-protocol-driven lighting controls. Its $19.99 UltimateREMOTE Home Control Kit entry-level package includes a radio remote control, a transceiver control module (takes radio frequency commands from X10 remote controls and converts them to X10 signals carried over household wiring), and a lamp module. You can get extra lamp modules, dimmer switches, and other additional lighting controls for around $10 to $30 each, as well as other automated home controls for heating, remote monitoring, and other applications. X10.com is a great site with lots of reasonably priced products for lots of applications (just learn to ignore the pop-up ads!).

A great resource for ideas about lighting control systems — and your home theater in general — is the magazine *Electronic House* (www.electronichouse.com). It's inexpensive, available on newsstands, and has helpful hints about how to approach your projects from lots of different angles (including lots of home-theater-specific articles). You can also find more X10-based devices at www.smart home.com.

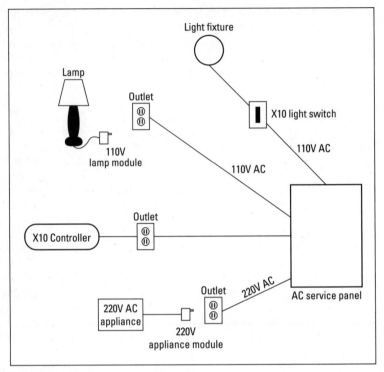

Figure 19-1: Plugging into an X10 network.

Controlling Your Home Theater Environment Remotely

Many lighting control systems can interface with or drive whole-home automation capabilities. Although whole-home automation is beyond the scope of this book (Dare we say it? Why not? Read our *Smart Homes For Dummies* book for a whole-home approach.), you can get whole-room automation with many systems.

Many of the better remote controls we discuss in Chapter 14 support home automation commands, including X10-based controls. And you can find that some manufacturers offer complementary products that work off the same remotes. For instance, Lutron's Sivoia (www.lutron.com/sivoia) motorized shade and drapery system is integrated with the firm's GRAFIK Eye, RadioRA, and HomeWorks lighting and home control systems. Each new control

Hidden advantages of lighting control systems

Although having a lighting control system for your home theater makes sense, expanding it to other parts of your home makes even more sense. In addition to setting the mood in your home theater, a lighting control system

✓ **Saves money on electricity bills:** Want to turn off all your lights at night and enter Sleeping mode? One button can do that, no matter the condition (on/off) of the lights at that time.

✓ **Adds security:** Automatically illuminating dark halls or that creepy space by the garage at night not only adds to peace of mind, but also reduces the likelihood of problems.

✓ **Supports your lifestyle:** Whether it's really making sure your kids' lights are out at 9:30, or automatically turning on your lights when you drive in the garage, a lighting control system can help support the way you use your home.

If you want to find out more about extending your lighting control system to the rest of your house, check out *Smart Homes For Dummies,* which we also wrote.

offers Open, Close, Raise, and Lower buttons, along with three programmable, preset stop locations for shades or draperies. With this, you can control the dimming of the lights and opening of the drapes, just like in a real theater.

Closing the drapes without leaving the couch

Motorized shade/drape kits are simple to install and can add a professional touch to your home theater. You can get electronic drapery kits that open and close on your command. If you have ever installed a drapery rod, a kit is basically the same thing with a motor.

For instance, the Makita Motorized Drape System (www.smarthome.com) is a self-contained system for your home theater drapes. You can get a single drape system or a double drape. You screw in the tracks, mount the drapes, and plug it in. You can customize the length merely by cutting the tracking. Pretty simple.

You can also get motorized window-treatment hardware from manufacturers such as BTX (www.btxinc.com), Hunter Douglas
(www.hunterdouglas.com), Lutron (www.lutron.com/sivoia),
and Somfy (www.somfysystems.com).

Turning up the heat from the comfort of your recliner

Automation isn't just lights and drapes. You can monitor and control temperature settings as well. Don't forget that you need to
maintain the temperature for all those electronic components per
manufacturer specs — usually above 55 degrees Fahrenheit at a
minimum. If your theater is located in a part of the house where
you might have to warm it up or cool it off in advance, then consider integrating the heating system in your home theater room
into your controller system, too.

Again, without getting waist deep in detail, you can get X10-
controlled heating and air conditioning modules that interface
with your environmental controls to 1) make sure they stay within
a specified range and 2) allow you remote control in case you want
to prep your theater.

Many of the firms mentioned for lighting control systems also have
similar systems for heating and air cooling. These systems are usually tack-on modules to their other systems and can cost as little as
$30 to $50. A really decent bidirectional X10 thermostat will probably run you $200. Check out www.smarthome.com and www.X10.com
for some good options. Again, whole-home options cost considerably more, because you start getting into multiple zones and probably several interface formats. But for your home theater, the ability
to preset your environmental controls from remote locations won't
cost much.

Getting Comfy

Finally, getting comfortable in your home theater means different
things to different people. To Danny's wife, it probably means
having about 20 large pillows from Pier One Imports lying around
the floor. To Pat's wife, it would mean having theater seats wide
enough for Opie the beagle to sit next to her (with some beagle-
proof fabric covering them).

Oh starry, starry night . . .

Fiber optics can add a really neat effect to any home theater. Here are some ideas, suggested by Acoustic Innovations (www.acousticinnovations.com):

✔ **Starlight fiber-optic ceilings:** To make your ceiling look like a nighttime sky, you can have fiber-optic ceiling panels applied to your existing ceiling. The panels not only make your ceiling more fun, but offer acoustical correction as well. However, you might find yourself spreading out a blanket on your home theater floor to watch the ceiling!

✔ **Infinite starfield panels:** What a better accompaniment to your *Pink Floyd Dark Side of the Moon* midnight show than an infinite starfield in your home theater. These are made of multiple polycarbonate mirrors and fiber optic lighting and create an illusion of infinite depth. (Not suggested for theater ceilings.)

✔ **Fiber-optic carpeting:** This carpet is filled with tiny points of light (50 fiber-optic points per square foot, to be precise).

✔ **Fiber-optic curtains:** These classic, velvety curtains can twinkle, too. Très chic.

All illuminators come complete with a remote locatable dimmer, speed control for twinkle, and an on/off switch. You even get to choose between a twinkle or color change wheel. Decisions, decisions.

Lucky for you, there are many options for home theater seating comfort: chairs, couches, and lounges; seating that's motorized or manual; some with storage and control compartments, some with speakers included . . . the list goes on.

You're probably looking at around $300 and up per seat for specialty theater seating, and seats can quickly get into the $2,000–$3,000 range if you start piling on the extras. You can really sink money into your seats.

Some things to keep in mind, no matter what you buy:

✔ **Sound implications:** You'll set up your sound system roughly so that no matter where you sit in your theater, you hopefully have a similar (breathtaking) aural experience. Three couches in a U-shaped configuration may sound right for you, but make sure that your speaker configuration is designed to handle it. You may need some additional speakers or different capability to support weird configurations. Seating configuration and speaker configuration simply go hand-in-hand.

Going Hollywood all the way

For those of you who want to really go all the way with the theater theme, you can buy all sorts of add-ons to create that atmosphere:

✔ **Personalized home theater intro:** Open up each showing with your own customized one minute video, just like in the theaters (your DVD player must be able to play DVD-R). For $200 or so from www.htmarket.com, you can personalize one of five home theater intros, from an awards night theme to a classic popcorn theme. How fun is that!

✔ **Specialty rugs:** You can get rugs festooned with stars, film reels, popcorn, and so on. The cost is about $50 per square yard on average (but there's a huge range).

✔ **Posts and ropes:** If you wanted that velour rope and stainless steel post look, you've got it. Expect to spend around $300 a post and $100 a rope. Maybe there is some poetic justice about making your boss wait in line at your home theater! Pat's going to buy a set of these the next time Danny is in town.

✔ **Popcorn machines:** Complete with the swing down popping bucket, these $700 to $900 machines will give you freshly popped popcorn and that movie theater smell. Check out www.popcornpopper.com for some cool models.

✔ **Wall sconces:** You can get cool theater lighting that will give you that interior decorated look, on a budget (about $200 to $250 a piece).

✔ **Film posters:** Decorate the outside of your theater with current and past movie posters, just like you see waiting in line to get your tickets. These run about $10 to $20 for current films, in their usual 27-x-40-inch formats. Check out www.allposters.com for new ones, or vintage ones at places such as www.moviemarket.com.

✔ **Sound Edgelits:** Add some of these table-top back-lit signs to let your viewers know which sound systems you have in your theater. These $225 signs sport Dolby Digital, THX, DTS, and other surround sound logos.

You can find these and more at places like www.hometheaterdecor.com and www.htmarket.com.

✔ **Visual implications:** Although high-backed theater chairs may look good in the showroom, they can block your rear surround sound speakers. If you want multiple rows, these high-backed seats may necessitate a tiered floor (so back row viewers see the screen, not the back of a chair).

✔ **Food:** Well, the "You can't take food into the living room" rule does not go over well with a viewing population trained on eating popcorn while they watch the movies. So you need to consider how you will handle food. You may want built-in trays or drink holders, or nothing. Maybe you need tables between chairs instead. All we ask is that you think about how you'll handle food when you are buying the furniture and rugs. No sense setting yourself up for yelling at the kids later.

You need to think about seating more than some other aspects of your home theater, because many people are used to viewing movies in bed, on couches, on the floor, and so on. You really need to think through how you define comfortable, and then design toward that.

Chapter 20

Moving Up to the High End

· ·

In This Chapter

▶ Defining *high end*

▶ Checking out integrated systems

▶ Doubling your lines

▶ Getting into scalers and interpolators

· ·

*T*here's a somewhat indefinable concept that we talk about throughout *Home Theater For Dummies* — the idea that you can move up to the high end when you're buying components and setting up a home theater. Everyone's got his or her own definition of *high end,* but for us, it means equipment that is designed to offer the ultimate reproduction of music and movies.

In this chapter, we introduce some really awesome high-end systems. The systems' designers are so single-minded in their pursuit of musical and video fidelity that they've created their own proprietary systems that they feel do a better job than standard mix-and-match components. When we say a system is *proprietary,* we mean that it is designed to work best (or in some cases only) with other components from the same vendor. So if you buy part of your home theater from one of these vendors, you'll probably end up buying all of it from them — at least on the audio side. These systems usually work with any display. When you buy a proprietary system, you are in effect taking a bet on this company's ability to do things better than the industry in general does — and its ability to stay in business and support you in the future.

Later in this chapter, we also talk about some of the *video processing* systems that let your top-of-the-line display really look as good as (or better than!) the movies you see in the theater.

Introducing High-End Home Theater

In the introduction to this chapter, we already started to define what we think high-end theater is. Just to recap, our definition of *high end* starts and ends with the philosophy of the designers and engineers who create the product (which can be speakers, a display, an A/V controller or power amplifier, or even an A/V receiver, though high-end systems usually go with separates).

See, anybody designing a piece of consumer electronics equipment has to balance a lot of different (and often conflicting) requirements: price, aesthetic considerations, size, performance, interoperability with other gear, and so on. High-end gear skews this very delicate balance toward the performance side of the equation, and as a result, the high-end components can be much more expensive, big, proprietary, and even ugly.

A few years back, there was a bit of a geographic divide (or at least, a perceived divide) between high-end and mass market A/V components. High-end vendors were located in the United States, Canada, and Europe, while big consumer electronics companies based in Asia were focused on high-volume, middle market products. We're not convinced that this perception was ever correct, but we're sure that it's not true today. Although many high-end manufacturers are indeed based in the "traditional" places, you can find some really awesome (and expensive) gear coming from those big Asian companies. Just because a company sells a ton of $299 A/V receivers doesn't mean that it can't build a great $3,000 receiver. So throw any perceptions of brand bias out the door, because you may be surprised by who's got the great selling products these days.

Separating Your Amps

Within the audio realm of the home theater domain, the most common step for manufacturers moving up to higher-quality products is to move from the all-in-one A/V receiver into separates. We talk a little bit about separates in Chapter 10, but in this chapter, we get a bit more detailed.

Basically, separate components take the many functions of an A/V receiver and divide them among several separate components. Doing this has two major benefits: greater flexibility and better performance.

A/V receivers are really pretty darned good these days, and there is such a thing as a high-end A/V receiver. These receivers (from companies such as Denon, Yamaha, and Marantz, to name just a few) compete performance-wise with most separates systems in their price range.

The functions of an A/V receiver are usually doled out to the following components:

✔ **A/V controller:** This device handles all the surround sound decoding and digital-to-analog conversions. It also switches audio and video (from source devices to the amplifiers or display) and performs the *preamplifier* functions (adjusting the power level of audio signals going to the amplifiers, to adjust the listening volume). A few A/V controllers include a built-in radio tuner, making them essentially A/V receivers without built-in power amplifiers.

Depending upon who's talking, you might hear these devices referred to as *surround sound processors, home theater pre-amps,* or something else entirely. If they decode the surround sound signals and switch between audio and video sources, they're an A/V controller.

✔ **Power amplifier:** These devices boost the power of analog audio signals coming out of the controller, in order to drive the speakers and create sound. As we just mentioned, you don't control volume with the power amplifier (the A/V controller does that). Basically, a power amplifier is a big box with an on/off switch, speaker terminals, and one or more RCA jack audio inputs on the back for connecting to the A/V controller. Most home theater power amplifiers are *multichannel* amplifiers, meaning they have five or more built-in amplifiers for powering all your surround sound speakers. Some systems are designed around *mono* power amplifiers, where you have an individual amplifier for *each* channel in the system. (You can also find 2- or 3-channel amplifiers to mix and match into a 5- or more channel system.)

✔ **Radio tuner:** We discuss these in Chapter 5. Just remember that the majority of A/V controllers don't have a built-in tuner, so if you want to listen to the radio, you need to buy a separate tuner. If you have digital cable or a DSS satellite dish, you might get around this requirement if you can receive radio stations through these systems (and like the channel line-ups they offer).

Connecting a separates system is really only minimally different from the process of hooking up a home theater that's based on an A/V receiver. Just as you do with an A/V receiver, you want to route all your source components through the A/V controller. All your analog audio, digital audio, and video connections connect directly from the source device to the A/V controller. (The only exception to this rule is this: If you don't have enough or the right kind of video inputs on your A/V controller — specifically if your controller doesn't have component video switching — you might connect the video cables from some of your components directly to the display.)

Your powered (active) subwoofer connects directly to the A/V controller, just as it connects to your A/V receiver. The rest of your speakers, however, are connected differently. You use an audio interconnect cable for each channel of your 5.1, 6.1, or 7.1 surround sound system, and route this signal from a set of Power Amplifier Out connections on the back of your controller to the appropriate Preamp In connections on the back of your power amplifier (or amplifiers).

Moving into Integrated Systems

One way that many high-end vendors create their high-performance systems is to create their own integrated ways of doing home theater. Some of these systems use proprietary connection systems (their own special cables) to link components, whereas others use standard connectors and cables but have components that are specially designed to work together.

These systems are basically the steroid-enhanced siblings of the inexpensive home-theater-in-a-box systems we discuss in Chapter 2. You buy a complete system from a single manufacturer, rather than picking and choosing between components from different vendors. It's a high-end, soup-to-nuts approach; the power amplifiers, A/V controllers, DVD and CD players, and speakers — everything but the display itself, in most cases — come as one integrated package from one company.

In the sections that follow, we talk about a few companies who have some of the leading integrated systems. These aren't the only manufacturers who build these kinds of systems, just a sampling.

Linn

Linn is a Scottish company (www.linn.co.uk) that's always done things its own way. For example, well after the introduction (and mass market success) of the CD, Linn plugged away with new and improved versions of its famous Sondeck turntable — while many other famous turntable manufacturers switched focus or went out of business. (Don't worry, Linn also makes a ton of digital gear these days.)

So you won't be surprised to find out that Linn has taken its own road with home theater audio products, too. Linn's AV 51 (which goes for somewhere around $30,000 depending upon what options you choose) includes Linn's AV 5100 series speakers and subwoofer, the AV 5101 Personal Controller remote control system, the AV 5103 System Controller (the A/V controller), and the AV 5125 multichannel power amplifier. You can add in a Linn DVD player, a Linn CD player, one of those awesome Linn turntables (can you tell Pat wants one badly?), and mix in your own video display unit. All these pieces and parts are designed to work transparently and seamlessly together.

In addition to the great sound, the AV 51 gives you an upgradeable system — just like you can upgrade a PC with new cards and software. You also get a dealer installation (you ought to for this much money), so you walk away with a fully set up system and a smaller bank balance.

Meridian

Meridian (www.meridian-audio.com) offers some of the coolest, highest-end A/V equipment available anywhere. One Meridian feature that we think really reflects the future of A/V gear is the computer-like construction. Meridian systems are even more modular and upgradeable than the Linn system we just mentioned. So if your current Meridian processor, for example, doesn't support a new surround sound format, you can simply have your dealer pop in a new card.

Meridian's products are known for being some of the finest in terms of dealing with digital audio signals (no surprise given its expertise in the field), and Meridian does a couple of things differently than most other A/V component vendors:

> ✔ **Smart Link:** Meridian has an all-digital connection called Smart Link for carrying DVD-Audio signals to the controller. In Meridian's own words (and we believe what they're saying), Smart Link allows "the full resolution of multichannel audio from DVD-A recordings [to] be losslessly transferred in the digital domain from player to surround controller to loudspeaker." That's a mouthful, but it means that digital audio signals remain digital until the very final link in the audio chain — the speakers. Meridian can do this because of Smart Link, and also because of the item we discuss next.

✔ **DSP loudspeakers:** Meridian builds active loudspeaker systems designed to connect and integrate with its lineup of CD/DVD players and A/V controllers. Like all active speakers, these have built-in power amplifiers, so you don't need a separate amp. The difference comes with the DSP that gives them their name. This digital signal processor allows Meridian to send fully digital audio signals to the speakers. So the digital chain is broken only when the speakers themselves convert this signal to analog internally. You benefit from a clean, interference-resistant digital connection. Additionally, the DSP speakers do all the things that normal loudspeakers do (such as *crossovers* that send different frequencies to different drivers within the speaker) entirely in the digital domain. There's even a separate amplifier within the DSP speakers for each individual driver.

All this modularity, flexibility, and digital audio goodness doesn't come cheap. Meridian's flagship speakers, the DSP8000, cost $40,000 a *pair.* They're not for the faint of heart or the shallow walleted. But the sound is simply awesome.

We're not telling you about $20,000-a-piece loudspeakers to make you feel bad if you can't afford them (we can't either, to be honest, at least not without second mortgages and angry wives). But these kinds of systems give you a feel for what's possible in home theater. And the technologies featured in these systems will eventually, in the words of Ronald Reagan, "trickle down" to more affordable gear. We certainly can't wait for DSP-based active loudspeakers and modular, upgradeable components to hit the Crutchfield catalog instead of the super-expensive boutique audio stores.

Exploring High-End Video Systems

It's not just the audio part of home theater that fits into the high-end category. If you've read earlier parts of the book (particularly the discussions of front-projection display systems in Chapter 13), you already know that high-end video systems (such as the $60,000 CRT projectors we keep mentioning) are out there on the market, waiting to be gobbled up by well-to-do home theater enthusiasts. If you want to go high-end with front projection, look for units from Faroudja (www.faroudja.com) or Silicon Imaging (www.silicon imaging.com).

In this section, we talk about a group of high-end devices called *video processors* that complement these displays (particularly projection systems) in many home theaters.

Improving resolution

If you go for a front- or rear-projection system or the biggest plasma display, you get a really big picture in a home theater. The problem is, the picture is so big that you begin to see the line structure of analog NTSC television broadcasts (and other low-resolution sources, such as VHS VCR tapes). These sources just don't have too much resolution, and you end up in a situation where a picture that looks okay on a 20-inch TV in the bedroom looks like a disaster on your fancy projection TV. Simply put, the 230 horizontal lines that make up a VHS picture will be so far apart on a big screen display that you can see them (and the black lines between them) without sticking your face up next to the screen. To say the least, this is an annoying situation.

To get around this, many high-end projectors (and other displays as well) make use of a device known as a *line doubler.* A line doubler, in its simplest form, takes the two fields that make up a frame in an interlaced video system and combines them. (We discuss frames and fields in Chapter 4, if you're not sure what we're talking about here.) These newly reconstructed frames are then sent to the display twice in a row, until the next pair of images comes along (⅟₃₀ of a second after the first). For example, with NTSC broadcast TV signals, the 480 interlaced scan lines of the broadcast come out of the line doubler (and head into your display) as 480 progressive scan lines. This makes for a much smoother image and helps hide those visible scan lines, because twice as many are displayed at a time.

To take advantage of a line doubler, your display must be able to handle progressive scan video. Look for displays with scan rates of 31.5 kHz or higher (we discuss scan rates in Chapter 12). Most HDTV-ready or progressive scan displays already have an internal line doubler built in. As you start moving into really high-end home theater installations, many experts like to bypass these by using a top-of-the-line external line doubler (or more likely, one of the devices we discuss in the next section).

Investigating top-of-the-line video processors

Some video processors do more than just double the lines of resolution. For example, *line quadruplers* that are on the market (as the name implies) quadruple the number of scan lines being sent to the display. These systems don't wait for four fields to come in and then repeat them four times (which is what you might think they do, given how line doublers work). Instead, line quadruplers do some math and *interpolate* what might come between a pair of lines (because there's no actual picture data for the new extra lines, the quadrupler uses various mathematical models to guess what might be there). For NTSC analog video signals, a quadrupler gives an output of 960 progressive scan lines (in other words, it doubles the 480i output to 480p, and then doubles that again). You need a display that can handle a scan rate four times as fast as the standard NTSC scan rate (which is about 15.7 kHz). So your display needs to be able to handle a 63 kHz scan rate.

The most advanced video processors available (usually called *image scalers*) can convert an incoming video signal to a cus-tomized scan rate — a rate that is most suitable for a particular projector or other display. In other words, these particular video processors don't do a simple doubling or quadrupling of a signal. For example, many CRT projectors can't handle the 63 kHz scan rate of a line quadrupler, so the image scaler creates a signal some-where between the 31.5 kHz of a doubler and 63 kHz.

Most image scalers also contain circuitry to perform *3:2 pulldown,* the process of removing artifacts found in video when a 24-frame-per-second video is converted to a 30-frame-per-second video (we discuss this in detail in Chapter 4). This feature is also found in many DVD players and a number of displays, but standalone image scalers often have superior systems for this process.

Some image scalers have modes specifically for fixed-pixel displays, such as DLP or LCD projectors and plasma flat-panel displays. Instead of a scan rate or a number of lines of resolution, fixed-pixel displays need a video signal that contains a certain number of hori-zontal and vertical pixels. For example, if you have a DLP-based projection system using Texas Instruments HD-2 chip (which has a resolution of 1280 x 720 pixels), you want a scaler that can output a 1280 x 720 video signal.

All the fixed-pixel displays on the market have their own internal scalers that can perform this image scaling. Many home theater enthusiasts (at least those who are spending $10,000 or more on a display) bypass these internal scalers and use an external image scaler that they feel does a better job of interpolating and creating video signals.

Relating scaled images and HDTV

You may have noticed that some video processors can output video at resolutions that would qualify as HDTV resolutions (720p or higher). So the question may have entered your mind, "What's the relationship between scaled images and HDTV?" Well, to begin with, we'll say that a scaled image (no matter how high the resolution and how good the system that created it) is not high definition. After a lower-resolution video signal is run through a high-quality scaler, the signal can look great — spectacular even. But no interpolation system (which is what all scalers are, in essence) can put information back into a video signal that was never there. Scalers can come close, but they can't match the real thing.

Having said that, we want to hasten to add that scalers make great companions to HDTVs and HDTV-ready displays. For this reason, the majority of HDTV displays on the market already have some sort of built-in internal scaler, which *upconverts* lower-resolution video sources to an HDTV resolution. External image scalers can often improve upon these internal systems and make everything you watch on your HDTV look better.

Using High-End Controls

One of the most common things folks add to a home theater is a high-end control system for providing local and remote control of your audio and video masterpiece. You can get a complete system that provides this control, and such systems are most often focused on whole-home control.

Crestron (www.crestron.com) is a well-known company in this space. Crestron doesn't make DVD players, A/V receivers, or projection displays, but their products (along with those of a company called AMX, www.amx.com) can be found in many high-end home theaters. Crestron offers a whole lot more than the remote controls we mention in Chapter 14. In a nutshell, Crestron builds whole-home control systems that use LCD touchpads to control just about any electrically operated device in a home. A Crestron system can raise or lower your drapes, dim your lights, adjust your HVAC (heating, ventilation, and air conditioning) system, *and* control all the devices in your home theater. And this list is by no means exhaustive. There's really not much you can't do with a complete Crestron system.

Specifically for home theater, Crestron makes several models of home theater control systems that incorporate wired or wireless touch pads and centralized controllers (not A/V controllers, despite the name). These pads and controllers interface with the IR or RS-232 ports on your A/V gear. Crestron's computer-like devices have enough intelligence that you can easily have them programmed to perform complex *macros* (or sequences of control actions). So with only a single tap of a virtual button, you can set into motion all the things you might do manually when turning on your home theater's systems and getting ready to watch a movie.

Crestron sells literally hundreds of components designed to control a home theater (and a home!), and we won't even try to run through them all here. This isn't off-the-shelf, DIY type stuff. You need to go through a Crestron dealer (many high-end home theater installers also install Crestron) to have a system designed for, and installed in, your home theater. All this automated goodness doesn't come cheap. The typical Crestron installation is over $50,000, and that *doesn't* count the home theater components themselves.

Part VI

The Part of Tens

The 5th Wave   By Rich Tennant

In this part . . .

Top-ten lists abound here! Look in this part of the book for our top-ten lists on all sorts of home theater topics. We start with tips and tricks about how to figure out if your present gear can fit into your home theater plans. We're sure some of it can.

Then, we discuss ways to accessorize your home theater with fun add-ons, like a theater-style popcorn popper without the $6 price tag per bag!

We also delve into the myriad ways that you can get more out of your home theater — by using it by the pool, in your car, in your backyard, and even in your own drive-in theater. Check out ten ways you can mount, store, hang, and otherwise set up your home theater gear around your house.

Then, find out where to go for more information — those extra special places where you can go to track down more ideas for your home theater experience.

Are you having fun yet? We are!

Chapter 21

Ten Accessories for Your Home Theater

Depending on where you put your home theater, you can envision adding all sorts of extras to flesh out your home operation. But in our minds, there are some things you've gotta have. We tried to list those here, so that you have a checklist next time you're online or at that home theater store.

Video Calibration Disc

Calibrating and setting up your video system is *so important* that we hesitate to even list this as an accessory. But unfortunately, lots of people think a video calibration disc is something you can get away without — or at least that it's a low priority. So we are making video calibration discs our *numero uno* accessory.

We talk about the subject of tweaking your video system rather extensively in Chapter 19, so we don't go over all the details again here. But we *will* say that if you just leave your TV or monitor in its factory state and with its factory settings, you're missing out on the best picture you can get — often by a large margin. And there's no easier way to dial in the settings on your video display than to use a calibration DVD, such as the AVIA Guide to Home Theater (www.ovationsw.com).

So get one for yourself, get one for your friends, and calibrate away.

Wireless Headphones

Ever want to use the home theater when your spouse, significant other, or roommate is asleep, working, or performing brain surgery in the other room? Ever get told to *"Turn it down,"* in no uncertain terms? Well maybe you need that marriage/friendship-saving device, the wireless headphone.

You can find some really cool models of headphones out there. Some will cancel out ambient noise (so the kids can scream and smash things and you won't hear a thing), others use some special digital signal processing to recreate 5.1-channel Dolby Digital surround sound. Some fit in your ear canals, and some totally cover your ear with a huge "can." Whatever you like, you can find it in the headphone world.

We love wireless headphones because they enable you to get more popcorn or let the dog out without catching a long cord on something and wreaking havoc. So wireless headsets, which use radio waves to connect to a base station plugged into the home theater receiver (like a cordless phone uses radio waves to connect to the phone base station plugged into a phone jack), are the way to go for us.

One of the cooler wireless headsets we've seen comes from Acoustic Research (the loudspeaker company, www. acoustic-research.com). They have a model (the AW791) that retails for about $200 and connects to your DVD player or other surround sound source using a standard optical or coaxial digital cable. It can also connect to stereo sources using RCA jacks, which can be handy if you don't have a headphone jack on your gear. This model gives you well-simulated Dolby Digital surround sound in your headphones. (See Chapter 11 for more about headphones.)

Dolby has a new capability called Dolby Headphone (www.dolby. com/dolbyheadphone) that can take up to five channels of audio from any source and make it sound like it's coming from that many speakers in a real listening room. The difference relative to stereo headphones is amazing. Look for the Dolby Headphone logo on the box.

Improving Your Game Console Connection

If you read Chapter 15, we discuss interconnect cables — the short run cables that hook A/V components together. Hopefully we convinced you of the importance of the hierarchy of these cables and of using the best cable you can in all situations. (In the video world, component is best, S-video is a close second, composite video lags way behind, and RF coax connections are back on the bench trying to get the coach to let them in the game.)

When it comes to game consoles, however, we do find that many people just use whatever cable came in the box. As Jeremy Piven says in that VHS masterpiece *PCU,* "Don't be that guy." (If you missed *PCU,* the whole line is: "You're wearing the shirt of the band you're going to see? Don't be that guy." Oh yeah, and we said VHS; the movie never even made DVD.) If you stick with the simple, composite video cable that comes in the box with the console, you strangle the gorgeous (and possibly hi-def) picture your system is capable of putting out. Use an S-Video cable or, if your TV can handle it, a set of component video cables. And let your games give your eyeballs a treat.

DVD Recorder

We discuss DVD recorders a bit in Chapter 6, but for most people, DVD recorders aren't quite in the mainstream. The main reason for this is a jumble of confusing (and noninteroperable) DVD recording standards on the market — DVD-R/RW, DVD-RAM, DVD+R/RW, and so on. Ugh, we know, and we wish these consumer electronics companies would cooperate once in a while, for the sake of their customers.

Despite this ugliness in the marketplace, we still think DVD recorders can be a pretty neat accessory to your home theater. PVRs — hard drive-based personal video recorders such as ReplayTV — are cool but eventually you run out of hard drive space. Some pretty cool DVD recorder/PVR combos hit the market as we write (early 2003), and unlike the PVRs, these combo devices (such as Panasonic's DMR-HS2) can record your shows on the hard drive or on a DVD. The combos give you the ability to archive old shows that you want to keep so that you can free up hard drive space for the new ones you haven't seen yet. Now that's convenient. Top this all off by transferring all those home movies to DVD, and you've got a winner.

Power Conditioner

Close your eyes and think about your electrical power lines. No really. Imagine a current flowing (or alternating) from Homer Simpson's nuclear power plant, over the high voltage lines of Springfield, across hill and dale, and finally ending up in a transformer on a pole outside your home. Think about all the other junk attached to that electrical power grid. Even within your home, tons of different electrical devices are connected to your power lines. All this stuff adds its own little bit of degradation to the nice clean, pretty, sine-wavy AC coming out of those turbogenerators at the power plant. End result: power at your home theater's outlets that may be of an incorrect voltage or that may be full of electrical noise that keeps all your A/V components from being their best.

At a bare minimum, you need (absolutely need) some surge protection in your home theater. But even with surge protection, you still may have issues. For example, if your voltage drops (not an uncommon occurrence), it may actually lower the output of your amplifier. You can also run into ground issues that cause hums in your audio and lines on your video display. So you might want to consider investing in a power conditioner that improves and stabilizes your AC power. For example, Monster Cable has some really cool (and cool looking) Home Theater Power Centers that provide surge protection, voltage stabilization, and noise filtering. The more expensive ones even have a cool, digital voltmeter readout on the front. Check them out at www.monstercable.com/power.

Shake It Up, Baby! (With Transducers)

If you are like us (and we feel that you are if you've read most of this book), then you like to get totally into what you're watching. After all, a home theater is supposed to help suspend disbelief.

With audio transducers from companies such as Clark Synthesis (www.clarksynthesis.com), you can get one giant, T-Rex step closer to the ultimate goal of suspending disbelief! You'll see these called many things — *bass shakers, tactile transducers,* or as one vendor calls them, *butt kickers.* They add an element that goes well beyond the sensation of a subwoofer and help to change your whole theater into a sensaround environment (remember *Earthquake* in the theaters?). The units are screwed onto the bottom of your furniture or into the frames of your floorboards.

These transducers are more friendly to the rest of the house than cranking up massive subwoofers that can seem to shake the whole neighborhood. Because the low end of the sound is effectively isolated to a more specific area, namely the couch or chairs, transducers virtually eliminate any bleeding of this sound into adjoining rooms or connected housing units.

Transducers are also great for houses that are built on concrete slabs. Unlike wood subfloors, concrete slab doesn't conduct bass well.

The sky is the limit with transducers. You can get low budget ones (such as Aura Bass Shakers for $100, www.aurasound.com) that do a fairly good job. If you want more power and precision, check out the Clark Synthesis models, which can run from $200 to $500 depending on the model (www.smarthome.com), or the Buttkicker from The Guitammer Company, Inc. (www.guitammer.com). The difference is astounding and noticeable. One thing to note: Some products support frequencies up to 200 Hz, and some go even higher (up to 800 Hz). We prefer keeping it low, say between 5 Hz and 200 Hz; otherwise, you find there is a constant background rumble that gets nauseating after a while. Keep the effect directed and precise — you'll like it better. To control the frequency sent to your transducer, consider an equalizer like Audio Source EQ, which runs about $120.

Consider using more than one; try, say, three across the bottom of your couch. The middle transducer would acquire its signal from the LFE/subwoofer out of the processor-receiver and the two side ones would derive their signal from the left and right front channels, respectively. With this setup, you can get a better sense of the action in three dimensions. If you are watching *U571,* for instance, when a depth charge goes off to the right of the submarine, you get a sensation from the right channel, and when the lower part of the compression from the bomb and water splash enters into the soundtrack, you feel the sub channel and right channel together.

 If you mount transducers directly to your furniture, you can get rubberized molded mounts for your chair or couch legs that isolate the noise and vibration to your furniture.

If you install more than one of these transducers, you probably would do well to power each unit with its own amp. Read the manufacturer's recommendations closely. For some of the cheaper models, powering them with anything over a 20-watt amplifier is probably not a good idea. Some of the fancier models call for an amplifier of at least 100 watts. You can find transducers that come bundled with an amplifier (active transducers); consider getting one of these if you have questions. In any case, the amp should have its own volume control so that you can tune the effect relative to the audio level. The hi-fi quality of the amp is not critical, so you can use relatively inexpensive amplifiers.

You can get shaker units that attach to the floor boards of your house and can shake the whole room. There are pros and cons to this. On the pro side, you don't have to worry about being on a particular piece of furniture in order to get the effect. On the other hand, you are shaking your foundation of your house (never really a good thing), and the vibrations can bleed into other areas of your house. So, before you experiment with your foundation, think about what surrounding rooms will be affected.

Motion Simulators

If moving with a movie is really your thing, and you've got a fairly open budget, then check out the Odyssee motion simulators from D-Box (www.d-box.com). Unlike bass shakers, which provide only vibration or "shaking" in response to the audio track and are in reality merely transducers that vibrate rather than move air, Odyssee is a sophisticated motion simulation system that lifts seating and occupants on an X-Y-Z axis (pitch, roll, and yaw) at up to 2Gs (think F-14 at full throttle) of acceleration.

Odyssee provides dramatic motion that is precisely synchronized with on-screen action, which draws in viewers even more by allowing them to accurately experience the accelerations, turns, and jumps that they could previously only imagine. When a car rounds a corner in a 007 chase scene, turn with it. If the *Top Gun* jet fighter suddenly moves into a climb, climb with it.

Just about everyone who's tried this system loves it, but the price tag will set you back. An entry level system runs $15,000 and up.

Turn That Down, I'm on the Phone!

You know the drill. You're lying on the couch, right in the middle of your favorite team's football game, and the phone rings. You scramble to find the remote and turn down the music, all the while saying, "Hold on, hold on, hold on." Or, you're playing the music or movie so loud that you can't even hear the phone in the first place.

Well, you can get products that automatically turn down the audio system volume when they detect a ringing phone, so that you can answer immediately. They even turn the volume down when you make an outgoing call!

One example is the Telemute II ($250 from www.smarthome.com), which has two volume controls — one for controlling overall output during nonmute operation and a second for controlling volume during muting events. It connects between the output of your power amplifier and loudspeaker system, and to the phone line. You can see a wiring diagram for this device on the Smart Home catalog Web site (www.smarthome.com/images/7848adgm.jpg).

You choose how low you want the volume turned down. When you hang up the phone again, the volume automatically reverts to the normal listening level. Now you can crank up your tunes without worrying about missing an important call!

Turn It Up! Turn It Down! Turn It Up Again! Argh!

Sometimes, you just want everything at a quiet but intelligible level (like when everyone else is sleeping). To help you in this endeavor, many A/V receivers (and some TVs) have a *compression* circuit built in to the digital signal processor that keeps the louds from being too loud, and the quiets from being too quiet (this is often called *night mode*).

If you're using older equipment that doesn't have this feature, you need a leveler (also called a levelizer or a stabilizer). This device automatically adjusts your volume to a reasonable level (even as the source material gets louder or quieter). If the source volume increases, a leveler will attenuate the signal down; if the source signal decreases it will adjust the signal up.

To use a leveler, you generally adjust the volume to where you want it, and the leveler keeps the volume at that level. An audio leveler connects between any line level stereo or mono audio source and an amplifier (with RCA output/input jacks) or between your TV or VCR outputs and the inputs to your stereo tuner. Levelers range in price from $70 to $300 (you can check out various units at www.smarthome.com).

No more having to juggle that remote constantly (at least not for changing the volumes). Keep in mind, however, that these devices are really not for serious movie watching, in which case you *want* to have all the loud parts loud and the quiet parts quiet. They are instead intended for nighttime viewing, when you just want to not wake up the whole family *and* still be able to hear the quiet parts.

Automation System

An excellent way to improve your picture is to minimize the light that comes from anywhere but your video screen — in other words, to minimize the ambient lighting by turning off light bulbs and closing drapes. You could get up to turn off the lights and pull down the shades. A little exercise (and that really is a little!) never hurts anyone. But how cool would it be to press a button — a single button — and have the lights dim, the motorized drapes lower, and the A/V system power up? Pretty cool, we think.

Sound kinda like *The Jetsons*? It's really not. Home automation isn't rocket science. You can put together a simple X-10 system that dims the lights (theater style even) and activates the drape motors for just a few hundred dollars. We like this stuff so much we wrote a book about it (*Smart Homes For Dummies*), and you can find out how all this automation stuff works there.

Automation systems are also a task where a good dealer can help out. The superstore isn't going to do this for you, but if you find a good home theater dealer/installer, chances are good that automation packages are part of what the folks there do.

Chapter 22

Ten Ways to Enjoy Your Home Theater Everywhere

*W*hat good is having a home theater if you can't take advantage of it when you leave the room? Well, actually, it's still great, but why not leverage your investment and enjoy your home theater everywhere! Here are ten great things you can do to really exploit what you've spent your money on. Some are really cheap, some are disgustingly expensive, but all are fun, fun, fun. Go get your money's worth!

Storing Your Electronic Content

Before you can take advantage of your home theater outside your home theater, you need a way to make the content portable. The obvious first approach to this problem is using the "sneakernet" system by picking up the DVD and carrying it to another room. (*Sneakernet* is an old computer term meaning you put on your sneakers and walk over to the other computer with a floppy disk instead of sending the files over your Ether*net* network.) However, suppose that you have some home video stored on your PC hard drive or a movie on your ReplayTV that you want to watch in your car. How do you take it with you?

You have several options:

- ✔ **DVD/CD writers:** Get a DVD/CD burner to create your own discs. It's easy, it's cheap, and it's a lot more permanent and higher quality than video or audio tapes.

- ✔ **Portable USB keychain storage:** Get a portable hard drive system that enables you to carry your content from one place to another. Portable USB storage devices are out there now that literally attach to your keychain like a Blockbuster ID tag. M-systems DiskOnKey (www.diskonkey.com) stores up to 512MB on its USB-accessible hard drives; we expect to see 1G+ devices soon.

- ✔ **Flash Memory Cards:** You can also use flash memory card systems, which came out of the consumer goods arena. Flash media (like Compact Flash cards, Memory Sticks, and SD Cards) is for transferring photos and other content among devices. These tend to be vendor-specific, so if you are going to rely on these, try to stick within the company's electronics product line. Sony (www.sony.com), for instance, offers the Memory Stick for transferring data from its cameras, video camcorders, and other devices to the PC. Sony even has televisions with a Memory Stick reader, so that you can play back memory stick content directly on the TV screen.

- ✔ **Removable hard drives:** There are also removable hard drives that promote moving information between places, like the NEO Home Jukebox from SSI America ($450, www.ssiamerica.com). This device enables you to carry up to 80G of songs (more than 9,000 songs in the MP3 format) between your car and home theater. The NEO Car Jukebox can be instantly docked to your home stereo using standard RCA connectors, which means that you can access your entire music collection at home or on the road. It can also slide into your PC into a special docking bay that hooks to your USB port.

- ✔ **Wireless:** Finally, you can add a wireless connection. We talk throughout the book about wireless speakers, remotes, and other parts of your theater than can be wire-free. You can also find inexpensive wireless *dongles,* or wireless connectors, which are devices you can use to connect to available ports on your home theater and computing devices to open them up to other systems. Examples of these wireless connectors include D-Link's D-Link Air USB 802.11b interface ($60) and X10's Entertainment Anywhere system ($69). If you have a USB, Ethernet or FireWire connection, on your devices, chances are you can find a wireless connector to make it easy to get data from Point A to Point B. You'll see more and more electronics having native wireless interfaces, making them open to the surrounding environment. SSI America, for instance, has a version of its NEO Car Jukebox ($150 extra) that can wirelessly connect to your PC over 802.11b so that you can transfer songs whenever your car is nearby. Rockford Fosgate (www.rockfordfosgate.com) has a similar 802.11b-based audio server product called Omnifi ($599). Cool!

Reaching Synchronization Nirvana

It's one thing to walk something between two places or manually transfer files from one place to another. It's another thing to have your devices do this for you. We think synchronization capabilities (the ability to keep your content up to date on multiple devices) are one of the most critical buying criteria for consumer goods, and such capabilities are often overlooked.

You see, we are *lazy*. We want everything done for us. We don't want to manually do anything, because chances are, we'll muck it up.

So when we saw that SonicBlue's ReplayTV (www.sonicblue.com) and AudioReQuest (www.request.com) have autosynching capabilities over the Internet, we got really excited. The AudioReQuest devices, for instance, have NetSync technology that allows you to store the music from a CD on *one* of your AudioReQuest devices, and it transfers those songs (and changes to your playlist of favorite songs) to *all* your other devices, automatically, in the background, for lazy people like us. Check for sync options on anything you buy.

Streaming from Afar

You don't even have to be in your home to enjoy your home theater. Using high-speed Internet connections, you can often access parts of your home theater, such as MP3 audio servers and even networked video devices like PVRs (TiVo or ReplayTVs), wherever you are in the world.

Having a broadband connection enables you to access your home theater remotely. More and more devices are offering an on-board Web server that gives you remote access to info over the Internet, just like accessing any Web site over a browser. The trick is setting up your network so that you can access your info and no one else can. We can't explain in this book all the details of things such as port forwarding for your router/home gateway and secure remote access, but we can tell you how some products allow you to stream your data elsewhere. For more information, check out the owner's manuals that came with your equipment, the FAQ section of your router vendor's Web page (we like Netgear routers — www.netgear.com), or look at good online sources for network configuration, such as practicallynetworked.com.

SnapStream Media's Personal Video Station ($80, www.snapstream.com), which we discuss in Chapter 8, has a Web-based interface that enables you to control and edit recordings from anywhere in the world. A built-in stream server lets you watch the videos over the Internet. Many of the hard-drive-based audio servers we discuss in this book also have an option to open that server to the Internet. They don't come configured that way for security purposes, but you can usually find a section about how to do it in the user manual. So you can listen to your playlists at work, too!

Taking Your Home Theater with You

The concept of synchronized, network-based audio and video storage described earlier in this chapter is what enables a whole class of devices that make your home theater portable. Whether it's listening to music on a portable MP3 player, watching a portable DVD player, or even enjoying movies on your PDA, you can enjoy your home theater on the go.

Among your portable video options are TV shows. What's cool about the SnapStream product mentioned earlier in the section, "Streaming from Afar," is that you can also move your favorite TV shows to your pocket PC (via the PocketPC module, $30) or your laptop. Forget about renting DVDs for that flight!

And you don't have to leave your entire sound system at home either. Many MP3 players synchronize with your PC's music lists — the same lists that drive your home theater system. Most CD storage devices use programs such as MUSICMATCH Jukebox (free, www.musicmatch.com) to act as a gateway to a whole range of portable MP3 players, such as the Rio line of products from SonicBlue (www.sonicblue.com). You can find almost any portable music device you want at www.mp3.com. The site lists the most popular units being sold, as well as provides reviews.

Creating Your Own Screen on the Green

Danny and his wife used to haul the TV set out to the front porch for evening movies on nice summer nights. But that went by the wayside when the TVs got bigger and Danny got older. Now, however, he can set up an outdoor theater by using his portable projector for his home theater, his DVD-equipped laptop as a source (or wireless connections to another source), a screen, and some outdoor speakers. (By the way, you really need to use an LCD or DLP projector to do this — it's just too hard to set up a CRT projector to consider one for portable usage.)

This application is a great excuse to go for the portable projector for your whole home theater. You need at least 1600 lumens for decent outdoor shots, preferably 2000 if you can get them. (If you missed it, we discuss lumens in Chapter 13.)

For sound, portable speakers from your system can work great. The WSP255 speakers from RCA ($200 from www.radioshack.com) are 900 MHz wireless speakers that you can disconnect from their power outlets and carry outside on battery power. However, if your property is big, you might be a little farther away than those speakers can reach, so consider permanent outdoor speakers.

You can find great outdoor speakers that are shaped like rocks and can put out some great sound (you can even get so-called 'sub-rocks' for subwoofer bass). Check out Stereostone at www.stereostone.com; these rocks start at $300 per pair and go up from there. You can even get planter boxes for plants that have speakers in their base.

 You can get Direct Burial Speaker Wire that you can bury in your yard in order to connect to your home network. Look for the UL rating for burial. (You can check out the Underwriters Labs Web site at www.ul.com, for more information.)

For the screen, you can sew together some sheets, spend a lot of money on outdoor screens, or do something in between, depending on how much you want to spend. Two king-size sheets sewn together will do — with a seam down the middle though. You can get inflatable screens (www.blimpsign.com), real cinema style fabric and foldaway frames (www.da-lite.com), or just some big white canvas painting tarps outfitted with grommets and bungee cords (www.homedepot.com). You can even use a piece of plywood or a flat side of your house! It depends how fancy you want to get.

Elvira, Mistress of the Dark, in 3-D

What's the best way to watch Elvira in her cult classic, *Encounter in the 3rd Dimension*? Why, only in 3-D of course. Delving into 3-D is lots of fun, but there are varying levels of quality depending on the system you use.

If you have an interlaced screen, then for a mere $99 from iO Display Systems (www.I-glasses.com), you can get a complete 3-D kit that will transform your home theater into a 3-D experience. You start with a video transmitter unit that connects between your TV and VHS or DVD player so that you can view these and most other 3-D videos and DVDs. You don your 3-D glasses, and voilà — prime 1950s entertainment. All you need is a carhop to go to for a malt afterwards. This is on Danny and Pat's "You gotta do this" list. (Some people report poor quality in using some 3-D systems — you have to make sure that the system you are using can support the display you are using, or else it will look horrible.)

For HDTV, Plasma, LCD, and most projection television systems, you need a 3-D system that works with progressive mode displays. (Some vendors are calling this 3DVD . . . that's cute!) For that you'll need a product like Sensio's 3-D Processor (www.sensio.tv). Sensio, a startup company developing products as of early 2003, has teamed with lots of industry players to make modern day 3-D films, based on present hits like *Shrek*. Its processor can handle films like *Transitions* in IMAX 3-D. The product, when out, will cost around $2,500.

Our take: Put your money into the projector, which you'll also be using inside in your home theater, and the audio. Don't worry too much about the screen for an outdoor theater, unless you've got money to burn; people will put up with whatever you do for video.

Screens can act like sails on a boat, and catch a lot of wind. Be sure to:

  ✔ Check the weather.

  ✔ Use sufficient ballast or other stabilizing lines to keep your screen from ripping or blowing away.

Building Your Own Drive-In

Sadly, one of the cultural icons of the 20th century is disappearing from our roadsides. And how much fun it is to pile in with a bunch of friends to watch an outdoor movie at the drive-in. So you can do your bit for Americana by building your own drive-in — it's not hard at all.

Putting aside the playground in the front of the drive-in screen and the snack bar, which you can add at your own leisure, the rest of the drive-in can be built using your home theater gear.

Your gear for the outdoor theater works well here, too, but you need one more item — an FM transmitter to broadcast the sound to all the cars. You can find a range of low-cost ($60 to $250) FM transmitter devices that are designed to rebroadcast audio from portable CD players, portable cassette players, or computer audio, to an unoccupied channel on the FM broadcast band. The range of the units can vary from 50 feet to ¼ mile, so check the fine print.

Most of these units use a stereo mini plug connection between the external sound source and the FM transmitting unit. To decide which FM frequency to use, you must find an unoccupied FM frequency based upon your listening to the FM channels at your location. You then tune the FM transmitter to an unused channel from 88 to 108 MHz, and start transmitting.

Causing interference to existing FM broadcasts is prohibited by FCC Part 15 regulations, so be sure to pick that spare channel carefully. As long as you use the FM transmitter unit in accordance with manufacturer instructions, you will be in compliance with FCC Part 15 rules and regulations.

We like the FM25B unit available from Ramsey Electronics ($270, www.ramseyelectronics.com). It's got great range and performance at a reasonable price. It connects directly to the line output from your CD player/changer, or to one of the tape-out connections on your receiver. Simple as that.

You're not going to get surround sound out of one of these FM transmitters — just like you don't get it at a real drive-in. But you *are* re-creating the experience.

In San Diego, where Pat lives, the houses are pretty much jammed together. If you live someplace like this, you might not be able to even fathom a home drive-in. If you've got some land, however, it is *really* cool.

Setting Up Your Car's Theater

There's a lot of focus on improving the entertainment systems in cars. It's hard to buy a minivan without falling for the built-in DVD/gaming option, or going for that "Executive" stereo package.

Certainly, you can share CDs, DVDs, cassettes, and other home theater source items with your car. There's nothing new about that. But we do want to say two things about your car:

- ✔ If you don't have anything in your car, adding something to it can be relatively inexpensive.

- ✔ If you want to do neat things with your car, the technology is finally getting cheap enough to do it.

You can go to any car-oriented e-commerce site and find a slew of add-ons for your car. You can get in-dash DVD players with Dolby Digital and DTS Surround Sound for less than $300. For another $200, you can add a widescreen (16:9 aspect ratio) 7-inch LCD screen to it. For $150, you can get a DVD/MP3 player. The list goes on, and prices are dropping all the time. Bottom line: Don't assume these cost a fortune. Check them out at your local auto stereo store and online at places such as Crutchfield.com (www.crutchfield.com), Parts Express (www.partsexpress.com), or CNET (www.cnet.com).

Kenwood ($700, www.kenwoodusa.com) makes a neat CD server for your car, the Music Keg (love the name), which is a hard drive-based CD player that links to your PC to grab your music from your home theater system. Its transportable 20GB DMS cartridge can hold up to 5,000 of your songs at standard MP3 compression — just drop it into its cradle, which connects to your home theater-connected PC via a standard USB cable. You'll probably need to upgrade to a compatible CD/MP3/WMA Receiver, which can run $500+.

But if you are serious about your car — and its link to your home theater — then the way to go is to put a PC in your car and link that via wireless to your home theater. G-Net Canada's (www.gnet-canada.com) Revolution Auto PC, for instance, is a $1,300 add-on (not including the LCD screen) that gives you just about all you'd want to drive your smart car. It includes an MP3 audio player, a DVD player, GPS navigation support, vehicle diagnostics, a digital dash software interface, as well as a full Windows PC that can run any application you want. Slap a simple USB-to-802.11b or Bluetooth dongle from D-Link on it, and you can network it with your home theater for easy transfers. They call this "the future of in-vehicle computing" — we tend to believe that!

The same FM transmitters we discuss earlier for your drive-in will work in your car, too. You can send any stereo signal from your portable CD player, DVD player, or other audio output to your car stereo — just by laying the devices on the seat. Cool!

Creating a Wet and Wild Theater

Ferris Bueller can sing in the shower, so why can't you? With some creativity, you can link your home theater investment into the wet and wild world of your bathroom or other watery locale.

We've already told you how to do whole-home audio and video, but the areas that are water-, steam-, and otherwise humidity-prone need some extra planning to come out right. (This has something to do with water and metal equaling rust and short circuiting, but we're no electrical engineers.)

Some whole-home audio vendors have kept this fact in mind and come up with more rugged versions of their volume controls and keypads that fit right into that moist and warm bathroom environment. Actually, they've designed these controls for outdoor use — for example, volume controls for outdoor speakers — so they usually refer to these models as their "weatherproof" product line. Well, it may not be storming in your bathroom, but if you've got several gallons per minute of hot water flowing, it will be more like a tropical rain forest than the rest of your house. You might want to consider using weatherproof products from companies such as Niles Audio (www.nilesaudio.com). Niles Audio has a line of weatherproof volume controls, special weatherproof covers to keep the humidity out of outlets when they're not in use, and even weatherproof speakers so that the moisture doesn't damage the cones on your woofers.

You really don't want to mess with zapping yourself with 110 volt AC. It will ruin your day. So before you start installing anything fancy in the shower/bath area, you really should check with an electrician to make sure that your wiring is up to snuff. Most locales require something called a *GFCI* (or Ground Fault Circuit Interrupter) to be installed for outlets in the bath and kitchen. These devices do exactly what they say they do; they interrupt the circuit (that's the 110 volt AC power) when there's a ground fault (which means that the power is going to the ground through your body). We have to be in the CYA mode here (if you don't know what that means, ask your mom) because requirements are different in every city, village, town, and hamlet. Make sure you talk to an electrician who's qualified in your area.

But for the ultimate in wet home theater enjoyment, you have to talk to Jacuzzi. We can't go to the Jacuzzi Whirlpool Bath (www.jacuzzi.com) Web site without crying — check our their La Scala hot tub with 42" plasma display. This is the ultimate for a home theater enthusiast — far more important than a great home theater. We're talking about our bathroom time here.

Taking a Dip with Home Theater

If you own a pool, undoubtedly you are thinking about extending your home theater audio and maybe even video capabilities to poolside. However, when you are in the pool, the audio can get lost as you play underwater.

Just as the higher-end hotels are now installing audio-equipped pools, you too can extend your home theater to underwater, with Aquasonic ($600, www.clarksynthesis.com). The AQ339 simply drops into the water and is hung by a tether half of the depth of the pool. The IQ339 is an in-wall version that uses a third-party hardware light niche to provide a safe, unobtrusive installation. With this high-quality speaker in your pool, you can experience high-fidelity underwater sound that's as loud and clear as sound produced by above-water speakers.

This portable underwater speaker attaches to the wire leads on most standard receivers or amplifiers. It comes with a 25-foot Euroflex jacketed 14-gauge underwater cable — long enough to prevent water damage to audio components. After the cable is connected, simply attach a rope-tether to the eyelet at the top of the unit and lower it into the pool away from diving boards and high-activity areas, halfway between the water surface and the pool floor.

Watching TV on the Plane

Talk about James Bond gadgets. iO Display Systems (www.I-glasses.com) allows you to take a DVD player and enjoy virtual widescreen TV anywhere, even at 33,000 feet! With their i-Glasses, you don't have to suffer through another long flight watching a bad movie on the plane's blurry video projector. With a 180,000-pixel image simulating a 52-inch screen from 6-1/2 feet away, it might be the best way to view any classic.

It connects to any standard video source, including almost every game console, and features rich stereo sound with bass boost. The system plugs into an AC outlet with the included adapter, or can be powered with the included rechargeable battery pack. The i-Glasses also offer RCA composite and S-Video inputs, RCA audio inputs, and a foldable frame for easy storage. Prices on the street run about $600 and up.

Chapter 23

Ten Tips for Storing Your A/V Gear

*L*ike any piece of furniture, buying your home theater equipment is the easy part; figuring out where to put it is the hard part. Nothing seems to fit just where you want it to, and few people are prepared for just how big that 64-inch, rear-projection TV really looks in the family room. (Answer: *Big!*)

Let's face it: Some people are more interested in how the system sounds, and some are more interested in how it looks (and we're not talking about the video quality here). Problem is that most people can't afford to have their equipment custom installed in their living room, and fewer can afford to have a dedicated media room where it fits in.

You should consider aesthetic issues early in your planning, because when you take the gear home and unpack it is the wrong time to realize that the black Bose speakers don't look so hot in the all-white dining room (and oh my, don't let anyone *ever* find out that you had the option to buy white ones and you chose black because it matched the rest of the black matte finish A/V gear).

Some considerations:

- ✔ Does your gear need to be out of sight when not in use?
- ✔ Do you want to show it off?
- ✔ Does your gear need to be "color sensitive"?
- ✔ Do you have the right electrical and communications connections nearby where you want the theater to be?

These are but a few of the questions to think about when planning how to store and use you're A/V gear. Here are ten ideas for keeping things under control in your household.

Frame It

A lot of people are seriously considering the flat panel LCD and plasma screens because they can be only 4 inches thick, which opens up a huge range of options in terms of hiding it. One option: Put a frame around it. Yes, an actual picture frame. As weird as this can sound, it can look very stylish. If you plug the screen into the appropriate source device, such as a PC, you can pick your favorite artist and cycle through his or her paintings when not displaying movies, or play on-screen dynamic content from your ReQuest CD server.

Mantle It

Most home theaters go into the living room, where the fireplace is often the central focal point of the room. Until recently, there was no way to integrate the TV into that same 'space.' However, with the advent of plasma screens, it became a possibility.

Mounting a plasma display above the fireplace can save space and be an attractive way to display the panel. You can place the TV screen on the mantel (a typical plasma table stand is 4 to 6 inches in depth). Or get a mounting bracket, as discussed later in this chapter.

However, you need to check your fireplace's heat emissions. Although plasma screens have their own cooling systems, they were not designed to keep up with external heat sources, too. There's no problem with the extra heat while the unit is off (unless it's like an oven up there). Heat is only an issue when the TV is on. If the temperature tops 90 degrees, then don't run the plasma for a long period of time while its environment is hot. Think about glass doors on your fireplace or making smaller fires when the TV is on.

Swing It

You can find a host of attachment options for mounting your TV screens. For your plasma screen, you might consider a swing out wall mount, especially if you are putting the screen in an area where, if flush mounted, everyone in the room might not have an optimal view. You can get a swing-out arm that fits snug to a wall (about 3.5 inches between the wall and the screen when not in swing-out use). You can adjust the pitch up 5 degrees or down 15 degrees. Typically, these arms can pivot 90 degrees left or right of center. You can horizontally traverse the screen 22 inches right or left of center. Finally, some mounts allow you to pull the screen more than 30 inches from wall. These mounts add about 1.5 inches of depth to the screen when it's pushed flush to the wall. Expect to spend between $500 and $800 for one of these mounts.

For large, direct-view TVs, there are assorted wall and ceiling mounts that can offer similar functionality, but these are more static and less flexible than the plasma mounts.

Lift It

Another option is a lift mount, so that you can conceal your screen in furniture or cabinetry and raise to view. These are run by remote control and fulfill the need to have the units totally disappear when not in use. Sizes and capabilities vary by the size of your unit, but these are a great compromise for anyone who is struggling with how to hide a unit, particularly a large plasma unit that simply does not fit with your, say, 1890s Victorian house. But such conveniences come at a very high price. You might find you spend more on your lift mount than your screen, because these mounts can cost up to $4,000 for some units.

Drop It

When you don't seem to have enough floor space for your gear, think about suspending it from the ceiling. If you're looking at front projectors, then you'll want to at least consider a motorized drop-down screen. There are a range of relatively low-cost options for rather large screens — and we mean large. These screens can get larger than 120 inches wide.

At the touch of a button, the projection screen drops out of the ceiling. You install the unit so that it's flush with the ceiling and hidden by a trapdoor. When you activate the unit, the door opens, and the screen emerges.

Some come with a low-voltage interface so you can use a contact closure from an automation system or the relay output of a projector to enable automatic screen movements to coincide with other AV equipment. So, you could have the screen automatically lower, for instance, when you turn off your projector.

The in-ceiling units run $1,500 and up; wall-mounted, motorized versions start around $500. You can get nonmotorized pull-down screens for as little as $65. Check out places such as www.avmall.com for a range of options.

Hide It

You can buy easy-to-install, remote control door mechanisms so that you can hide your equipment behind doors or fake pictures. These are usually available in either two- or four-door models, and have rails along which the cabinet doors can ride. Check for units that have inputs for contact closure control. These inputs allow easy integration with X10 and other home-automation systems so that you can have a 'home theater mode' in your home-automation system, where the lights dim, the A/V gear sets itself to the right settings, and your screen opens in front of you. Pretty cool. Expect to spend up to $1,000 for this level of sophistication, though.

Build It

Finding any sort of furniture to store your A/V gear in used to be a huge problem. The stereo, tape deck, DVD player, and so on were not the problem — it was the huge TV. Not many pieces of furniture were designed to hold a 60-inch TV.

Now, however, you can choose from a good selection of ready-to-assemble home theater furniture kits. These typically have some sort of particle board or press wood base with a laminate on top. You can find a range of styles at some of the online furniture stores, such as www.furnitureonline.com, or your local furniture store or warehouse club.

Here are some things to look for:

✔ **An expandable *bridge:*** This is the part of the unit that straddles the top of the TV set. It allows you to get bigger TV sets and not have to swap out your furniture.

✔ **A staggered unit:** The center TV section should stand out from the sides so that the whole piece looks smaller in a room by staggering the effect.

✔ **A good cable management system:** Look for holes to run cabling from one shelf to the next, or built-in power cabling.

✔ **Good back panel access:** You'll want to check out the back of your equipment every once and a while, and you don't want to move a whole cabinet to do so. Units with lighting in the back get extra points from us.

Buy It

The problem with ready-to-assemble furniture is that it can look, well, *college,* for lack of a better term. You can step up to a higher quality with assembled furniture, available at your local furniture store or online. Starting generally at about $1,000 and going up, you can find all kinds of all-wood or all-metal cabinets, casings, armoires, and so on that are specifically designed for audio and video components. You may even find some nice cabinets at your local unfinished furniture store — cabinets that you can stain yourself to match your existing furniture.

We can't tell you what to look for in your furniture tastes, but think about whether you want doors with speaker cloth hiding your speakers (which might slightly muffle the sound, but may improve the acceptability of your system in your spouse's eyes) or felt-lined drawers for your remote controls. Planning on hiding the equipment behind some doors? Think about air circulation and whether your remotes are IR or RF. (If they use IR, you need IR sensors mounted outside the cabinet, which we discuss in Chapter 14.) Shop around because you'll find that you have more options than ever. Watch for the shipping costs!

Customize It

Certainly, if we all had our druthers, we'd have someone come to our homes and build something especially for us. And you'd be surprised at how little this can cost, when you add up everything.

Keep in mind what you want to access a lot (like your CD and DVD drives) and what you hope you'll hardly touch (like your modulators or amps). It makes a difference what you hide behind doors and make inaccessible.

Building in your gear gives you a lot of options. Consider using ceiling- or in-wall-mounted speakers for your surround sound system. If you have an unfinished basement and your theater is on the first floor, take advantage of that by running the wiring under the floor and up the risers where necessary.

Customizing your own area does not have to cost a lot more than buying the equipment, and you can do it in phases, too. Danny's Maine home theater has been in development for six years, while waiting for plasma screen prices to come down (they were $30,000 when he started, and now plasma TVs start off in the $3,000 to $5,000 range).

Rack It

Racks come literally in all shapes and sizes. They are great for keeping your gear well organized; and the better organized and stabilized your gear is, the fewer connection and other problems you have.

We put money into our racks, because we have dealt with nonracked gear in the past, and we've found that using a rack (as opposed to just putting your gear on shelves) makes it about a million times easier to access, connect, and reconfigure your A/V system.

You can get inexpensive rack systems starting at a couple of hundred dollars. We like the type that is designed to simplify your access while minimizing your chances of mucking this up. For instance, the AVRack from EAS, Inc. ($500+, www.avrack.com) rotates 360 degrees — shelving, cabling, and all — so you can get to the back of the gear, from the front of your unit. That's great. The company's slogan, "Install with ease, access with ease," lives up to its billing. Other things to look for: cable management, power supplies, and expandability.

 Depending on how much equipment you've got, consider getting a rack mounted cooling fan to expel heat from the system. Check out the Cool-stack, a one-unit high, true rack-mount ventilator, from Active Thermal Management ($275, www.activethermal.com).

Chapter 24

Ten Great Sources for Getting More Information

*W*e can in no way cover the entire home theater industry in one book. So, we're leaving a few nuggets for other publications to cover. It's only fair.

Here's a listing of those publications that we read regularly (and therefore recommend unabashedly), and which you should get your hands on as part of your home theater project. Most publications allow you to purchase back issues of their magazines, so you can have a library at your fingertips in about a week. You know what they say: You can never be too rich or read too much about home theater before you become too poor.

The Web sites mentioned also have a ton of information online, but you might have to try different search keywords to find what you are looking for. Topics vary substantially from site to site. All sites are free.

Home Theater Magazine

Phone: 800-264-9872 or 850-682-7644
Web site: www.hometheatermag.com

Home Theater Magazine is one of the main sources for information about home theater. It is a very high-end publication and will certainly expose you to a range of systems, from budget to those on the finer side of home theater. It's not unusual to see $30,000 projectors reviewed, for instance. Don't let that scare you, however, because almost every issue has something to offer, no matter the budget. And you can always find out the leading trends in the industry, which is important, because there's nothing like buying yesterday's technology on sale and thinking you got a great deal. (How *about* that sale on Betamax VCRs, huh?) The accompanying Web site offers archives of prior articles.

The same folks also publish a dynamite *Home Theater Buyer's Guide Annual Directory,* which lists more than 5,000 source devices, controllers, speakers, home-theater-in-a-box packages, video displays, and all sorts of accessories. An annual subscription costs $12.97 for 12 issues — quite a deal. The annual buyer's guide is $5.99.

Stereophile Guide to Home Theater

Phone: 800-666-6471 or 850-682-7644
Web site: www.guidetohometheater.com

Stereophile Guide to Home Theater focuses on the high-end sector of the home theater market. The guide's cadre of industry experts is dedicated to providing in-depth gear reviews on everything from projectors to line conditioners to DVD players to HD tuners. Instructional how-to columns on fine-tuning your system, special features, and software reviews help you get the most out of your system. An annual subscription costs $15.97.

Stereophile

Phone: 800-666-3746 or 850-682-7644
Web site: www.stereophile.com

Like their home theater-oriented publication, *Stereophile* is devoted to the high-end of the market, concentrating on the better audio equipment and recordings available. Again, that does not mean there is nothing for the budget-minded — it's found in the feature stories and advice columns on topics like placement of speakers for maximum effect. If you are going to buy some new audio gear, check the reviews out here. An annual subscription runs $12.97.

Sound & Vision

Phone: 800-876-9011 or 212-767-6000
Web site: www.soundandvisionmag.com

Another respected home theater publication that captures the essence of home theater and its various components is *Sound & Vision*. This publication regularly has helpful articles in very layman's nontechie language about how to set up your speakers, tune your system, and so on. The buyer's guides are ample and feature checklists. All in all, this is a very friendly publication for the beginner, with meat for the enthusiast.

The accompanying Web site contains archived issue content, and its S&V Forums are a great place to ask questions. The editors moderate the forums, which are heavily trafficked.

A one-year subscription to the printed publication is $24.

Electronic House Magazine

Phone: 800-375-8015 or 508-358-3400
Web site: www.electronichouse.com

Electronic House is one of our favorite publications because you can read a lot of very easy-to-understand articles about all aspects of an electronic home, including the home theater domain. It is written for the consumer who enjoys technology.

Although only a portion of each issue deals with home theater topics, *Electronic House* magazine provides a very easy-to-understand coverage of the key issues of the systems that comprise a home theater, including audio, video, remote controls, speakers, wiring, lighting, and other home theater components. Each issue also devotes time to neat new things on the market — most within the budget of any family — such as new remote controls, cool new consumer devices, and accessories for your entertainment system. *Electronic House* also offers an *Electronic House Planning Guide,* which walks you through all sorts of issues of upgrading your home for the 21st century.

We think that, after you start reading this magazine, you'll want to expand your interests beyond home theater, to the whole home at large. (Then you'll want to buy our *Smart Homes For Dummies* book, too!)

Crutchfield

Phone: 800-955-9009 or 434-817-1000
Web site: www.crutchfield.com

This is the perennial catalog that sits by the toilet, for constant perusing while in the, er, office. *Crutchfield* offers a free catalog of all sorts of A/V and home theater gear, and it's great for just getting ideas about what's out there. Its companion Web site is very simply laid out and offers a Home Theater and A/V Info Center. For instance, you can find some great photos of the various connectors at www.crutchfield.com/infocenter/home/S-5x6V1F3d9Aa/ connections_gallery.html (this URL might change, so look around for their Home A/V Connections Photo Gallery if you can't find it). Overall, we pick up our *Crutchfield* when we want to know, "Does anybody have something that will. . . ."

CNET.com

Web site: www.cnet.com

CNET.com is a simple-to-use, free Web site where you can do apples-to-apples comparisons of home theater and electronic equipment. You can count on seeing pictures of what you are buying, editor ratings of the equipment, user ratings of the gear, reviews of most devices, and a listing of the places on the Web where you can buy it all — with the actual pricing along with it. It's a one-stop resource for evaluating your future home electronics purchases. What we especially like is the ability to compare, side-by-side, different devices, so we can see who's got which features. Overall, a solid stop on your Web research trip.

Home Theater Forum

Web site: www.hometheaterforum.com

Home Theater Forum is a massive Internet messaging site where people interested in home theater gather to discuss their issues and solutions. You can find areas for discussion of home theater basics, construction, DIY solutions, sources, displays, and so on. You really should check it out, if for no other reason than to see that lots of other people just like you are also trying to figure out what's going on in home theater.

The site includes a Member Home Theater section where you can see all sorts of different implementations of home theater in different environments, complete with listings of the equipment and components they use to drive their setups. This is great for getting ideas about what other people have done — ranging from grad students in their dorms to retired people with their life savings. The Member Home Theater section is a true smorgasbord of ideas.

Home Theater Talk

Web site: www.hometheatertalk.com

Home Theater Talk is another great site. This site is run by none other than our esteemed technical editor, who was an admin on the Home Theater Forum for several years before striking out on his own. Home Theater Talk isn't as big as Home Theater Forum, but it has a nice friendly atmosphere — it's the "neighborhood pub" of online home theater sites.

AV Science

Web site: www.avsforum.com

Similar to Home Theater Forum, AV Science's AVSForum.com is an online community of technical enthusiasts who indeed wallow in the minutest details of a home theater installation. But think of it this way: It's a collection of "the guy next door who knows how to install A/V gear" — a proverbial hothouse of information and opinions that you can tap to help solve your problems.

The site is organized in folders according to interests. If you want information on how to tune your ReplayTV unit, there's a whole group devoted to that, for instance. There are also places where people are selling their old gear. As the techies buy the latest gear, they sell off their leading-edge stuff from a few years back — at great prices. The manufacturers themselves monitor this site for feedback from customers about what they want in their next versions. It's got that much to offer.

eBay.com

Web site: www.ebay.com

Although eBay started out as a place where people could sell everything in their attics, it has really matured into a place where all sorts of equipment is bought and sold. Companies are selling excess gear here. Old home theater gear is available in the listings. Even new stuff is being sold online. You never know what you are going to find here, and it is a "let the buyer beware" type of environment. You, indeed, get what you pay for. Nonetheless, you can get a good handle for street prices for used gear here, and we've known people who have grown their home theater by trading up equipment through eBay, spending a fraction of what they would have if they had bought new components in the stores.

Other Sources

Almost any major retail store chain where you might go to purchase home theater equipment has a Web site. These sites often contain information centers about home theater and are a good stop before going to meet the geeks at the store. For instance, Circuit City has a starter section on the basics of home theater. Sears has its Electronic Advisor.

In addition to these information boutiques, here are some other sites for you to sample:

Magazines:

- ✔ *Home Theater Builder* (www.hometheaterbuilder.com)
- ✔ *Audio Video Interiors* (www.audiovideointeriors.com)
- ✔ *Widescreen Review* (www.widescreenreview.com)
- ✔ *The Perfect Vision* (www.theperfectvision.com)

Web Sites:

- ✔ Remote Central (www.remotecentral.com)
- ✔ PC Gamer (www.pcgamer.com)
- ✔ Game Spot (www.gamespot.com)
- ✔ Guide to Home Theater Web Sites (hometheater.sandler.org)

Organizations:

- ✔ CEDIA (www.cedia.net)
- ✔ Consumer Electronics Association (www.ce.org)
- ✔ Audio Video Intelligent Association (www.avia.org)

Industry:

- ✔ Dolby (www.dolby.com)
- ✔ DTS (www.dtsonline.com)
- ✔ THX (www.thx.com)

Index

• *W* •

• *Z* •